Cultural warfare and trust

Manchester University Press

Cultural warfare and trust
Fighting the Mafia in Palermo

CARINA GUNNARSON

MANCHESTER UNIVERSITY PRESS
Manchester and New York

distributed exclusively in the USA by Palgrave

Published by Manchester University Press
Oxford Road, Manchester M13 9NR, UK
and Room 400, 175 Fifth Avenue, New York, NY 10010, USA
www.manchesteruniversitypress.co.uk

Distributed in the United States exclusively by
Palgrave Macmillan, 175 Fifth Avenue, New York,
NY 10010, USA

Distributed in Canada exclusively by
UBC Press, University of British Columbia, 2029 West Mall,
Vancouver, BC, Canada V6T 1Z2

British Library Cataloguing-in-Publication Data
A catalogue record for this book is available from the British Library

Library of Congress Cataloging-in-Publication Data applied for

ISBN   978 0 7190 7672 5   *hardback*

First published 2008

17 16 15 14 13 12 11 10 09 08   10 9 8 7 6 5 4 3 2 1

Typeset by R. J. Footring Ltd, Derby
Printed in Great Britain
by Bell & Bain Ltd, Glasgow

Dedicated to my parents, Sven and Soon-Joo

Contents

Tables

Acknowledgements

Many colleagues and friends were involved with this project. First of all, I would like to thank my financial sponsors. The Swedish STINT accorded a scholarship that enabled a preliminary study of the anti-Mafia movement in Palermo. The Swedish Research Council granted a research fund that financed the project and the language check. Borbos Hansson and Rektor at Uppsala University gave financial contributions to numerous research trips to Palermo.

A lot of persons in Palermo offered help and advice during my research trips. First and foremost, I would like to warmly thank the school principals, teachers and other staff, and students who opened their doors, dedicated a lot of their time, and in other ways helped me and my research assistants to carry out this research project. And special thanks to the students who took part in the Letter Project.

I am more than grateful for all the advice and support I have received from Carmela 'Mimma' Valido. She closely followed the project from the very beginning and generously offered her advice on different aspects of my work. She also gave some important keys to Palermitan life and included me in her wonderful family. In addition, I would also like to thank Francesco Cultrera at Centro Pedro Arrupe, Anna Puglisi and Umberto Santino at Centro Peppino Impastato, Patrizia Ardizzone, Enrico del Mercato, Giovanni Leone, Gianluca Lo Coco, Ivana Manone, Carla Monteleone, Paolo Pavone, Claudio Riolo, Roberto Rovelli and Santo Li Vecchi at the ISTAT office in Palermo, and numerous other interlocutors who have generously shared their knowledge with me. My research assistants in Palermo, Pasqualino Ferrarotto and Cono Ferrarotto, organised the Letter Project, including translations, the formulation and distribution of the supporting material as well as the collection and interpretation of the letters. Cono also organised the distribution of the second questionnaire; Leonardo Alagna helped me to organise the distribution of the first questionnaire.

Many colleagues, most of them at the Department of Government at Uppsala University, commented on different parts of the project: Per Adman, Shirin Ahlbäck Öberg, Ellen Almgren, Hanna Bäck, Katarina Barrling-Hermansson, Li Bennich-Björkman, Christina Bergqvist, Hans Blomkvist, Gelu Calacean, Marco Foffa, Stefano Guzzini, Sverker Härd, Magdalena Inkinen, Ann-Chatrin Jungar, Leif Lewin, Åsa Lundgren, Gunnar Myrberg, Erik Noréen, Sven Oskarsson, Charles Parker, Olof Petersson, Bo Rothstein, Roxanna Sjöstedt, Per Strömblad, Anders Westholm, Sten Widmalm and Daniel Wohlgemuth. I am particularly grateful to Hanna Bäck and Magdalena Inkinen, who co-authored Chapter 8. Christian Lundahl at the Department of Education, Uppsala University, helped me with the formulation of questions in the questionnaire and inspired the Letter Project. At the end of the study, I received extremely valuable advice from Alfio Mastropaolo, Arnaldo Bagnasco, Rocco Sciarrone and Loredana Sciolla, of the University of Turin, that helped me to improve the manuscript for this book.

The ECPR Standing Group on Organised Crime offered contacts with colleagues interested in Mafia-related issues. Felia Allum, Monica Massari and Rino Coluccello gave useful advice and encouraged me in my work. Vera Husfeldt of the IEA and Bruno Losito at CERISDI in Rome helped me to locate the Italian version of the IEA questionnaires. I am grateful for useful comments from Vera and all kinds of advice from Bruno over the years. Michael Hawthorne, University of North Carolina at Pembroke, and Michael L. Berbaum, University of Illinois, Chicago, my teachers at the ICPR summer programme in quantitative methods in 2004 in Ann Arbor, Michigan, shared their knowledge of panel studies.

Anna Holmlin Nilsson and class 8F, Mörbyskolan 2002/03, and headmaster Pia Blandano and class 2D at Scuola Antonio Ugo 2002/03, helped me to organise pre-tests of the questionnaire. Bodil Aronsson Cavaliere and Mauro Cavaliere helped me with some of the Italian translations; Ralph Footring and Jessica Trask corrected my English. Jonas Mertanen designed the questionnaires, rendering them more reader-friendly. Peter

Knutar, Susanna Hammelev Jörgensen and Per Åsberg at the Department of Government patiently helped me with all sorts of computer-related matters.

Without the following persons my stays in Palermo would definitely have been more boring. Thank you Stefano Garitta, Salvatore 'Totò' Pernice, Michele Mazzola, Mario Bernardi, Barbara Grandi, Gabriella, Leo, Alessandra, Marcello, 'Totò' Cangelosi and his Margherita, Vincenzo and Maria Schillaci, Giuseppe Ciminna, Marco Pavone, Giuseppe 'Pippo' Vaccaro, Paolo Pavone and Luca Toni for unforgettable moments! I would also like to thank the Rusignolo family at Hotel Letizia for company and shelter, Al Ferro di Cavallo for delicious Palermitan food and Coffee Time in Via Tommaso Gargallo for its coffee.

Last, but not least, I would also like to thank my publisher and the staff at Manchester University Press for their professionalism.

1

Introduction

Can you tell me, Socrates, whether virtue is acquired by teaching or by practice; or if neither by teaching nor practice, then whether it comes to man by nature, or in what other way? (Plato, *Meno*)

Is it possible to fight persistent values of distrust? Is it possible to support the development of generalised trust between citizens through public action from above, through civic education?

Fukuyama once described the accumulation of social capital as 'a complicated and in many ways mysterious cultural process. While governments can enact policies that have the effect of depleting social capital, they have great difficulties understanding how to build it up again.'[1] Stolle said that questions about how the norms of reciprocity and values of trust are generalised and institutionalised represent 'the most underresearched area in social capital studies, supporting only a few hypotheses, all of which need more development and empirical testing'.[2] There is also wide disagreement among scholars as to whether social capital is created from above, by institutions, or from below, from civil society.

Research shows that the existence of social capital in a society – or, in the context of the study described in this book, more specifically generalised trust – could be decisive not only in the prevention of crime, but also for economic development[3] and an effective democracy.[4] Moreover, the presence of generalised trust in society leads to better government, more redistribution and economic growth and less corruption.[5] The existence of generalised trust in society is connected to positive outcomes such as personal happiness, safer neighbourhoods and solutions to various problems of collective action. As Uslaner describes it: 'life in a trusting society is pleasant, life in a country where a majority distrusts other people is highly contentious. Where mistrust runs rampant, daily life can be a struggle to survive.'[6] Generalised trust is related to optimism and possibilities for change. 'Generalised trusters' 'believe that they can right wrongs and leave the world a better place than they found it'.[7] Generalised trust is also necessary for the establishment of civil society, as it makes people more inclined to participate voluntarily in different kinds of collective institutions, such as political parties and trade unions, or any other kind of organisation that is beneficial for democracy in general.[8] In a cross-national survey of 24 societies, Inglehart showed a close link between generalised trust and subjective well-being and the long-term survival of democratic institutions.[9] Increased knowledge about the origins of generalised trust is also crucial for new democracies or states where trust has been destroyed by warfare or massive violations of civil rights, for example in Rwanda and the former Yugoslavia.

Although generalised trust and cooperation are highly desirable for any society – and many societies are indeed marked by high levels of trust and cooperation – societies may fall into a negative cycle of distrust and non-cooperation, which is difficult to break. The situation is described by Rothstein as a 'social trap', or a situation where individuals, groups or organisations are unable to cooperate owing to mutual distrust and lack of social capital, even where cooperation would benefit all.[10] The logic of a society that has fallen into that social trap is that even persons who have strong incentives for fair play will continue to be disloyal, as they will assume that everybody else will continue to cheat, that is, to defect from the cooperative line. Rothstein emphasises that such behaviour is not based on any specific personal characteristics but on rational calculations and expectations about other people's behaviour. As long as we suspect that most people will cheat others, our incentives to cooperate will remain weak. The challenge is to change citizens' perceptions of society in order to break the vicious circle of distrust.

Why vicious circles of distrust are difficult to break is frequently explained with reference to Hardin's example, 'the tragedy of the commons'. In his example, we are asked to imagine a common meadow that is threatened by over-grazing. No herder can limit the grazing of anyone else's flock. If individual herders limit their own use of the common meadow, they alone lose. Yet unlimited grazing destroys the common resource on which the livelihood of all depends. All parties would be better off if they could cooperate and come to an agreement to limit grazing. But, in the absence of a credible mutual commitment, each individual has an incentive to defect from the cooperative line and become a 'free rider'. The message is that without trust between citizens, it is difficult to establish the cooperation needed and citizens find themselves in a vicious circle of non-cooperation. Speaking in game theoretic terms, the strategy of non-cooperation is a stable equilibrium. Trust is the lubricant for social relations: without trust, there can be no cooperative equilibrium; with it, there can be a stable cooperative equilibrium. In a situation where trust and resources are scarce, and values of individualism and non-cooperation are strong, the use of clientelistic relations is likely to be more beneficial for realising one's immediate and short-term interests. From a long-term perspective, however, the outcome is sub-optimal, since non-cooperation leads to less development, less democracy and a poorly functioning economy and state.

In his study of Italy, Putnam argued that lack of social capital and weak mutual understanding explained the poor performance of democratic institutions and weak economic development in southern Italy.[11] The economic, political, social and cultural divide between northern and southern Italy is nothing new to scholars in Italian studies. The 'southern question', *la questione meridionale*, has marked Italian politics ever since unification in 1860. Despite massive public investment and cash flows into southern Italy after the Second World War through the regional development fund Cassa per il Mezzogiorno, economic development in the south remained weak. The gap between north and south widened rather than narrowed between 1950 and 1975.[12] In 1990, the youth unemployment rate reached 44 per cent in the south, in contrast to almost 15 per cent in the centre–north. In the same year, the south's gross domestic product (GDP) was, in proportional terms, only 59 per cent of that of the rest of the peninsula – lower than it had been in 1970 or 1980.[13]

Putnam traced the origins of these differences to medieval Italy. Whereas governance in the north stimulated the development of horizontal relations, the rule of the king in the south was more favourable to the development of hierarchical and vertical relations. In northern Italy, a practice of self-government was established in the communal republics during the eleventh century. These communes had sprung from voluntary associations and, as communal life progressed, a vibrant organisational life developed. The norms and networks of civic engagement that emerged explain why the economy developed and governmental performance improved, Putnam argues. At the same time as communal life in the north spread beyond the traditional elite, feudal authority was strengthened in the south. The Norman kingdom established in southern Italy from the eleventh century fostered the development of mutual distrust and conflict, and the different regimes that ruled between 1504 until 1860 destroyed horizontal ties of solidarity in favour of vertical ties of dependence and exploitation. Hence, as early as the fourteenth century, two different models of governance had already settled on the Italian peninsula.[14] These differences laid the ground for a tradition of cooperative behaviour, or 'civicness', in the north, whereas a tradition of non-cooperation and distrust became dominant in the south, Putnam argues. Putnam's explanation for the differences in economic and democratic performance in northern and southern Italy today rests on the assumption that the *social context* for institutions was more favourable in the north than in the south.[15] The social context itself is determined by some key factors, including civic networks, trust and norms of reciprocity. History determines which of these two stable equilibria – cooperation or non-cooperation – characterises any given society.

Institutionalists have criticised Putnam for presenting a static view of political culture. It is argued that his model does not sufficiently take into account the fact that the degree of civicness is also influenced by political policies, the behaviour of governments or their policy performance in more recent times.[16] Focusing on more recent explanations for the differences between the 'two Italies', Pasquino argues that the behaviour of government matters more than civic traditions. If Emilia-Romagna in the centre–north scores high on Putnam's civic community index, some weight has to be attributed to politics, and in particular the fact that the local government has known how to invest in and exploit the existence of social capital.[17] The 'path dependency' of Putnam's model has also been criticised. If everything was 'decided' in medieval times, then why should we care about political action today? And why is the present situation conditioned more by events during those times than by more recent events? It is argued that a more convincing explanation for the lack of good governance and 'civicness' in southern Italy is the patronage system and the clientelism established by the Italian state during the post-war period.[18]

Another factor that has not been sufficiently considered in Putnam's explanatory model is the presence of the Mafia. The effects of organised crime on democracy are often ignored in the literature on social capital, but of course central in the literature on southern Italy. Although southern Italy has enjoyed formal democracy, democratic practices have been undermined and distorted by the presence of the Mafia. In this context, similarities exist between the Mafia and the ability of authoritarian regimes to limit the civil rights of citizens by preventing the development of civil society and by keeping citizens in a state of atomisation and isolation. In the past, the Mafia actively hindered the development of cooperation between citizens, by killing those who openly opposed it and by creating a culture of domination, threat and fear. Despite the presence of formal institutions in Sicily, the influence of the Mafia continues to greatly distort the mechanisms of democracy. The Mafia also undermines citizens' possibilities to express their legal, civil and democratic rights in these areas. As described by Siebert, the Mafia creates a culture of fear that leads to conformist behaviour, which in turn implies a mental surrender to the Mafia's exercise of power:[19]

> Where the Mafia rules, there is a fear of leading a private life, of boasting personal spaces that could arouse suspicion. Caution, in the private and personal sphere, suggests conformism; fear, in the public sphere, requires that personal rights be waived. Hence those who have the right to vote do not exercise it, or vote against their convictions, and those who have the right to apply for public work contracts withdraw for no apparent reason, or cheat.... Connivance with Mafia terror is wide-ranging and also includes various forms of consensus; what, however, typifies the surrender of the individual both in a private and in a public sphere is mortal anxiety, evoked and re-evoked systematically by violent and brutal threats.[20]

This book will focus on institutional explanations and analyse more recent political efforts to break the heritage of the past, that is, to turn the vicious circle of non-cooperation into a virtuous circle based on trust and cooperation, and to change citizens' perceptions of society. While there is quite extensive knowledge today of the mechanisms that rule the two states of equilibrium – cooperation and non-cooperation – there is less knowledge about *change*.[21] We will now turn to our case study, Palermo, and have a look at the political efforts made during the 1990s to change Palermo's trajectory.

Cultural warfare

After the killings of two judges, Giovanni Falcone and Paolo Borsellino, in 1992, Palermo's mayor, Leoluca Orlando, was re-elected in 1993 on a strong anti-Mafia platform, with 75 per cent of the vote. Orlando successfully used the moment of emotion provoked by the assassinations of the two judges to launch a new programme for Palermo, focusing on three sectors: culture, public schools and infrastructure. The major aims of Orlando's political programme were to reclaim control over the city's territory, to restore citizens' rights and to promote a civic consciousness based on the rule of law. Efforts were made to improve Palermo by renovating buildings and monuments, and restoring green areas in the city centre. Better public transport and illumination of the city centre were other examples of those efforts. Orlando's anti-Mafia platform consisted of breaking the Mafia's territorial and mental control. Orlando also emphasised the importance of making a distinction between Mafia values and Sicilian culture:

> Speaking about the Mafia is an effective way of fighting it. The Mafia is identified with Sicily: the Mafiosi would like Sicilians to become their cultural accomplice. They think that Mafia and Sicily identify with one another. But the Mafia is Sicily's worst enemy because it has used the history of Sicily against Sicily, the identity of Sicily against Sicily. The culture of Sicily against Sicily. This is why it's a good thing to speak about the Mafia and remember that the Mafia is not Sicily.[22]

There is no doubt that Orlando was able to put Palermo on the right track, starting with the so-called 'Palermo spring' during his first period in office (1985–90) and continuing with the 'cultural revolution' during the first years of his second term as mayor (1993–2000), thanks to his charisma and massive public support. Many consider his school policy one of the most successful parts of Orlando's programme. New schools were built, enrolment procedures were improved, efforts to fight drop-out were reinforced, the use of 'double turns'[23] was stopped, new teaching methods were introduced, the project 'School adopts a monument' was launched and more attention was given to education in good citizenship and the rule of law. A central part of the programme was also to stimulate cooperation and trust between students and to instil a belief in the possibility of *change*.

Orlando's warfare on organised crime during the 1990s included efforts within the cultural, political and economic spheres, at the same time as his administration was trying to solve some of the city's most urgent infrastructural problems. One important part of the cultural programme during this time was work to fight the Mafia through schools. We will focus on only one aspect of his wider programme, namely the establishment of generalised trust through the state schools.

Palermo may thus be understood as a cultural battleground, where the Mafia and state compete for power, legitimacy and territorial control. The weakness of the state explains both why citizens look to the Mafia instead of the state for security, protection or other services and how the Mafia originally established its territorial power. The Mafia, of course, strongly opposes any attempt to break its territorial power and continues actively to oppose any actor who threatens its position. This is particularly strongly resented in poor areas where the local Mafia conditions everyday life. Consequently, the presence of the Mafia may also explain why the state continues to remain weak in some specific areas. Mafia leaders use ideology and symbols to maintain their territorial control. Traditionally, Mafia members have promoted the image of themselves as brave and generous men of honour, *uomini d'onore*, and supported the ideal of a self-made man who is dependent on nobody and nothing except his own capacity for success. Mafia leaders have also used religion or myths in order to render their criminal acts more legitimate, for example the old myth of 'Beati Paoli' (discussed in Chapter 4). The darker side of the mental control exercised by the Mafia is the fostering of a culture of fear and distrust, which denies citizens their democratic rights and hinders their incentives to cooperate. The presence of the Mafia breeds distrust as persons who are 'protected' by it do not hesitate to take advantage of those who are unprotected.

Encouraging the development of generalised trust between citizens and enhancing their ability and motivation to co-operate – breaking the vicious circle of distrust – therefore constitute important aspects of the fight against the Mafia and were also important parts of the programme launched by Orlando's second administration. Two cultural models were here at play: one that favoured change, and one that strongly opposed it. School policy in Palermo represented a cultural battlefield, where the dominant role model offered by the Mafia was challenged.

Generalised trust and school

The role played by civic education in the processes of state formation is, of course, not new. The sociologist Stein Rokkan analysed the importance of schooling in the processes of state- and nation-building in Europe. The historian Eugene Weber showed how the French army turned peasants into French citizens.[24]

There are two strong theoretical reasons for focusing on the educational system. First, despite the importance of school, theorists on social capital have not yet studied the effects of schooling on generalised trust. Research has rather focused on the importance of associations or public institutions like government, administration or welfare systems. Although there is strong evidence that a higher level of education is a predictor of generalised trust, research on the effect of school or civic education on generalised trust is still scarce. Given the central role of school in the lives of most young citizens, there is good reason to study its effects on generalised trust. For most people, school represents their first important encounter with public institutions. Many teachers describe the early years of secondary school as crucial, since students turn from children into adolescents during this time and take their first steps as independent young citizens. In a Palermitan context, where youth unemployment is high and organised crime may offer an alternative career path, top priority has been accorded the fight against school drop-out.

Second, a weakness in the literature on social capital is that researchers have mainly analysed the values of adults, while there is strong empirical evidence that generalised trust is established early in life. It has also been shown that interpersonal trust is stable over time, more stable than trust in government.[25] There are strong theoretical reasons for studying young citizens and, more specifically, the effects of school on their values. Even if changes do occur during adulthood, as a result of, say, job experiences, family events, social experiences or changes in society, these do not interfere, in general, with the basic pattern established early in life. When a young person reaches adulthood, much of the foundation for political life, such as affect, cognition and participation, is already in place. In his study of the United States, Uslaner points to early socialisation and education as the most important determinants of interpersonal trust: the higher the level of education you have, the more trustful you are.[26]

Whereas theories of social capital have ignored studies on the early formation of values, civic education has enjoyed a renewed interest among scientists during recent years. There is strong disagreement within the literature on the effects of civic education, however, especially regarding what particular aspects of it have an impact: is it the cognitive element or perhaps factors related to the 'hidden curriculum' (e.g. classroom climate, school climate/culture or active involvement in community projects) that matter? There has also been a change in the aims of civic education over time. Whereas, in general, civic education in the past aimed to increase students' knowledge of politics and national history, today 'civic education has turned into a more hands-on experience where the emphasis is on learning civic skills and various forms of engagement'.[27] Despite this increased interest in civic education, its impact on generalised trust has not yet been studied; the focus has rather been on the impact of school policy on political knowledge, values of good citizenship or 'vertical trust' (trust in the political system and institutions – see Chapter 2), or future political behaviour.[28]

There seems to be an important bridge to build between the two discourses. While research on social capital has acknowledged the importance of education on generalised trust, specific school factors have not yet been studied in this regard. On the other hand, research on civic education has not yet studied its possible effects on generalised trust, but rather has focused on its impact on political knowledge.

This study

This book focuses on a top-down action to change a predominating political culture of distrust, that is, by civic education at a grass-roots level. The book analyses political efforts to change young citizens' attitudes and values in some of Palermo's most deprived and Mafia-dominated areas. Is it possible to generate generalised trust through school?

It is important here to define 'generalised trust' more precisely. While Putnam's initial definition of social capital was broad and included networks, norms and trust, the concept has evolved and more precise definitions have been introduced. A common distinction is often made between structural social capital and attitudinal social capital. Whereas structural social capital is related to networks, for example membership of associations, attitudinal social capital refers to attitudes about trust and reciprocity. This book will focus on attitudinal social capital, here defined as attitudes of generalised trust.

It has become increasingly clear that not all forms of trust are beneficial for democracy. Trust between members of a Mafia group or even of motorcycle clubs like the Hells Angels or the Bandidos differs from trust between members of a voluntary organisation. In the case of the former, trust and loyalty extend only to fellow members of the particular grouping, and distrust and hostility mark their relations with non-members. A distinction between 'bridging social capital' and 'bonding social capital' is commonly made in the literature. Bridging social capital is the broader concept, and encompasses people across diverse social cleavages, whereas bonding social capital is more restrictive and tends to reinforce exclusive identities within homogeneous groups and to exclude people from other groups.[29] Bonding trust is particularised, and encompasses only a limited group of people, who are personally known to one another. Bridging trust is similar to generalised trust; it is broader and encompasses people who are not personally known to one another. A person with generalised trust believes that most other people can be trusted, whereas a person with particularised trust trusts only a limited number of people who are personally known to him or her. The trust we are interested in here is generalised trust, which includes people who are not personally known.

The book describes a project that involved the collection of both quantitative and qualitative data in Palermo between 2000 and 2005. Both descriptive statistics and multivariate regression analyses are reported. Pupils' attitudes to public institutions and their perceptions of other people are described in order to provide a general overview of 'the landscape'. The quantitative analysis is combined with a qualitative study based on some 200 letters from students in four classes. The so-called 'Letter Project' started as an experimental study but turned out extremely well. The students enjoyed writing the letters, and the content gave vivid insights into the challenges they faced in their daily lives. Not least, the letters gave important qualitative information on how these young citizens reasoned about trust. Four classes were invited to participate in the Letter Project: two from schools in poor socio-economic areas; one class from a mixed area; and one class from a school in one of Palermo's most well-to-do neighbourhoods. The classes that participated in the Letter Project were also part of the two questionnaire surveys reported here.

The main research question of this book – *is it possible to support the development of generalised trust through civic education?* – was addressed through a panel study of the anti-Mafia programme (or legality programme) in seven public schools at lower secondary level in Palermo, Sicily. Two surveys were distributed to the students, in 2002, during their first semester at lower secondary school, and in 2005, during their last semester of compulsory schooling. The questionnaires were thus distributed to the same classes and students on two different occasions. At these seven schools, almost 400 students initially participated in the study. Four of the schools were situated in some of Palermo's most deprived areas. The selected areas shared several characteristics: a high density of criminality or dominance by the Mafia; a low social and economic level of development; the weak presence of government agencies or other associations; and relative isolation from Palermo (as described in Chapter 3, even though one of the areas was in the city centre, there was little connection with the city *per se*, and little movement between areas). Two schools situated in areas with more mixed profiles (i.e. comprising middle-income as well as low-income households) and one school in a high-income district were included to enable comparisons to be made between different socio-economic settings.

The focus of the book is on institutional explanations for the development of generalised trust, and in particular on variables at the school and classroom levels. In the literature on civic education, factors such as openness of the school structure and the classroom climate have been identified as important explanatory variables. Does it matter for the development of generalised trust whether the school structures are perceived as open or not? The importance of the implicit or hidden curriculum is another factor that is widely recognised in the literature on civic education. Several studies highlight the impact of classroom climate and the impact of interaction patterns between students and their teachers on students' values. Does the interaction pattern between students and their teachers affect students' development of generalised trust? We have also borrowed and adapted explanations from the literature on social capital theory. One of these factors is the fairness of institutions. Does it matter if school is perceived as just and fair by students? Emotional engagement, flexibility and adaptation to the situation (what has been called 'the logic of care' – see Chapter 8) are other factors that may have an impact on generalised trust. If the school environment is caring, does that have any effect on generalised trust? The nature of social interaction between students at school is another factor that may contribute to the development of less selfish and more socially engaged attitudes and values. Does it matter if peer interaction is marked by violent attitudes or not?

In our analysis, we will also include other school factors that may have an effect on students' generalised trust, for example school activities, excursions and extracurricular activities. We will also study the impact of several variables that relate to students' families. In the literature it is argued, for example, that children who are provided with a trusting parental environment and who are socialised in an open, self-respecting and tolerant atmosphere are more likely to be trusting. Examples of family-related variables are the parents' educational level, the families' socio-cultural level, the parents' involvement in schoolwork and the families' interaction with neighbours. Various individual features of the student will also be included in the analysis. To what extent do personal factors such as commitment to schoolwork, ambition within school and political interest influence students' values of generalised trust? Do media habits influence generalised trust? Are students who engage in organisations more trustful than other students? Another factor that might have an impact on generalised trust is gender; that is, are girls or boys more trustful or more inclined to change?

The plan of the book

Chapter 2 starts with a discussion of the different definitions of trust (bridging versus bonding trust, generalised versus particularised trust, moralistic versus strategic trust, vertical trust). This is followed by a presentation of theories from two different discourses: the literature on social capital and that on civic education. What are the sources of generalised trust? The chapter discusses major explanations of the origins of generalised trust, as these relate to organisations, family, the economy and institutions. The literature on civic education is also reviewed. Factors in the school environment that may influence students' values are discussed, such as the formal curriculum, the school and classroom climate, and teachers' experience, educational background or personal values.

Chapter 3 discusses the research design and the methods used to select areas, schools and classes. Which areas, schools and types of classes participated in this study? The chapter also discusses the composition of the questionnaire, drop-out rates (internal and external), how trust was measured, the questions' validity and reliability, and practicalities related to the organisation and distribution of the questionnaire (see also Appendix).

In Chapter 4, different aspects of the Mafia are discussed. The first part consists of a description of the organisation in itself, as an institution parallel to and independent of the state. The focus is on the Sicilian Cosa Nostra, although we will make some comparisons with other Italian Mafia groupings. The second part consists of an analysis of the Mafia's relation to the state. It is argued that the relation between the Mafia and the state should be understood as an exchange relation, although some sectors are more penetrated by Mafia interests than others. We will thereafter turn to a discussion of the Mafia's territorial control and the weakness of the state. In the Italian case, the Mafia's power is closely related to its control over a specific territory, including control over the citizens who are living in that area. In the fifth section, the Mafia's mental control will be discussed. Whereas parts of the literature have emphasised cultural explanations of the Mafia's power, it is here argued that the Mafia has actively used some Sicilian values as a means to render its activities more legitimate. The sway of the Mafia is not only a consequence of distrust: it is also a promoter of distrust.

Chapter 5 describes the anti-Mafia policy of Mayor Leoluca Orlando, particularly the school policy. What were the most important aspects of Orlando's cultural warfare against the Mafia? What were its objectives? Which were the strategies chosen? To what extent may the programme be described as a success or a failure? The chapter starts with a brief outline of the anti-Mafia movement. It continues with a description of civic education in Italy and the school policy in Palermo that sought to break the Mafia's territorial and mental control.

Chapter 6 presents descriptive statistics on students' trust in public institutions. Distrust of government institutions is frequently mentioned in literature pertaining to the Mafia, and is often referred to in literature on southern Italy in general. In this chapter we will present descriptive statistics that focus on students' attitudes to the state and its agencies, that is, their vertical trust. To what extent do students trust political institutions, for example the president, the mayor of Palermo, the political parties? What is their degree of trust in the police and the courts? Do they trust school? The statistics are based on the total samples of the two school surveys, distributed in October–November 2002 and February–March 2005. We will also present descriptive statistics regarding students' attitudes to the police and the conception of *omertà*. Differences or similarities between different socio-economic areas will be highlighted. The results are related to the international and national studies done by the International Association for the Evaluation of Educational Achievement (IEA), which included samples of 90,000 students in 28 countries.

Chapter 7 offers a descriptive analysis of students' level of generalised or interpersonal trust. In the literature on Italy, southern Italians are often described as less trustful than people in other parts of Italy. The theme was presented by Banfield in the late 1950s, supported by Almond and Verba's comparison between five states, and later resumed in Putnam's study of Italy.[30] This chapter aims to give a description of students' trust in others. As in the previous chapter, the statistics are based on the two questionnaires, distributed in 2002 and 2005. Statistics will be presented for total samples and by socio-economic area. We will use different types of questions in order to analyse students' perceptions of other people. We will use two standard questions on trust that are frequently employed in international and national surveys and that are closely related: 'Generally speaking, do you believe that most people can be trusted or that nobody can be trusted?', and 'Do you believe that most people try to help each other or that people generally only think about themselves?' We will thereafter analyse students' trust in different specific categories of citizens. How much trust do students have in family (*familiari*), relatives (*parenti*) and neighbours?[31] How much trust do they have in their classmates, teachers, school principals and school staff? Furthermore, what is their degree of trust in Palermitans, Sicilians, Italians or foreigners?

Chapter 8 is co-authored with Hanna Bäck and Magdalena Inkinen.[32] In this chapter we will turn to our panel data and multivariate regression analysis in order to explore possible change between the two surveys. The analysis will be based on an index of trust that measures students' trust in persons who are not personally known to them. We focus on variables at the school level and the classroom level, for example openness of school structures, fairness of institutions, caring school environment, peer interaction, openness of classroom climate and aspects of the school programme. Is it possible to see whether any of these institutional school variables have an impact on students' generalised trust?

Chapter 9 presents the Letter Project, which adds qualitative information to the study. Students in four selected classes were invited to write private letters on different themes during their three years at lower secondary school. A total of 222 letters were received, on four themes: 'A normal day in my life', 'My district', 'Relations with other people' and 'Reflections on important events at school'. The analysis of students' letters will be organised according to different themes. The first consists of students' description of school life, including their perception of school, interaction with teachers, social interaction with peers and experiences of school excursions. The chapter also includes students' narratives about trust in other persons and their descriptions of the residents and the area where they live. How do these young people reason about trust? Do they believe that people in general can be trusted, or are they cautious when dealing with other people? What motivates their perceptions on trust?

The concluding chapter contains a summary of the most important empirical, theoretic and methodological findings to be drawn from this study and points at areas for future research. We will not reveal these here.

Notes

1 F. Fukuyama, *Trust: The Social Virtues and the Creation of Prosperity* (London: Hamish Hamilton, 1995), p. 11.

2 D. Stolle, 'The sources of social capital', in M. Hooghe and D. Stolle (eds), *Generating Social Capital: Civil Society and Institutions in Comparative Perspective* (New York: Palgrave Macmillan, 2003), p. 20.

3 Fukuyama, *Trust*.

4 R. Putnam, *Making Democracy Work: Civic Traditions in Modern Italy* (Princeton: Princeton University Press, 1993).

5 E. M. Uslaner, *The Moral Foundations of Trust* (Cambridge: Cambridge University Press, 2002), chapter 8.

6 Uslaner, *The Moral Foundations of Trust*, pp. 10–11.

7 Uslaner, *The Moral Foundations of Trust*, pp. 79–80.

8 W. Mishler and R. Rose, 'Trust, distrust and scepticism: popular evaluations of civil and political institutions in post-communist societies', *Journal of Politics*, 59:2 (1997), p. 419.

9 R. Inglehart, *Culture Shift in Advanced Industrial Society* (Princeton: Princeton University Press, 1990).

10 B. Rothstein, *Social Traps and the Problem of Trust* (Cambridge: Cambridge University Press, 2005).

11 Putnam, *Making Democracy Work*.

12 J. Chubb, *Patronage, Power and Poverty in Southern Italy: A Tale of Two Cities* (Cambridge: Cambridge University Press, 1982), pp. 28–9.

13 P. Ginsborg, *Italy and Its Discontents 1980–2001* (London: Allen Lane, Penguin, 2001), p. 22.

14 Putnam, *Making Democracy Work*, chapter 5.

15 Putnam, *Making Democracy Work*, p. 11.

16 G. Pasquino, 'The politics of civic tradition eclipsed', *APSA-CP* (newsletter of the American Political Science Association's Organized Section

in Comparative Politics), 6:2 (1995), pp. 8–9; S. Tarrow, 'Making social science work across space and time: a critical reflection on Robert Putnam's Making Democracy Work', *American Political Science Review*, 90:2 (1996), pp. 389–97; M. Huysseune, 'Institutions and their impact on social capital and civic culture: the case of Italy', in M. Hooghe and D. Stolle (eds), *Generating Social Capital: Civil Society and Institutions in Comparative Perspective* (New York: Palgrave Macmillan, 2003), pp. 211–30.

17 Pasquino, 'The politics of civic tradition eclipsed', pp. 8–9.

18 Huysseune, 'Institutions and their impact on social capital and civic culture', pp. 211–29.

19 R. Siebert, 'Mafia and anti-mafia: the implications for everyday life', in F. Allum and R. Siebert (eds), *Organized Crime and the Challenge to Democracy* (London: Routledge, 2003), pp. 39–54.

20 Siebert, 'Mafia and anti-mafia', p. 42.

21 Rothstein, *Social Traps and the Problem of Trust*.

22 L. Orlando, *The Mafia: 150 Years of Facts, Figures and Faces* (City of Palermo: Cliomedia Officina, CD-ROM).

23 'Double turns' involves the organisation of education as morning and afternoon/evening shifts. Because of a lack of school infrastructure (there are too few classrooms to accommodate the whole population of pupils) two sets of pupils attend school at different times. It is widely believed that this has a detrimental effect on school attendance rates, especially for those pupils allocated to afternoon/evening attendance.

24 S. Rokkan, *State Formation, Nationbuilding, and Mass Politics in Europe: The Theory of Stein Rokkan* (Oxford: Oxford University Press, 1999); E. Weber, *Peasants into Frenchmen: The Modernization of Rural France, 1870–1914* (Stanford: Stanford University Press, 1976).

25 Of the young people who participated in the Niemi–Jennings socialisation study in 1965, 64 per cent had the same level of trust in 1982 as in 1965. See Uslaner, *The Moral Foundations of Trust*, pp. 162–5.

26 Uslaner, *The Moral Foundations of Trust*, pp. 90–1.

27 M. Hooghe and D. Kavadias, 'Determinants of future willingness to vote. A comparative analysis of 14 year olds in 28 countries', paper presented at the 3rd ECPR General Conference, Budapest, 8–10 September 2005, pp. 3–4.

28 Questions on interpersonal trust were, for example, not included in the international study by the International Association for the Evaluation of Educational Achievement (IEA) that was distributed in 1999 in 28 countries to 93,000 students. See for example R. G. Niemi and J. Junn, *Civic Education: What Makes Students Learn* (New Haven: Yale University Press, 1998); J. Torney-Purta, R. Lehmann, H. Oswald and W. Schultz (eds), *Citizenship and Education in Twenty-Eight Countries: Civic Knowledge and Engagement at Age Fourteen* (Berlin: International Association for the Evaluation of Educational Achievement, 2001); P. A. Beck and K. M. Jennings, 'Pathways to participation', *American Political Science Review*, 76:1 (1982), pp. 94–108.

29 R. Putnam, *Bowling Alone: The Collapse and Revival of American Community* (New York: Touchstone, 2000), pp. 22–3.

30 E. C. Banfield, *The Moral Basis of a Backward Society* (New York: Free Press, 1958); G. A. Almond and S. Verba, *The Civic Culture: Political*

Attitudes and Democracy in Five Nations (Boston: Little, Brown, 1963); Putnam, *Making Democracy Work.*

31 The terms *familiari* and *parenti* are not easily translated. *Familiari* refers to next of kin and the like (not necessarily restricted to blood relations), whereas *parenti* is a broader term.

32 Hanna Bäck is a postdoctoral fellow at the Department of Political Science and Research Methods at the University of Twente in the Netherlands. Her work deals with issues such as political participation, parties and government formation, democratic institutions and state administrative capacity. Magdalena Inkinen is currently working for the Swedish National Agency for Higher Education. Previously she was a researcher at the Department of Government at Uppsala University, with a special interest in education, gender equality and development in South Asia.

2

The origins of generalised trust

Researchers have identified several distinctions between various forms of social capital. While social capital has been defined in relation to norms, attitudes and patterns of interaction, inter-personal relationships are its central component. Hooghe and Stolle make a distinction between structural and attitudinal social capital: whereas structural social capital is related to networks, for example membership of associations, attitudinal social capital refers to attitudes to trust and reciprocity.[1]

Furthermore, different forms of structural social capital may have different effects on democracy. Not all organisations are promoters of democratic values and democracy. For instance, a group could develop very strong ties between its members, while denying membership to other citizens. The Hells Angels are frequently cited as an example of 'bad' social capital, where strong loyalties develop within the group but violence is used against competing groups as a way of maintaining the organis-ation's power. Another extreme example is the Mafia family, the *cosca*, where group members are bound together by a dense tissue of family, kinship and friendship ties. Ethnically or religi-ously defined clubs are other examples of organisations that might create distrust towards other citizens.

The distinction between bridging (inclusive) and bonding (exclusive) social capital is a basic one in the literature on social capital. While bridging social capital refers to a broader social capital that encompasses people across diverse social cleavages, bonding social capital is more restrictive and tends to reinforce exclusive identities within homogeneous groups and to exclude people from other groups.[2] Bonding trust is related to particularised trust, which encompasses trust in a more limited group of people who are personally known to one another. Bridging trust is similar to generalised trust; that is, it is broader and encompasses people who are not personally known to one another. People with generalised trust believe that most other people can be trusted, whereas people with particularised trust trust only a limited number of people who are personally known to them. Generalised trust extends beyond the boundaries of face-to-face interaction while particularised trust results from experiences of cooperation and repeated interaction with the immediate circle of cooperators, for example family members, community members, or fellow members of a voluntary association. Personalised trust is often described as 'thicker', and is based on personal relations 'that are strong, frequent and nested in wider networks'.[3] 'Thin' trust is broader and includes persons met through chance encounters – say in a public space, in a coffee shop or at the supermarket. Putnam argues that thin trust is more 'useful than thick trust, because it extends the radius of trust beyond the roster of people whom we can know personally'.[4]

While such distinctions focus on the nature and the possible effects of different kinds of social capital, Uslaner has suggested a distinction between strategic and moralistic trust; this distinction relates to the motives behind a person's trust in other people.[5] Strategic trust is determined by previous experience and relates to people we have already met (i.e. we know whether or not this person is trustworthy). Moralistic trust, in contrast, involves a moral commitment to treat people as if they were trustworthy, and is not based on direct experience. While strategic trusters cooperate only with people they already know, moralistic trusters are needed for civic engagement. Uslaner's distinction shares some similarities with bridging and bonding trust. Strategic trust is related to particularised trust, while moralistic trust is closer to the definition of generalised trust.

Another definition refers to vertical trust or political trust, that is, the trust citizens have in the political system and societal institutions. Several theorists suggest that vertical trust is multidimensional. Norris argues that political trust could, for example, refer to the political community, regime principles, regime performance, regime institutions or political actors.[6] Political trust could also vary considerably between different public institutions (courts, parliament, police, local government, schools, banks, army, etc.). Vertical trust may thus refer to the trust a citizen has in different dimensions of the political system and its institutions.

This book looks at attitudinal components of social capital, namely trust and norms of reciprocity. The kind of trust we are interested in here is specified to generalised trust, that is, trust between members of society. The terms 'interpersonal trust', 'generalised trust' and 'horizontal trust' are often used as synonyms to denote trust in people who are not known on a personal basis. Uslaner's distinction between moralistic or strategic trust is very interesting, although difficult to measure since it requires knowledge about a person's inner life and his or her individual reasons to trust others. It will be raised in Chapter 9, in relation to the Letter Project.

The blessings of generalised trust

The positive effects of generalised trust have been widely affirmed in the literature on social capital.[7] Horizontal trust correlates with several outcomes that are highly desirable for any society. High levels of trust are even associated with economic growth, since economic transactions are accomplished at lower cost in trusting environments. Individuals in trusting societies spend less time and resources on exploitative economic transactions such as paying bribes. A low-trust environment will discourage innovation if more time needs to be devoted to time-consuming struggles with partners, employees or suppliers than to modernisation and improved procedures.[8] A high level of trust also encourages income redistribution between rich and poor. Uslaner has shown that trust is important for donations or benevolence. As trust declines, so does people's willingness to make contributions to causes supporting other people.[9]

As argued by Putnam, trust makes democratic institutions work. Trust makes people more inclined to cooperate, which enables them to engage actively in associations and public life. In turn, through such engagement, members learn how to cooperate and to overcome dilemmas of collective action. Even if people pursue their self-interest, it is a self-interest that is open to the interests of others and that considers broader public needs.[10] Or, as Uslaner put it, 'Generalized trusters are connected not just to other people, but to their communities'.[11] Trust and 'civicness' make representative institutions strong, responsive and effective. Moreover, research has shown that the existence of generalised trust is connected to outcomes such as personal happiness and safer neighbourhoods.[12]

If generalised trust is highly desirable in society, then what do we know about its origins? We will start by discussing institutional explanations for the development of trust. The focus will be on top-down explanations, since a top-down intervention forms the core of this study. We will thereafter move on to discuss the importance specifically of classes in civic education and other school factors in the creation of generalised trust. This is followed by an examination of a variety of other factors potentially related to generalised trust – competing explanations – including participation in voluntary associations, educational level, family environment, neighbourhood environment, economic disadvantage, personal factors and gender.

What are the origins of generalised trust?

Even though it is generally acknowledged among theoreticians of social capital that interpersonal trust and vertical trust are two different concepts, significant discussion remains as to how they are related to each other. Generalised trust is viewed either as a cause of vertical trust or as an effect of vertical trust. Putnam argues for a bottom-up process where vertical trust flows from people's horizontal trust in each other. The causal mechanism is that people's engagement in voluntary associations teaches them how to cooperate and trust other people, which eventually leads to increased vertical trust in the government.[13]

In contrast, Braithwaite argues that the two concepts are mutually reinforcing, but that the causal direction is top down rather than bottom up: strong institutions breed trust, whereas weak institutions breed distrust.[14] Eek and Rothstein similarly argue that horizontal trust is caused by vertical trust:

> The logic is that when people lose their trust in a person representing an important institution (i.e., an authority), they reason that if the authority is a 'bad' (e.g. immoral, unfair, untrustworthy) person,

> than [*sic*] other people might just as well be equally 'bad' ... if an
> authority does not obey the law, why should anyone else bother?...
> it is not equally logical that it should work the other way around
> ... if someone else on the street is a 'bad' person, it does not
> necessarily suggest anything about authorities.[15]

In their experimental study, participants were presented different scenarios to describe encounters between other people and authorities. They were then asked to indicate whether or not their vertical and horizontal trust had been influenced by what they imagined they had observed. The participants found that 'when an authority ... accepted a bribe in order to provide help to another person, it had damaging effects on people's vertical and horizontal trust'.[16] On the other hand, they also found that when the authority refused to accept a bribe, it had positive effects on vertical trust, but participants also said that trust in the authority spread to other people who were not present in the scenario.

As stated in Chapter 1, this book will analyse institutional explanations for the development of trust. We will, therefore, develop in the next section the argument about which institutional factors might matter.

Institutional explanations

The degree of repression in society is a factor that has a strong influence on social capital and trust. Authoritarian governments in particular build their strength by planting distrust between citizens and by undermining their civic engagement. People become isolated and mistrustful and consequently unable to engage in organised activities.[17] Studies of generalised trust in Czechoslovakia and post-war Germany, for example, have suggested that the credibility of government can influence interpersonal trust. While trust was lost in Czechoslovakia after the Communist take-over in 1948, the opposite pattern was found in post-war Germany. In West Germany, starting from a very low level of trust in 1948 (when only 9 per cent said they could trust most people), trust continuously increased thereafter, reaching 39 per cent in the mid-1970s.[18]

Levi has pointed at several ways in which the state can create interpersonal trust, for example by punishing law-breakers and providing information and guarantees to its citizens: 'If citizens doubt the state's commitment to enforce the laws and if its information and guarantees are not credible, then the state's capacity to generate interpersonal trust will diminish'.[19] Government institutions can also build trust by the establishment and respect of bureaucratic arrangements that reward competence and honesty on the part of civil servants. Fair procedures such as sanctions for law-breakers, universalistic welfare policies, credible courts and the involvement of citizens in policy-making are other important factors; another is the behaviour of the political opposition, which can feed distrust or trust among citizens. Moreover, citizens should be treated with respect; politicians should stick to their commitments. Neighbourhoods that are badly treated or neglected by government officials may develop feelings of resentment and distrust towards all agents of government.[20]

Democracies usually score higher on measures of generalised trust, but there are significant differences between democracies in their ability to generate civic capacity.[21] Tarrow focuses on aspects of governance as an explanation for regional differences in the Italian case. He describes a system where prefects bought elections for the government's candidates in the south after the unification of Italy in 1860, and 'they often arrested unfriendly candidates and closed down local governments which displeased them'.[22] The interaction of the national government with the local elite differed between northern and southern Italy. It co-opted the local elite into patron–client relations in the south and interfered in other ways, unlike in the north. Tarrow consequently argues that the difference between northern and southern Italy was 'a public culture shaped by more than a century of political and administrative dependency'.[23]

Tyler discusses the importance of procedural justice for the legitimacy of legal authorities. Most people have two separate ideas of what justice is: one concerns the outcome or substance (what you get); the other concerns the process (how you are treated). The majority think that it is important that the system complies with both. Procedural justice demands that government officials are perceived as unbiased and that they treat people with respect. An unfavourable outcome can be accepted as long as people think that the process that led to it was fair. The way people are treated by legal and political authorities also has implications for their group identity and self-esteem.

'People are unlikely to feel attached to groups led by authorities who treat them rudely or ignore their rights.'[24] Departing from Tyler's argument, Stolle argues that citizens who feel they are taken seriously by politicians – if they are listened to and respected – develop a belief in people in general. If politicians are perceived to act fairly, honestly and responsively, citizens will feel more secure and consequently will be encouraged to trust their fellow citizens.[25] Personal experiences of impartial, just and fair social and political institutions are thus important for the development of generalised trust in society. The character of service delivery and the impartiality of the street-level bureaucrats, as well as perceived possibilities to cheat the system, lead to differences in institutional trust, which in turn influence generalised trust. Citizens who experience unfairness, dishonesty, unresponsiveness, lack of respect and corruption in their contacts with public institutions transfer these experiences and views to people in general. Trust and reciprocity are therefore dependent on the character of political institutions.[26]

Emotional engagement, flexibility and adaptation to the situation are other factors that may affect generalised trust. After the tsunami catastrophe in South East Asia in December 2004, when 600 Swedish tourists lost their lives, many were upset by the lack of empathy not only shown by the minister for foreign affairs but also as manifested by civil servants working on the ground.[27] Many victims were confronted by rule-abiding civil servants who stuck to the protocol instead of adapting to the catastrophic situation by relaxing formal procedures. Of course, the Ministry was not ready to handle a crisis of this dimension and some people may have had too high expectations of what the Swedish state could actually do. Nevertheless, many accounts and testimonies revealed that inflexibility and a lack of emotional engagement had marked the civil servants in charge. One of the victims said in an interview one year after the tsunami:

> The personnel at the Ministry for Foreign Affairs were fettered by a formal system of responsibility and were scared to death: they didn't dare do anything on their own. They belittled themselves, ceased to be fellow human beings.[28]

Stenesöta argues that we expect people working in the public service sector, for example medical professionals, social workers and teachers, to be not only fair or impartial, but also to be engaged and to show compassion. 'The logic of care' adds an important value to discussions about the fairness of institutions, since it emphasises the emotional value of caring and adapting to circumstances. 'The caring state' complements the idea of the rule-abiding bureaucracy. 'The logic of care' is relevant in situations where there is a physical encounter between civil servants and citizens and where there are some margins of manoeuvre for civil servants to make their own judgements and decisions. The situation should also be characterised as a dynamic process rather than a static situation.[29] The logic of care does not imply that care is necessarily fairly distributed to anyone; it means, rather, that it is delivered to those who are needy in a particular situation. In an emergency, we would expect doctors first to help those who are seriously injured, instead of paying equal attention to all.

We will now turn to the literature on civic education in order to identify possible school factors that may have an impact on generalised trust. Although the literature on civic education has not particularly discussed the impact of education on generalised trust, we will see some similarities with the literature on social capital.

School factors

The effect of civic education on students' political knowledge and attitudes is a widely discussed topic in the literature. A popular belief in earlier research was that civic classes had little or no effect at all on students' political knowledge or political attitudes. For example, studies from the mid-1960s showed that high-school classes in American government and civics had little or no effect on students' political knowledge.[30] Niemi and Junn went beyond the formal curriculum in their study from 1998 and saw that participation in civics courses, the timing of the courses, the number of topics and the discussion of political events did have significant effects on political knowledge. Small-scale studies with an experimental design have shown that civic education may increase students' knowledge.[31] Furthermore, participation in extracurricular activities has sometimes been understood as a contributor to participatory attitudes and to actual participation.[32]

The arguments about universal government welfare policies and procedural justice are easily translated to a school-related context with the help of the literature on civic education. In an early study, Oppenheim argued that more important than what individual teachers do to change students' attitudes is the climate that characterises school as a whole: its organisational structure, patterns of hierarchy and participation, and type of discipline. Pupils at schools where drill and rote learning of factual material were emphasised had lower scores on knowledge-based tests and expressed less support for democratic values: 'The students take their cues not from what the teachers say, but from what the teacher does, how he behaves, and what his own attitudes appear to be'.[33] White similarly points at the importance of trust in school, arguing that one of the primary tasks of school is to *show* trust. Negative signals such as distrust of students, or different categories of students, should be avoided even if there is reason to distrust some individual students. Although control systems are necessary in all schools, there is always a risk these will be perceived negatively by students.[34]

The implicit or hidden curriculum is widely recognised as an important factor in the literature on civic education. Bricker studied how citizenship was taught to students in American schools by analysing the so-called 'hidden curriculum' of the classroom. Bricker focused on how liberal values were implicitly transmitted to students, for example by stimulating students to work individually and by encouraging their individual achievements.[35] The first study by the IEA found that students participating in classroom discussions had higher scores on anti-authoritarian measures and knowledge tests than students who were only memorising dates or facts about politics. Analyses by Torney-Purta *et al.* support the claim that classroom climate has an effect on students' values: 'Nearly every discussion of education for democracy begins with a statement that one must "practice what one preaches" and in particular create a democratic school culture.'[36]

Social interaction in general, particularly outside the narrow family circle, is another factor that may contribute to the development of less selfish and more socially engaged attitudes and values. Various types of informal interaction between friends and peer groups may also have an impact on students' degrees of trust. School may be understood here as a social arena constructed by teachers and students, where informal peer interaction between students needs to be considered.

We will now turn to discussion of other explanations for the development of generalised trust. These variables will later serve as control variables in the analysis in Chapter 8.

Competing explanations

Participation in voluntary associations

Putnam argues that trust in society is the consequence of citizens' engagement in different kinds of associations and organisations. Participation in organisations breeds trust between citizens, develops their cooperative skills and lends citizens a public spirit that goes beyond their immediate self-interests, which is all favourable to democracy. To quote Putnam:

> Participation in civic organizations inculcates skills of cooperation as well as a sense of shared responsibility for collective endeavours. Moreover, when individuals belong to 'cross-cutting' groups with diverse goals and members, their attitudes will tend to moderate as a result of group interaction and cross-pressures.[37]

Putnam's argument is that the lack of trust and mutual confidence in southern Italy explains why the democratic institutions there are less efficient and why economic development in the region is low. While northern Italy developed horizontal networks, relations in southern Italy remained vertical and were marked by distrust. However, later research has produced only weak empirical evidence to support the causal mechanism between organisational engagement and generalised trust. Stolle's studies of Sweden, Germany and the United States showed that trusting people were self-selected as members of voluntary associations in a disproportionate way. She also found that the effects of this self-selection on generalised trust were more important than the membership effects.[38] In fact, a causal mechanism linking membership of organisations to civic engagement is missing in Putnam's analysis. How was trust originally created in the north? Which factors associated with membership of associations made citizens become civic? According to Tarrow, the mere presence of associations does not explain the development of civicness, but their internal dynamic must also be considered.

The *explanandum* is missing in Putnam's analysis. Although the early Italian city states had associations, nothing says that they were civic or horizontal in character. 'After a short period as voluntary associations, most of them produced closed urban oligarchies, fought constantly over territory and markets and left the urban poor vertically compromised.'[39]

Despite the weakness in Putnam's explanatory model, we would still like to include students' participation in organisations as a control variable. Do students' activities have any effect on their generalised trust? Does it matter whether students attend music or dancing lessons, play sports like football or volleyball, or engage in social activities like the Scouts, church groups or any other kind of social groups outside school? Do they become more trustful of other citizens if they join these groups?

Educational level

Education is believed to widen people's horizons and make them more accepting of other people. Both Putnam and Uslaner have pointed to the importance of education for the development of generalised trust. Putnam's findings suggest that education is the most powerful predictor of trust, membership of organisations and other forms of social and political participation. Education is a far better predictor than income and social status of civic engagement and it is more likely that highly educated people are joiners and trusters. The relationship between education and trust is curvilinear: the last two years of college education has twice as much effect on trust and membership of associations than the two first years of high school. The four years of education between 14 and 18 'have *ten times more impact* on trust and membership than the first four years of formal education'.[40] In our case, students had the same educational level. But we would still like to analyse whether their parents' educational level matters for students' development of generalised trust. Are high levels of generalised trust related to parents' higher educational level?

Families' socio-cultural level

Another possible source of trust is the family. Children with a trusting parental environment and who are socialised in an open, self-respecting and tolerant atmosphere are more likely to be trusting. Misztal, among others, has discussed the role of the family in the development of trustworthy personalities. Early childhood experience of trust leads to the formation of an inner sense of trustworthiness, she argues, that eventually provides the ground for a stable self-identity. Trust is normally something already developed as early as infancy and is not easily lost thereafter. Early trust is a by-product of the family's activities and its values. Infant trust is rewarded and stimulated by the experience of trustworthiness in the family and it 'encourages the development of a more optimistic trusting approach to the world and others'.[41] Uslaner also argues that a person's trust in others is largely dependent on the level of trust exhibited by parents and a nurturing home environment. Attitudes of particularised trust are established early in life and shape generalised trust.[42]

Family values are therefore factors that are highly relevant to the analysis, even if they are difficult to study. In this study we will not be able to analyse whether the students' home environment is marked by a caring and trustful climate. Instead we will use a variable that is often used in the civic education literature as an indicator for the family's socio-cultural level, that is, the number of books at home.

Neighbourhood environment

Strömblad has analysed the impact of environmental factors on political engagement in poor residential areas in Sweden. Strömblad argues that factors such as resources and motivation may depend on social context. Informal contacts between neighbours can be viewed as a resource, for example, in that it may provide a person with knowledge that would not otherwise have been available. Therefore, the social composition of an area may also affect an individual's political engagement.[43]

Related to the discussion about socio-economic differences is the discourse on contextual factors that may have an impact on citizens' values. Uslaner has pointed at the importance of environment on trust:

> Just as having to cope with daily struggles in Banfield's Montegrano or today's Bosnia or Albania can destroy optimism and trust, so living in a more friendly environment can build optimism and trust.... If most people who live around you trust others, you are likely to be trusting, as well.[44]

We would like to analyse the implications of neighbourhood environment on students' level of generalised trust. Does it matter what kinds of interaction students' families have with their neighbourhood? Do students who come from families who are engaged in friendly interactions with neighbours express a higher degree of generalised trust? Does it matter for trust whether students' families help or receive help from their neighbours, or if they visit each other or discuss matters of concern?

Economic disadvantage

Another explanation points at structural and economic disadvantage as a predictor of trust. The existence of social capital is here believed to be tied to economic success. It is argued that differences in social capital are indeed mainly caused by structural and economic differences. Regions that lack social capital will also have fewer natural resources, or they may have other disadvantageous structural conditions that hinder both economic development and the development of generalised trust.[45]

Income inequality is another factor that may have an impact on trust. Boix and Posner, focusing on the problem of collective action, argue that a lack of cooperation is more evident in societies marked by social and political inequality, since there will always be incentives for the poor to defect from cooperative arrangements that maintain the status quo. Moreover, in an unequal society, the richer parties will endeavour to undermine any political efforts by the poor that aim to change the system. One reason why cooperation was easier to establish in the north of Italy was that society was more equal, whereas inequality ruled in the south. The feudal lords in southern Italy crushed any cooperative initiatives that threatened their political and economic status.[46] Uslaner's analysis of the United States shows that the degree of trust fluctuates over time and that there is a strong correlation between trust and variations in income equality. When inequality increases, trust goes down. When inequality decreases, trust goes up.[47]

Resource scarcity and income inequality may, of course, be explanations for the lack of trust at the national, regional and local levels. As already described in Chapter 1, southern Italy is poorer than the northern part of the country. Income inequalities within Palermo remain important, too. In some areas of central Palermo, particularly in the old town, *centro storico*, refuse collection is sporadic or non-existent, and some houses still are abandoned or in ruins as a result of the bombings at the end of the Second World War, more than 60 years ago. Unemployment varies between 19 per cent in one of Palermo's richest areas (Libertà) and more than 50 per cent in some of the poorest. According to the census in 1991, 43 per cent of the youth in the poor area of Borgo Nuovo were unemployed, compared with 23 per cent in Libertà.[48] Although the renovation of many buildings in Palermo's old town has increased considerably in recent years, differences between the areas remain.

Although we will not use income inequality at the explanatory level, we will highlight differences in levels of trust between low-ranked and high-ranked areas in Palermo in the descriptive parts of this study (Chapters 6 and 7). Are citizens in low socio-economic areas less trustful than those in higher-ranked areas?

Students' personal ambitions and interest in society

We will study to what extent personal factors such as commitment to schoolwork, ambition within school and political interest influence students' values of interpersonal trust. Another factor that may have an effect on students' trust is their media habits and their interest in society. Putnam has evidence to suggest that newspaper reading is associated with high social capital, whereas television viewing correlates with low social capital. The relation holds even after controlling for education, income, age, race, work status, gender and place of residence. 'Pure readers' are 55 per cent more trusting than 'pure viewers'. Every hour spent watching television is related to less social trust and less membership of associations.[49] Of course, television is an important aspect in youngsters' lives, even if its effects on their values and behaviour remains controversial. In this study, we will focus on media habits that manifest an interest in society. Are students who follow the news on the radio or on television or in the newspapers more trustful than other students?

Gender

Studies of gender differences and trust are rare in the literature on social capital. The discussion appears to have focused more on differences between various kinds of organisations rather than gender differences regarding levels of trust. It has been shown that women tend to engage in peripheral organisations that are smaller and focused on domestic and community affairs, while men engage in core organisations which are large and related to economic institutions.[50] There are also important differences between men and women in terms of their voluntary engagement: while men engage in voluntary work related to sports and recreation, women engage in the fields of health, education and social services. As women's organisations tend to be more private in character (they often involve picking up children from school, organising baby sitting or taking part in child-care circles), they do not always qualify as formal associations and are therefore often neglected in studies on social capital.[51] Economists analysing gender differences in game theory have found that men exhibit more trust than women, while women show higher levels of reciprocity.[52]

Considering the local context in Palermo, it is interesting to include gender in the analysis. The Mafia culture strongly values attitudes supportive of the idea of a strong man, while females have a more marginal role. A local study done by a lower secondary school close to Palermo found important differences between students' perceptions of masculinity and femininity. According to that survey, successful men were expected to be 'decisive', 'secure' and 'strong', while the values attributed to a successful woman included 'sweet', 'elegant', 'beautiful' and 'pleasant'.[53] The practical experience of social workers in the poor urban areas of Albergheria and Brancaccio in Palermo suggests that women are more active and more open to change than men; women visit the centres and participate in social services' activities. Other explanations for the absence of men have been suggested by social workers. The men may be busy with work, or trying to find work. Another reason why women attend the different activities organised at the social centres may be that women have access to fewer meeting places than men, who could easily meet in any bar in the neighbourhood. Social workers also suggest that it may be more difficult to work with men's values, since they are less motivated than women to change a system that is convenient to them.[54]

The present research project will test for any observable gender differences in attitudes towards trust. Of interest is the investigation of previous research theses which have contended that girls are more likely to change their level of generalised trust than are boys.

Conclusion

In this chapter I have discussed different dimensions of social capital. In *Making Democracy Work*, Putnam defined social capital as norms, attitudes and interaction patterns. Hooghe and Stolle have suggested a distinction between structural and attitudinal social capital. This book focuses on attitudinal social capital, and specifically generalised trust. Several types of trust were discussed in the chapter (particularised trust versus generalised trust, bridging trust versus bonding trust, vertical trust and horizontal trust, strategic trust and moralistic trust) and it was specified that this study will analyse the development of generalised trust, that is, trust in persons who are not personally known.

There is disagreement about the causal direction between vertical and generalised trust, that is, whether generalised trust is a cause or an effect of vertical trust. In spite of this disagreement, the positive effects of generalised trust are generally acknowledged in the literature. High levels of trust are positively correlated with economic growth, democracy, personal happiness and security. Generalised trust is positive not only for the individual but also for society as a whole.

Our major research interest is to see whether institutions matter for the development of generalised trust. Is it possible to stimulate the development of generalised trust through civic education? From the institutionalist literature, we identified several important variables, which were further developed with the help of the literature on civic education. Previous research in civic education has pointed at different aspects of school that may have an impact on students' political knowledge and awareness, for example school programmes, classroom climate, school climate, formal activities at school, extracurricular activities, involvement in community projects, interaction between students, the school's interaction with parents, leadership, teachers' skills and education, and so on.

In our study we particularly focus on variables at the school and classroom level. *Openness of school structures* was measured by asking students whether they considered it easy or not to confide their problems to school staff (school principal, teachers or school psychologist).

Rothstein and Stolle highlighted the importance of impartial, just and fair social and political institutions for the development of generalised trust. *Fairness of institutions* was measured here by asking students whether they estimated their teachers to be 'fair', whether teachers were 'only interested in the best and most intelligent students', or whether they felt they were 'badly treated by teachers'.

Emotional engagement, flexibility and adaptation to the situation are other factors that may have an impact on generalised trust. Following Stenesöta's argument, we expect public sector workers such as teachers to be not only fair and impartial but also to be engaged and to show compassion. *Caring school environment* is here measured by using two indicators: 'Teachers pay attention to my situation' and 'Teachers make me feel at ease'.

The importance of the implicit or hidden curriculum is another factor that is widely recognised in the literature on civic education. Several studies, for example that by Torney-Purta, highlight the effects of classroom climate and the patterns of interaction between students and their teachers on students' values. *Openness of classroom climate* was measured using questions that had previously been used in the IEA international study.[55] The questions asked: to what extent teachers encouraged students to express their opinions; to what extent students felt encouraged to develop personal ideas and opinions on various topics; whether they felt free to openly express their thoughts in class; and whether they felt free to propose discussions on current problems.

The effect of civic education on students' political knowledge and attitudes has been a widely discussed topic in the literature on civic education. In our analysis, we will include students' participation in a variety of activities organised by school. The nature of social interactions between students is another factor that may contribute to the development of less selfish and more socially engaged attitudes and values. The impact of *peer interaction* was measured by asking students about their school environment: was swearing frequent among students, were there often quarrels between students, or did they feel badly treated by other students?

Drawing inspiration from the literature on social capital, we also added several variables that related to students' families and the students themselves. These will eventually be used as control variables in the regression analysis in Chapter 8. The *family-related variables* that will be included in the analysis are the parents' educational level (ranging from elementary school to university education), the families' socio-cultural level (measured as number of books at home), the parents' involvement in school work (participation in meetings at school and engagement in homework), and the families' interaction with neighbours (with what frequency do neighbours help, visit or talk with each other?). Various *individual features* of the students will also be included in the analysis. Does it matter whether the students are members of organisations? Does personal ambition in school, measured as the students' degree of interest in their studies, matter for the development of generalised trust? Is generalised trust affected by the students' interest in society, as indicated by their media habits (reading news articles, watching news on television, listening to news on the radio)? Gender will also be included as a control variable. Are girls or boys more trustful, or more inclined to change?

Another explanation that was discussed in this chapter was the impact of economic disadvantage on trust. According to this theory, the existence of social capital is believed to be positively correlated with economic success. Regions that lack social capital also have fewer natural resources, or they may have other disadvantageous structural conditions that hinder economic development or the development of generalised trust. Although we will not use income inequality at the explanatory level, we will endeavour to highlight possible differences in levels of trust between low-ranked and high-ranked areas in Palermo in the descriptive chapters of this study. Are students from low socio-economic areas less trustful than the more privileged students in the intermediate and high-ranked areas?

Notes

1 M. Hooghe and D. Stolle, 'Introduction: generating social capital', in M. Hooghe and D. Stolle (eds), *Generating Social Capital: Civil Society and Institutions in Comparative Perspective* (New York: Palgrave Macmillan, 2003), p. 2.

2 Putnam, *Bowling Alone*, pp. 22–3.

3 Putnam, *Bowling Alone*, p. 136.

4 Putnam, *Bowling Alone*, p. 136.

5 Uslaner, *The Moral Foundations of Trust*, ch. 2.

6 P. Norris (ed.), *Critical Citizens: Global Support for Democratic Government* (Oxford: Oxford University Press, 1999), pp. 9–12.

7 According to Widmalm's study of social capital in India, however, high levels of bonding trust likewise facilitate political cooperation and protect citizens from employers who try to 'exploit citizens in a corrupt or clientelistic manner'. S. Widmalm, 'The utility of bonding social capital', *Journal of Civil Society*, 1:1 (2005), p. 75–95.

8 S. Knack and P. Keefer, 'Does social capital have an economic payoff? A cross-country investigation', *Quarterly Journal of Economics*, 112:4 (1997), pp. 1252–3.

9 Uslaner, *The Moral Foundations of Trust*, p. 206.

10 Putnam, *Making Democracy Work*, p. 88.

11 Uslaner, *The Moral Foundations of Trust*, p. 192.

12 B. Rothstein and D. Stolle, 'Social capital and street-level bureaucracy: an institutional theory of generalized trust', paper presented at the ESF Conference, Exeter, 15–20 September 2001, and at the 1st General Conference of the European Consortium for Political Research (ECPR), Canterbury, 6–8 September 2001, p. 4.

13 Putnam, *Making Democracy Work*.

14 J. Braithwaite, 'Institutionalizing distrust, enculturating trust', in V. Braithwaite and M. Levi (eds), *Trust and Governance* (New York: Russell Sage Foundation, 1998), p. 344.

15 D. Eek and B. Rothstein, 'Exploring a causal relationship between vertical and horizontal trust', QoG Working Paper Series No. 4 (Quality of Government Institute, Göteborg University, 2005), p. 6.

16 Eek and Rothstein, 'Exploring a causal relationship between vertical and horizontal trust', p. 6.

17 J. L. Gibson, 'Social networks, civil society, and the prospects for consolidating Russia's democratic transition', *American Journal of Political Science*, 45:1 (2001), p. 53.

18 B. A. Misztal, *Trust in Modern Societies* (Cambridge: Polity Press, 1996), p. 198.

19 M. Levi, 'A state of trust', in V. Braithwaite and M. Levi (eds), *Trust and Governance* (New York: Russell Sage Foundation, 1998), pp. 85–6.

20 Levi, 'A state of trust', pp. 86–93.

21 D. Stolle, 'Communities, citizens and local government: generalized trust and the impact of regional factors: a study of three regions in Sweden', paper presented at the 95th annual meeting of the American Political Science Association, Atlanta, 2–5 September 1999, p. 8.

22 Tarrow, 'Making social science work across space and time', p. 394.

23 Tarrow, 'Making social science work across space and time', p. 395.

24 T. R. Tyler, *Why People Obey the Law* (New Haven: Yale University Press, 1990), p. 164.

25 Stolle, 'Communities, citizens and local government', p. 9.

26 Rothstein and Stolle, 'Social capital and street-level bureaucracy', p. 9. See also B. Rothstein, *Just Institutions Matter: The Moral and Political Logic of the Universal Welfare State* (Cambridge: Cambridge University Press, 1998), pp. 140–3.

27 Katastrofkommissionen, *Sverige och tsunamin – granskning och förslag*, SOU 2005:104 (Finansdepartementet: Stockholm, 2005), pp. 361, 388–90.

28 T. Lerner, 'Vi uppmuntras att inte ta ansvar', *Dagens Nyheter* (23 February 2006). Author's translation.

29 H. Stenesöta, *Den empatiska staten: Jämställdhetens inverkan på daghem och polis 1950–2000* (Statsvetenskapliga Institutionen, Göteborgs Universitet, 2004), pp. 49–50.

30 Niemi and Junn, *Civic Education*, p. 3.

31 Niemi and Junn, *Civic Education*, pp. 13–18.

32 A. Holland and T. André, 'Participation in extracurricular activities in secondary school: what is known, what needs to be known?', *Review of Educational Research*, 57:4 (1987), pp. 437–66; Beck and Jennings, 'Pathways to participation'.

33 A. N. Oppenheim, *Civic Education and Participation in Democracy: The German Case* (London: Sage, 1977), p. 36.

34 P. White, *Civic Virtues and Public Schooling: Educating Citizens for a Democratic Society* (New York: Teachers College Press, 1996), pp. 60–1.

35 D. C. Bricker, *Classroom Life as Civic Education. Individual Achievement and Student Cooperation in Schools* (New York: Teachers College Press, 1989).

36 J. Torney-Purta, J. Schwille and J-A. Amadeo (eds), *Civic Education Across Countries: Twenty-Four National Case Studies from the IEA Civic Education Project* (Amsterdam: International Association for the Evaluation of Educational Achievement, 1999), p. 14.

37 Putnam, *Making Democracy Work*, p. 90.

38 Analysis of self-selection effects requires longitudinal data, which are rare, as they are costly and time-consuming to collect. Stolle, 'The sources of social capital', p. 25.

39 Tarrow, 'Making social science work across space and time', p. 393.

40 R. Putnam, 'Tuning in, tuning out: the strange disappearance of social capital in America', *Political Science and Politics*, 28:4 (1995), p. 667.

41 Misztal, *Trust in Modern Societies*, p. 160.

42 Uslaner, *The Moral Foundations of Trust*, p. 77.

43 The interaction may vary in both intensity and form. It may be more or less voluntary or superficial, or based on professional contacts or friendship. See P. Strömblad, *Politik på stadens skuggsida* (Uppsala: Acta Universitatis Upsaliensis, 2003), ch. 2.

44 Uslaner, *The Moral Foundations of Trust*, p. 85.

45 Stolle, 'Communities, citizens and local government', p. 6.

46 C. Boix and D. N. Posner, 'Social capital: explaining its origins and effects on government performance', *British Journal of Political Science*, 28:4 (1998), pp. 688–9.

47 E. M. Uslaner, 'Trust, democracy and governance: can government policies influence generalized trust?', in M. Hooghe and D. Stolle (eds),

Generating Social Capital: Civil Society and Institutions in Comparative Perspective (New York: Palgrave Macmillan, 2003), p. 181. See also Uslaner, *The Moral Foundations of Trust*, ch. 6.

48 *Censimento generale della popolazione e delle abitazioni* (Rome: ISTAT, 20 October 1991).

49 Putnam, 'Tuning in, tuning out', p. 678.

50 J. Miller McPherson and L. Smith-Lovin, 'Women and weak ties: differences by sex in the size of voluntary organizations', *American Journal of Sociology*, 87 (1982), p. 883.

51 V. Lowndes, 'Women and social capital: a comment on Hall's "Social capital in Britain"', *British Journal of Political Science*, 30:3 (2000), p. 534.

52 A. Chaudhuri and L. Gangadharan, 'Gender differences in trust and reciprocity', Working Paper (Department of Economics, University of Melbourne, 2003).

53 Based on discussions with the school's principal and a selection of teachers, 10 February 2000.

54 N. Rocca, Centro Sociale di San Severio, Albergheria, interview, 26 February 2000; and I. Manone, Centro Padre Nostro, interview, 2 February 2000.

55 See Torney-Purta *et al.*, *Civic Education Across Countries*, pp. 137–40.

3

Methods

Our point of departure was that Palermo represents a case where change is *least likely* to occur. If change occurs in this area, despite the hostile environment, we can be fairly optimistic about the possibility of changing people's attitudes elsewhere. The project focus was therefore on the school programme (described in Chapter 5) in four of Palermo's most deprived areas, as 'the worst of the worst case scenarios'. The selected areas share several characteristics: high density of criminality and Mafia dominance, low socio-economic level and weak presence of government agencies or other associations. Three of these poor areas are on the periphery of Palermo, while the other is closer to the city centre. One of the areas received more political attention than the other districts in the study after the assassination of a local personality. Two schools in areas with more mixed profiles (districts with both middle-income and low-income residents) and one school in a high-income district were included in the study as a way of enabling comparisons between different socio-economic settings.

The selection of areas was based on comparisons of statistics on employment, unemployment (and specifically youth employment and unemployment rates), educational level, literacy rates, number of foreigners per 1,000 inhabitants, number of square meters per person, number of square meters per apartment and frequency of higher education in the 14–29-year age group.[1] Areas were ranked according to their value on each indicator and an average ranking score was computed for each. It should be noted that the selection of areas is not as clear-cut as it may at first seem, as differences within areas are very important. Micro-economic realities may change quite dramatically within the space of a few blocks in some areas. One example is the Politeama district in central Palermo. While the area around Viale della Libertà is one of Palermo's most commercial and wealthy districts, the neighbouring area round the harbour and Ucciardone prison is poor and inhabited by a completely different social strata than Libertà. It was evident that more in-depth knowledge about the localities would have a bearing on the selection of the different schools. The analysis of statistical indicators was therefore combined with numerous interviews and discussions with teachers, researchers, social workers and personnel at the Palermo office of Istituto Nazionale di Statistica (ISTAT, the Italian National Statistical Institute) as a way of getting a more correct assessment of the socio-economic status of each area. Through these discussions, advice was also received about the selection of schools. On visits to the areas, their status was readily apparent.

Following our statistical analysis, three of the selected schools were situated in areas that had an average ranking that classified them in the lowest (first) quartile. Three other schools were operating in areas that had an average ranking falling in the third quartile. Another school was situated in an area that ranked high on almost every statistical indicator, in the top (fourth) quartile.

Still, micro-level analysis of the territory proved that one of the schools was operating in a very difficult neighbourhood, despite its ranking in the third quartile. A strong presence of the Mafia and low-level criminal behaviour marked the school's surroundings. Illegal games, clandestine betting, usury, rackets, smuggling of cigarettes and drug dealing are common. The neighbourhood of this school was visibly poor, although the area had an average ranking that was higher than the three other schools in poor neighbourhoods.

The sample therefore consists of four schools in poor neighbourhoods, two schools in intermediate neighbourhoods and one school in a high-ranked neighbourhood. The schools selected within the first category are denoted A1–A4, those in the second category are denoted B1 and B2, and the last school is denoted C1.

Instead of focusing on schools in Palermo, an alternative research strategy would have been to focus on smaller cities or villages, as these might be more isolated from external in-fluences. Indeed, it might be argued that Palermo represents a city where habits and behaviours are more likely to change and where citizens are freer to choose their own lifestyle. Still, many of my interlocutors in Palermo commented that mobility between the different areas of the city was quite limited. This definitely holds true for three of the four poor neighbourhoods (the other of which was in any case in the city centre), where the isolation from the rest of Palermo was strongly felt. The geographic distances may have been short, but poor public communications rendered trips to these areas time-consuming enterprises. Several informants also talked about the psychological distance many citizens felt from the rest of Palermo. A voluntary worker in one of the areas said that many of the inhabitants in the area 'were afraid' of Palermo. They did not know where to go or what to see – the opera house, the churches or other cultural attractions – they were unaware of Palermo.

Selection of level, schools and classes

We decided to study the school programme at lower secondary school (*scuola media*), as it represents the last years of compulsory schooling. While there are several examples of studies at a higher secondary level, fewer studies exist of younger students' attitudes. An example of the former is the study organised by Centro Studi Cesare Terranova in 1993/94 of students at the higher secondary level in Palermo, between the ages of 15 and 24. That study included questions relating to citizenship, political participation, legality, rule of law, perceptions of the Mafia, the state and its institutions.[2] Leone has studied perceptions of legality and rule of law in a sample of 1,546 respondents aged 20–60 years in 25 different areas of Palermo.[3] Sciarrone studied students' attitudes at higher secondary level in the city of Corleone, one of the Mafia's strongholds.[4] Rovelli has studied the attitudes of Palermitan university students, in a study similar to this.[5] Thus, there appears to be a lack of studies on young students' attitudes, particularly of those who have not yet completed their compulsory schooling. It should also be mentioned that several schools conduct their own studies of students' attitudes.

Students are aged 10–11 when they enter lower secondary school and 13–14 when they leave. A sample of older students, staying on after their compulsory schooling, would likely have been biased towards more motivated and ambitious students. A study focusing on the compulsory, lower secondary level necessarily gives a more varied sample of students. Another advantage of studies at lower secondary level is that students are still grouped together in classes (each class is taught by a variety of subject-specific teachers, including one for civic education, who is often the history teacher). It is therefore possible to study the impact of factors such as classroom climate on students' attitudes.

Schools were selected according to 'the snowball method'. In discussions with teachers, school principals, social workers and others, many frequently mentioned some schools as interesting examples. Three of the schools participating in the study (A1, A2 and A3) were so-called comprehensive institutes (*istituti comprensivi*), that is, schools that offer education at both primary and lower secondary level, while four schools provided education only at lower secondary level (A4, B1, B2 and C1).

The classes were selected in cooperation with schools. We endeavoured to include classes of differing abilities in the study. Efforts were made to select a variation also with respect to teachers' experience, motivation and degree of cooperation in the class council (*consiglio di classe*).[6]

Students do have the possibility to follow different educational orientations at lower secondary level. The primary option at the start of this project was between normal time (*tempo normale*) and prolonged time (*tempo prolungato*). Students following a normal programme spend 35 hours per week at school, as compared with 38 hours per week for the prolonged programme. In Italy as a whole, classes with normal time were in the majority in 1996/97 (71 per cent of all classes, with the other 29 per cent in the prolonged programme).[7] In this study, classes following a normal programme represented 85 per cent of the sample and prolonged classes 15 per cent (Table 3.1). At least two classes following a normal programme were selected from each school, with the exception of school A1, where most classes followed a prolonged programme and so this requirement could not be met. In addition, students also have the option to select between 'bilingual' classes (students specialise and have more lessons in foreign languages than other classes) or other educational orientations, for example extra studies in music or information technology. In our sample, three classes had a musical orientation.

Table 3.1 Classes participating in the project

School	Programme				
	Normal time			Prolonged time	
	Normal	Bilingual	Musical	Normal	Bilingual
A1		1		2	1
A2	1		2		
A3	1	1	1		
A4	2	2			
B1	2				
B2	2				
C1	2				
No. of classes	10	4	3	2	1
Percentage of class sample	50	20	15	10	5

Students' motivation may vary somewhat between different school programmes. The selection of classes for inclusion in the study had to be made at the start of the first year of lower secondary school, when most students were new and unknown to the school staff. According to schools' experience, bilingual classes had a tendency to attract more ambitious students, and for this reason some bilingual classes were added to the study sample.

Composition of the questionnaire

Some of the questions in the students' questionnaire were drawn from the questionnaires distributed by the IEA.[8] As the IEA questionnaires were designed for 14-year-olds, some questions had to be adapted and simplified for the study sample (aged 10–14 years). Some questions relating to the Sicilian context were added to the questionnaire to add local flavour to the project. Some questions were based on questionnaires elaborated by the Department of Psychology in Palermo. Questions relating to school climate and classroom climate were mainly drawn from questionnaires developed by the Swedish National Agency for Education.[9]

The adequacy of the questions was tested in two pilot tests, one in Scuola Antonio Ugo in Palermo in September 2002, and one in Mörbyskolan in Stockholm in October the same year. Discussions with students were organised immediately after these tests about the adequacy and formulation of the questions.[10] School principals and teachers in the seven selected schools in Palermo were also invited to comment and make suggestions for the questionnaire. In most cases, however, discussions were limited to principals or a teacher assigned by the principals.

The students' questionnaires included questions on:
- the families' socio-cultural status (parents' education and cultural level)
- interpretation of concepts (citizenship, friendship, traditional Sicilian values)
- attitudes towards other citizens (family, relatives, neighbours, teachers, classmates, school staff, Palermitans, Sicilians, Italians, people in general)
- attitudes towards political representatives and institutions (president of Italy, president of the Sicilian region, the mayor of Palermo, courts, police)
- students' interest in political activities (political engagement and participation inside and outside school), both now and in the future
- lifestyle and habits (participation in school activities, participation in activities outside school).

We made a special effort to refrain from intensive questioning about students' families or their personal perceptions of the Mafia, as we feared those questions would prove provocative to some students. Questions on parents' educational level, reading habits (newspapers and books), possession of books and engagement in students' homework were included to get an idea of students' lives and the cultural climate at home.

A short school questionnaire was handed out to school principals in Palermo after the second test in 2005. It mainly included questions about the school programme and school principals' personal views on civic education. Where possible, discussions with school principals or teachers at each school were carried out.

A limitation of this study is that we were not able systematically to explore teachers' experiences or teaching methods. Questions about classroom climate were though included in order to capture students' perception of teachers' willingness to help and interact with students in class. Nor were parents' attitudes or perceptions included in the study. Nevertheless, questions on parents' involvement in school, engagement in homework, educational level and reading habits may to some extent compensate for this omission, and give a hint about parents' values and interest in school-related issues.

Measuring trust

In our study, we combined general questions with questions about students' trust in specific groups: categories of citizens whom students did not know personally, people living in the area, Palermitans, Sicilians, Italians and foreigners. Questions were also asked about how much trust students had in people they met frequently and probably knew more or less well: how much do you trust your family (*familiari*), your relatives (*parenti*), your neighbours, teachers, classmates, school principal and school staff?

Five different indexes were constructed in order to see patterns between areas, schools and change over time:

1 trust in known people 1 (family, relatives, neighbours, people in your neighbourhood – '*il quartiere*')
2 trust in known people 2 (school principal, teachers, school staff, classmates)
3 trust in unknown people (Italians, Sicilians, Palermitans, foreigners)
4 three general questions on trust and cooperation ('Generally speaking, do you believe that most people can be trusted or that nobody can be trusted?', 'Do you believe that most people try to be honest or do you believe that most people are not honest?', 'Do you believe that most people try to help each other or that people generally think only about themselves?')
5 adapted Sicilian sayings on trust, sincerity and cooperation ('Real friendship does not exist', 'To live well it's better to mind one's own business', 'If you need something, it's better to rely on yourself than on other people's help', 'When people cooperate, they never achieve positive results', and 'Nobody does anything unless he gains something from it').

Index 1 is interpreted as examples of particularised trust. Indexes 3 and 4 are indexes of generalised trust. The last index can be understood as an example of Sicilian stereotypes. These statements were inspired by traditional Sicilian proverbs but adapted to modern Italian to better fit students' comprehension level. Factor analysis confirmed a common dimension for items within each category. Index 2 is less clear-cut than the other indexes, in that students would have varying degrees of personal knowledge of the range of persons in the school environment, and so this index may tap both particularised and generalised trust.

In addition to these closed questions, open questions in the questionnaire on students' perception of their neighbourhood and of Palermo gave important qualitative input about students' perceptions of other people. One of these questions was phrased 'Do you like the area where you live?' The three (closed) response alternatives – 'Yes', 'Some things yes, some things no' and 'No' – were followed by the request 'Explain why you like or don't like it'. Likewise, a question on Palermo was asked. In many cases students gave long, colourful descriptions of their neighbourhood and its inhabitants. People's behaviour was frequently commented on and they were, for example, described as honest, dishonest, non-civilised, mean, uneducated, friendly and so on. Students also seemed quite aware of which people they should not approach, that is, those who were 'dangerous' or 'mean'.

The general questions in index 4 have been widely used in different national and international surveys in the last few decades.[11] However, there is an on-going debate about the validity of a general question such as 'Generally speaking, do you believe that most people can be trusted, or can't you be too careful in dealing with people?', as used in those surveys. The question is abstract in nature (it is not related to context or a concrete situation) and it does not work everywhere. Moreover, it has been questioned to what extent the question measures generalised moral sentiments or whether it reflects personal attitudes that are based on life experiences.[12] Taking these concerns into account, and considering the low age of the respondents in this study, we decided to use the third index – based on students' trust in Italians, Sicilians, Palermitans and foreigners – as it is more concrete and therefore more easily apprehended.

The samples

The project is based on two surveys of students' values at lower secondary level in seven Palermitan schools. A panel design was used in order to evaluate possible effects of the anti-Mafia programme. A first questionnaire was handed out in October–November 2002, at the beginning of the students' first year in lower secondary school, and a second questionnaire in February–March 2005, during the last semester of compulsory schooling. The first sample consisted of 386 students; the second was somewhat smaller, at 315 students. The core of the study consists of the panel of 246 students who participated in the test on both occasions (the panel is described further below). The project also included a qualitative study of around 200 letters from students in four classes; this will be referred to as the Letter Project. The methodology for the Letter Project will be described in Chapter 9.

The response rate for the sample was 89 per cent in 2002 and 76 per cent in 2005. These relatively high response rates were achieved because questionnaires were handed out in the classroom and immediately collected after the test. The samples for the two waves are broken down by socio-economic level, school and gender in Tables 3.2, 3.3 and 3.4.

Sample drop-out between the two waves (2002 and 2005) was largest for the low-income areas, particularly for schools A2 and A3 (Table 3.3). In those schools many students did not show up at the second test; students had moved, changed class or were otherwise absent on the day we visited the school.

There was no particular change between the two waves as regards gender. On both occasions, more boys than girls participated in the survey. At the first survey, 54 per cent of

Table 3.2 Total samples by socio-economic level

Socio-economic level	2002	%	2005	%
A: low-ranked areas	252	65	197	62
B: intermediate area	85	22	76	24
C: high-ranked area	49	13	42	13
Total	386	100	315	100

Percentages rounded to the nearest whole number.

Table 3.3 Total samples by school

School	2002	%	2005	%
A1	68	18	58	18
A2	58	15	40	13
A3	66	17	42	13
A4	60	15	57	18
B1	47	12	44	14
B2	38	10	32	10
C1	49	13	42	13
Total	386	100	315	100

Percentages rounded to the nearest whole number.

Table 3.4 Total samples by gender

Participants	2002	%	2005	%
Boys	210	54	174	55
Girls	176	46	141	45
Total	386	100	315	100

Percentages rounded to the nearest whole number.

the respondents were boys, compared with 55 per cent at the second survey (Table 3.4).

The sample information presented here relates to all students who participated on the separate occasions. We will be mostly interested in those 246 students who participated in both tests – the study panel (Chapter 8) – as they will allow us to see whether their attitudes changed over time (before and after having been exposed to the anti-Mafia school programme, or the legality programme as it later became known).

The panel

The purpose of the study was to analyse the effects of the anti-Mafia programme, or the legality programme (described in Chapter 5), on students' attitudes. The study follows the panel design shown in Table 3.5, where A, B and C represent the different socio-economic areas/categories.

Table 3.5 Research panel design

Area	$t-1$	Exposure to programme	t
A	0^1	✓	0^2
B	0^1	✓	0^2
C	0^1	✓	0^2

$t-1$ denotes the survey in 2002; t is used to denote the survey in 2005.
0^1 denotes first survey, or first observation of students' attitudes.
0^2 denotes second survey, or second observation of students' attitudes.

Despite significant discussion with people involved in the education sector in Palermo, we were unable to identify a control group that could serve as a point of comparison for the three socio-economic categories. An ideal control group would have been a class that did not receive any of the anti-Mafia programme, but all schools are obliged to follow the national and regional laws that make the programme mandatory. It would have been controversial for those I spoke to in Palermo to point out a school where the programme had been weakly implemented or not implemented at all. However, we suspect there will be significant variation between schools in the delivery of the programme, depending on their capacity and working environment. The focus of the study will therefore be on differences between schools.

In total, 246 students participated in the test on both occasions, which means that 64 per cent of the initial sample participated in the two waves (which is about normal for panel studies).[13] Some differences are observable between the socio-economic categories: a higher percentage of students in the high-ranked area participated in both waves than was the case for the two categories of lower-ranked areas.[14] The breakdown of the panel sample by socio-economic area is given in Table 3.6.

Were there any differences between schools as regards the percentage of students who participated in both tests? The highest percentage was found in the high socio-economic category, 78 per cent, as mentioned above. In three of the schools, A1, A4 and B2, the percentage of students who participated in the test on both occasions varied between 68 and 71 per cent. In the other three schools, A2, A3 and B1, the proportion was

Table 3.6 Panel by socio-economic area

Socio-economic level	Numbers participating in both surveys (2002 and 2005)	%
A Low-ranked areas	153	62
B Intermediate areas	55	22
C High-ranked area	38	15
Total	246	100

Percentages rounded to the nearest whole number.

Table 3.7 Panel by school

School	Numbers of participants	%
A1	46	19
A2	32	13
A3	35	14
A4	40	16
B1	33	13
B2	22	9
C1	38	15
Total	246	100

Percentages rounded to the nearest whole number.

Table 3.8 Panel by gender

Gender	Numbers of participants	%
Males	129	52
Females	117	48
Total	246	100

Percentages rounded to the nearest whole number.

lower and varied between 55 and 58 per cent. The differences may indicate a difference as regards the *stability* of the classes, but may also be random. For example, in one of the classes several students were absent at the second test because of their football training. A breakdown of the panel sample by school is given in Table 3.7. As shown in Table 3.8, more boys than girls were part of the panel (which was 52 per cent male).

Participation in the survey

The decision to use questionnaires, as opposed to interviews, clearly disadvantaged students with weak reading skills. Moreover, the students participating in the study were very young, only 10–11 years old when the first observation was made, in 2002. The questionnaire was long and most students needed two hours to complete it. Additionally, the students had little experience of this kind of test. Some questions were difficult to understand because of their abstract and negative wording. Some students had handicaps of varying degrees. It was obvious that some students had reading difficulties and advanced slowly through the questionnaire. This problem was partially managed by us providing reading assistance, through the reading aloud of questions. A few students caused significant disruption during the test and were asked to leave the classroom.

The majority of the students were highly motivated, however. In several classes we received applause and in one class we were even asked to sign autographs. Many students kissed our cheeks when leaving the classroom; one student said he would come to Sweden for a visit. Most students insisted on completing the test, despite individual difficulties. Many students spontaneously said the questions were good and relevant (*delle buone domande*). The dominant impression was that most students felt privileged to participate in the study. Their enthusiasm was partly animated by the fact that their answers would result in a book. Directly after the first test, one girl said that she was emotionally touched by the questions (*'mi sono emozionata'*).

Notes

1 Data taken from *Censimento generale della popolazione e delle abitazioni*.

2 C. Lo Presti, C. Morrocchi and M. Pezzini, *Quali valori tra i giovani: Risultati di un'indagine tra gli studenti di Palermo* (Milan: FrancoAngeli, 1999).

3 G. Leone, *Cultura della persona e senso della legalità oggi a Palermo* (Palermo: Cooperativa Grafica Siciliana, 1994).

4 R. Sciarrone, 'Corleone Italia: la cultura civica dei giovani', in P. Viola and T. Morello (eds), *L'associazionismo a Corleone: Un inchiesta storica e sociologica* (Palermo: Istituto Gramsci Siciliano, 2004), CD-ROM.

5 R. Rovelli, *Valori e modelli di comportamento: Un indagine sugli studenti dell'università di Palermo* (Palermo: I.l.a. Palma, 1997).

6 The class council (*consiglio di classe*) is for teachers who are teaching the same class. They are supposed to meet and discuss each class and its specific problems. There are no student representatives involved at lower secondary level in Italian schools.

7 *Statistiche della scuola media inferiore. Anno scolastico 1996/97* (Rome: ISTAT, 1999), p. 12.

8 I am grateful to Vera Husfeldt, IEA head office in Berlin, and to Bruno Losito, IEA Italian coordinator at CERISDI, Rome, for providing the questions in Italian.

9 Skolverket [Swedish National Agency for Education], *Attityder till skolan 1997*, Rapport 197 (Stockholm: Liber, 1997).

10 I am grateful to students in II D in Scuola Antonio Ugo, 2002/03, Palermo, to their school principal, Pia Blandano, to students in 8F at Mörbyskolan, 2002/03, Stockholm, and to their teacher, Anna Holmlin Nilsson, for constructive advice on how to improve the questions.

11 For example, the World Values Survey, the General Social Survey and the American National Election Studies.

12 In the light of the students' young age and comprehension skills in the present study, that question was in any case amended slightly, to 'Generally speaking, do you believe that most people can be trusted or that nobody can be trusted?'

13 Gibson, 'Social networks, civil society, and the prospects for consolidating Russia's democratic transition', pp. 55–6.

14 Low-ranked areas, 61 per cent; intermediate areas, 65 per cent; high-ranked area, 78 per cent.

4

The Mafia

Organised crime is sometimes analysed as a parallel institution to the state: a separate organisation with its own rules for regulation of conflicts and its own activities. Organised crime may, however, interact with the state at different political levels. This may be based on an exchange relation, where different services are exchanged between the two actors, the state and the criminal group. An exchange of favours is an example that applies at both local and national levels. The interest at the national level may be to exchange mobilised votes for guarantees of impunity, political passivity or the obstruction of proceedings against organised crime. At the local level, organised crime may mobilise votes in exchange for public contracts or other favours. There may also be a relationship of exchange between law enforcement agencies and organised criminal groups, whereby politicians interfere with the judiciary in order to influence legal proceedings. A more threatening scenario is when criminal groups or organised crime penetrates the state, that is, is present within the state. This may vary from small-scale penetration on different levels or within parts of the public sector to a full-scale penetration, where the state itself becomes criminal.[1]

This chapter analyses four different aspects of the Mafia. The first section below describes the organisation itself, as a parallel and independent institution to the state. The second analyses the Mafia's relation to the state. We will thereafter turn to a discussion of the Mafia's relations to local territory. In the Italian case, the Mafia's power is closely related to its control of a specific territory, including control over the local citizenry. We will go on to argue that the Mafia is not only a consequence of the weakness of the state but also a cause of the state's weakness. In the following section, the Mafia's mental control will be discussed. Whereas parts of the previous literature have emphasised cultural explanations for the Mafia's power, it is here argued that the Mafia has actively used some Sicilian values as a means to render its activities more legitimate. The Mafia's power is not only a consequence of distrust: it is also a promoter of distrust. We will make some comparisons between various Italian Mafia groupings but concentrate on the Sicilian Cosa Nostra.

The Mafia as a parallel institution to the state

The Italian Mafia is not a homogeneous entity. There are four main Mafia groups working on Italian territory: Cosa Nostra, the Neapolitan Camorra, the 'Ndrangheta in Calabria and the Apulian Sacra Corona Unita. A less well known Mafia group is Stidda, which is an outgrowth of the Sicilian Cosa Nostra.[2] During recent years there has been an increase in foreign organised crime groups that operate on Italian territory, notably ones originating from Albania, North Africa, Nigeria and China.[3] Cosa Nostra is the strongest Mafia group in Sicily, but has expanded its activities to new areas in Lazio and Rome, Campania and Liguria. Some Cosa Nostra groupings have established activities in France (Grenoble), Belgium and Tunisia.[4]

In the literature on the Mafia, stereotypes are often presented: the traditional rural Mafia, the modern entrepreneurial Mafia, the 'good' old Mafia or the 'bad' modern Mafia. The Mafia should not be analysed as a homogeneous entity, as the different groupings may vary between different geographical settings. The degree of organisation may also vary over time, especially in terms of the degree of centralisation. A common characteristic of the Italian Mafia groups is their flexibility and capacity to change their organisation or activities in accordance with the prevailing circumstances at any particular time.[5] After the intensive law enforcement response following the assassinations of judges Giovanni Falcone and Paolo Borsellino in the 1990s, the Mafia became less visible and more careful in its internal communications; cellular phones were avoided and short hand-written notes were instead used by its leader, Bernardo Provenzano. Cosa Nostra also ceased with its killings of public officials and the so-called 'illustrious corpses' disappeared.

Generally, the Cosa Nostra is more centralised and hierarchical than the other Italian Mafia groupings. Sicily as a whole is divided into at least 12 regions, *mandamenti*, which are ruled by different Mafia groups. Mafia leaders from each region are represented in a regional council, the Commission.[6] The Corleone Mafia ruled the regional Commission for some 25 years under the leadership of Salvatore ('Totò') Riina (captured in 1993) and Provenzano, who was caught by the police in April 2006 in a country house near Corleone. Under the leadership of Provenzano, the organisation strengthened both its centralised and horizontal character. While decisions regarding its internal and external relations were centralised, responsibility for local questions was delegated to 'entrusted representatives' (*rappresentanti di fiducia*). The *mandamenti* regularly contributed to a common fund, which served to finance activities and relations useful for the Mafia as a whole.[7]

The Neapolitan Camorra is less hierarchical and less structured in its organisation than its Sicilian counterpart. During the 1970s, there were attempts within the Camorra to establish a more structured organisation. The Calabria-based 'Ndrangheta similarly lacks a coordinating mechanism between different Mafia families. During the 1990s, however, it also tried to create a more centralised structure in order to reduce conflict between families and facilitate coordination. Although the Cosa Nostra is more homogeneous, more centralised and more hierarchical than the other Mafia groupings, the different families enjoy relative autonomy in activities on their own territory.[8]

The internal cohesion of the Mafia should not be overestimated, however. Sciarrone suggests that it should not be perceived as an internally cohesive organism, but as a social contract, based on an interweaving of relations of cooperation, exchange and conflict between actors who have divergent interests. The notion of 'organised anarchy' is more apt when describing the Mafia, as it is 'extremely disjointed and disorderly rather than organically structured'.[9]

The Mafia and politics

The strength of the Mafia lies in its capacity to create networks. It is able to recruit new members and at the same time protect itself from infiltration by law enforcement agents. The Mafia has important skills in creating networks on different levels and exploiting them for its activities. It establishes relations of mutual dependence, engages in exchange of services and establishes itself as a mediator, protector or guarantor.[10] The Mafia repentant Antonino Calderone described the organisation as 'a spider' that builds webs of friends, acquaintances and obligations.[11] The exchange relation may be developed both with citizens and with representatives of the state.

The clientelistic pattern of political mobilisation at national, regional and local levels is repeatedly underlined in the literature as essential to the Mafia's power. The collusion between Mafia interests and parts of the political elite is crucial in this regard.[12] Quoting Della Porta and Vannucci, 'there has been no more striking a case of interaction between politics and organised crime in any Western democracy' than in Italy.[13] Vannucci suggests that the relation between politicians and Mafiosi can be 'visualized as a hidden market within which the operators trade many different commodities: protection, public measures, classified information, use of violence and intimidation'.[14]

From the 1948 elections onwards, the Mafia almost exclusively supported the Christian Democratic Party, Democrazia Christiana. It eventually started to infiltrate the party with its own candidates. Ten years later, the Mafia was represented in all municipal administrations and was well prepared for the political struggle at the national level and the elections in 1958. Through Italy's use in elections of the preference vote, the Mafia also successfully managed to sanction or block the careers of political candidates within the ranks of the Christian Democrats.[15] The Mafia's support for that party lasted more than 40 years, until the demise of the First Republic in the early 1990s. Graziano analysed the relationship between politics at the centre and organised crime in the periphery, and pointed to the usefulness of cooperation for both. While the centre enjoyed stable political support in the south – because votes were mobilised by local bosses – local Mafia leaders gained influence in national and local decision-making.[16] Vannucci quotes the Parliamentary Anti-Mafia Commission's report from 1993 as follows:

> In practice, the link between institutions and the Mafia has developed over many years as a relationship between two different sovereignties: neither one has assaulted the other so long as each kept within its limits.[17]

But the Mafia has also penetrated state institutions. Even if the Mafia is an institution outside the state, it also exists inside the state and is involved in numerous activities, for example the use of public finances and the procurement of public contracts, through the control of preference votes and through its assumed influence on policy-making.[18] The Mafia is political in the sense that it uses its power to influence the policy-making process and to constrain or force others to behave and act in specific ways. Pragmatic power – supporting and promoting its candidates within institutions, and exerting some control over political and administrative bodies – is used to try to influence political and administrative decisions and policy-making.[19] In the early 1990s, according to a report from the Public Prosecutor's Office in Palermo, the number of politicians and officials in stable relationships with the Mafia had increased to the extent that Mafia groups had contacts with key officials and employees in 'every local authority office of interest'.[20]

The influence of Cosa Nostra on politics seems more developed in Palermo and Sicily than in other regions in southern Italy. This may be explained by the stronger organisation of Cosa Nostra than the other Mafia groupings, but is also related to the fact that Sicily is an autonomous region, with its own finances. This regional autonomy gives the Sicilian Mafia the possibility of more direct control over the region's finances than in the other regions in southern Italy, which is why Sicily, and Palermo in particular, continues to be the main operating territory for Cosa Nostra.[21] In contrast, decisions about the financing of public works in Calabria, for example, is 'reached via discretionary powers in the capital, through secret negotiations with the leading national construction businesses, from which the local [Mafia] bosses are excluded'.[22] The construction sector is one traditionally controlled by Cosa Nostra. According to the Anti-Mafia Commission's report in 1993, the Cosa Nostra controlled all public contracts in Sicily.

If the political protector fails to deliver to the Mafioso what has been promised, the Mafia generally uses intimidation, followed by violence if necessary, to impose its interests. Violence is normally used only as a last resort, after all other forms of intimidation, or if the person has behaved in such a way that only death can pay the debt back; a 'brutal threat, an attack, or wounding or murdering [of] a politician would soon put an end to the dispute'.[23] Murder as a means to block political candidates was frequently used during the 1950s, when the Mafia started its infiltration of the Christian Democratic Party but, as mentioned above, disappeared after the murders of Falcone and Borsellino.[24] Threats or violence may still be applied to anybody who opposes, or threatens, the Mafia's activities or interests: politicians, prosecutors, police officers, journalists, writers, business entrepreneurs, social workers and so on.

Despite the exchange relation between Cosa Nostra and political representatives, and the penetration by the Mafia of parts of the public sector, it should be emphasised that the political establishment as a whole has neither accepted nor co-operated with the Mafia. There has also been strong opposition to the Mafia infiltration within the Christian Democratic Party itself.[25] It should be recalled that the Italian state has launched forceful campaigns against the Mafia and if 'so many in its ranks have lost their lives, this is due also to the fact that not every politician and state official was supporting them'.[26]

The relation between political bodies and the Cosa Nostra has also varied over time. According to the analysis made by the Parliamentary Anti-Mafia Commission in 1993, the relation was asymmetric, to the Mafia's advantage.[27] This relationship changed in favour of the state during the years that followed the assassinations of Falcone and Borsellino in 1992, as an effect of the Maxi trial and the law enforcement response to the murders. After the fall of the First Republic in 1992, new parties and new political groupings emerged. Even if many parties initially expressed their commitment to fight the Mafia, this conviction became less clear and less explicit after the mid-1990s. One Palermitan journalist described the situation as 'marmalade' – it was no longer evident who was for or against the Mafia, even if everybody claimed to be against it.[28] Few would deny, however, that Silvio Berlusconi's centre-right alliance was the inheritor of the clientelistic networks of the Christian Democratic Party.

The Mafia and territorial control

Despite the internationalisation of Italian Mafia groups, the control of a local territory remains a vital element in the Mafia's power. Control over territory gives several advantages: a place where criminals can find a safe haven from law enforcement agencies, where recruitment of labour is possible, where money can be laundered and where people's loyalty gives the Mafiosi protection. In cases where organised crime seeks political cooperation, control over a specific population (i.e. voters) represents a power resource, which may be mobilised to increase the political influence of criminal groups. The local territory is a safe haven from where contacts with other criminal networks or groups are directed and organised.[29] Criminal organisations will do their utmost to ensure that the state remains weak in their particular area. Although criminal groups are increasingly transnational, 'Most illegal markets in which goods are produced and services are provided have a local basis'.[30] Local trading networks are used to connect to the global market flows.

The different Italian Mafia groupings are distinguished by their capacity to control a specific geographical territory. Despite the increasing internationalisation of their activities, Mafia groups are still firmly rooted on local ground and dependent on local resources. The power of the Mafia leaders stems from domination of a territory, 'which they cling to, even if it means going underground'.[31] Controlling a territory means imposing a certain way of behaviour and thinking on its citizens. It also means that any competition that could threaten the current state of affairs will meet resistance from the local boss. Quoting Orlando: 'For a boss to be a boss, he *must* remain in his territory and all his men must be aware that he is there, even if only very few trusted lieutenants know his precise whereabouts'.[32]

The Mafia's territorial claims are often, but not always, precise and the division of territorial powers between different groups has created a political geography of the Mafia.[33] The central purpose of a Mafia leader, and indeed a Mafia family, or *cosca*, is to gain a monopoly of power and protection in a specific territory and to cling to this power. Controlling the territory is essential and is often related to important economic gains. Mafia leaders who control a territory are free to act as they choose within it. They enjoy important protection and it enables them to control the local business in that area. Controlling the territory means taking the right to extort firms that have set up in the area. It enables ostensibly legitimate Mafia businesses to establish local monopolies in particular sectors of the economy by the use of threats and violence towards competing companies.[34] Those companies paying protection money to the Mafia will expect the Mafia to police the territory and to discourage potential competitors.[35] Extortion is particularly important for the establishment of Mafia leaders' power over a specific local territory, through which they establish their fief, or *signoria*, and their personal power.[36]

The local territory also represents an important recruitment ground. Organised crime is heavily dependent on labour, for example spies, assassins, drivers, doctors and so on. Many tasks may be accomplished by casual labour. Some missions are given to people who have to pay back debts. Occasional employment may occur when there is a need for special expertise, for example a chemist or a translator. However, delicate assignments, such as the elimination of a rival, are normally given to people with stable and long-term ties to the Mafia.[37]

Gambetta identifies an important functional aspect of territorial control, namely information gathering:

> The area where we were born or have lived longest is the best in which to begin operations, for there we know every resident and every street corner. Simply frequenting the right places – bars, shops, the bank, the church – is sufficient to bring useful information to our attention…. We are likely to have a higher concentration of friends and relatives here than elsewhere, and they represent cheap and trustworthy sources of information. Women talk to other women, children to other children, and report back to us. In small territories new faces stand out; often under the traditional guise of hospitality strangers are questioned, and their business, role, accent, and common acquaintances are determined.[38]

Moreover, territorial control is an important resource for any Mafia leader trying to escape law enforcement agencies. The Corleone boss Totò Riina managed to evade the law for 23 years. During that time, he lived openly in Palermo. He had been living in the same apartment since 1987 but was finally caught in central Palermo in January 1993.[39] The local attachment to a specific geographical area remains fundamental to the Mafia's power and is essential for the functioning and reproduction of its organisation.

Control of territory is important during the establishment and the expansion of a criminal group. In the first phase, what Armao calls 'entrenchment', is when the Mafia group tries to conquer a territory by violence or negotiations; this may involve other criminal groups as well as public officials and other representatives of the state. When a territory is finally controlled, the colonisation of other areas follows. The Mafia group may, for example, expand to the city, the neighbouring regions or into new states. In this way Cosa Nostra spread from Sicily to southern Italy and the north. The Japanese Yakuza and the Chinese Triads have followed the same developmental path. When moving into new areas, 'Mafia clans prefer to entrench themselves in cities where there is a solid community from their own country, which enables them to blend in and to facilitate the reproduction of practices of extortion and of totalitarian control already achieved at home'.[40]

In summary, the main reasons why the Mafia is interested in territorial control are: the associated economic power; cheap labour; and as a safe haven where law enforcement agencies can be avoided in times of crisis. Territorial control is also important for expansion into new territories. Normal activities such as civic education or the establishment of a playground will be strongly opposed by the local Mafia boss, as these are perceived as challenges to the Mafia's territorial power. Those who openly oppose the Mafia's power will be threatened or killed, unless their activities stop.

Weakness of the state – cause or consequence of the Mafia?

The Parliamentary Anti-Mafia Commission wrote in its report that the Mafia's access to local institutions was strongly facilitated by administrative weakness: 'Where public administration is inert or careless, where administrative controls do not work, a favourable environment for the interweaving of politics and the Mafia is automatically created.'[41] Mafia groups have better opportunities to expand when the state is weak or lacks the capacity to guarantee public order, when there is a need for protection of individuals and their property, or when there is a need for a guarantor to ensure that contracts are maintained. The logic is that the citizen who cannot trust the state or public agencies to access specific services will ask for help and protection from other actors, in this case the Mafia: 'Inefficiency and arbitrariness on the part of the state take away protection from the domain of citizens' rights and transform it into a market'.[42] In an area dominated by the Mafia, the Mafia to large extent replaces vital government functions, for example the distribution of water and electricity or the provision of security in exchange for Mafia-imposed 'taxes', or *pizzu*.

When the state is weak and the output of services unsure, private connections are also useful, as they render the bureaucratic system more flexible and responsive to the individual citizen. Having the right contacts may be particularly important in societies where the financial burden or time needed to deal with the bureaucracy may be costly for the individual citizen. Contacts may be used for a variety of reasons: for finding a house or apartment, getting a job, setting up a locality for your business or organisation, getting a pension, a hospital bed, a licence or a diploma.[43] Falcone, a Sicilian himself, described the importance of contacts in a system that does not favour skilled or ambitious persons but the ones with good private connections or contacts:

> Sicily has made *clientelismo* a way of life. In this context it is difficult for straightforward professional abilities to emerge. What counts is a friendship or a connection used to get a leg up. And the mafia, which always expresses the quintessence of Sicilian values, end up making what are every citizen's rights look like favours.[44]

On the other hand, the infiltration of the public sector by the Mafia also hinders the state from exercising its proper functions.[45] It undermines democracy, distorts the rule of law and makes the state less efficient. The presence of organised crime has reinforced political corruption and bad governance. Political corruption, on a more general level, leads to the satisfaction of particular interests at the cost of the general interest; that is, it leads to discretionary management of public spending, increased costs for public works and low quality of projects, as public contracts are offered to 'companies without the necessary qualifications, equipment and expertise'.[46] Hence, the presence of the Mafia and political corruption may be understood as a *cause* of the weakness of the state. Moreover, the poor functioning of public institutions also leads to a widespread scepticism among citizens and businesses regarding the reliability and impartiality of bureaucratic procedures, a scepticism that leads to the erosion of the state's political legitimacy.[47]

The Mafia actively opposes any actor who threatens its interests or territorial control. Consequently, the Mafia may also be an explanation for why the state continues to remain weak in a specific area. The political protection offered by the state and the Mafia are here addressed to the very same clients and may be understood as a zero-sum game: what one gains, the other loses. An example from Weber clearly illustrates this relationship. Responding to a question on the ability of the Camorra to offer security, a Neapolitan builder gave the following answer: 'Sir, the Camorra charges *X* Lire each month, but guarantees security – the State takes ten times as much, but does not guarantee anything'.[48] The Mafia's territorial claim thus represents an example of how the interests of the state and the Mafia are in opposition to each other: the power of the one undermines the power of the other. The territorial control exercised by the Mafia may also be a consequence of the collusion of Mafia interests and those of corrupt politicians: 'by guaranteeing impunity and territorial control … corrupt politicians have reinforced the power of organized crime'.[49]

The Mafia and mental control

Researchers from different fields have pointed at cultural explanations for the Mafia's power: egoism, suspicion and distrust of others, exaggerated individualism, strong attachment to blood relatives, instrumental view of friendship, a strong belief in honour, fatalism, pessimism and a negative view of the state and its representatives. Cultural explanations have dominated the analysis of both the Mafia and Sicily since the unification of Italy, but have also been emphasised by more modern authors.[50] This dominant discourse, the so-called 'Sicilianism', underlined the folklore origins of the Mafia, and understood it as an outgrowth of traditional Sicilian ways of acting and thinking. Spokespersons for this discourse were not only Mafia members and their associates but also a cross-section of those in power, be they in the church, state, press or university.[51] The Mafia was often interpreted as an anthropological phenomenon, and it was frequently argued that it shared a set of values and attitudes that were common in Sicily. Following this line of argument, references were often made to old sayings or proverbs as evidence of the Sicilian mentality, without, however, any acknowledgement of the difficulty of estimating their value – proverbs may, for example, vary according to their diffusion, acceptance and degree of legitimacy.[52] There may also be important differences between generations in the understanding of these proverbs.[53]

More recently, those who have researched the Mafia have increasingly contested such cultural explanations for its power. The mythology around the Mafia – its ideology of *omertà* ('silence', particularly in relation to law enforcement agencies), family values and so on – has been interpreted as a functional tool and served as a way of increasing its ultimate aims: money and power.[54] Santoro understands Mafia leaders as producers, users and manipulators of symbols.[55] This symbolic production is not necessarily individual and intentional, but may also be collective and unconscious, he argues. The symbolic values used by the Mafia in initiation rites and in the spreading of myths also represent a symbolic structure through which the Mafioso organises and perceives society. Santoro's point is that when explaining the Mafia and its capacity for reproduction, it is necessary to identify how the cultural structure is produced, how it functions, how it is diffused and how it interacts with and transforms sub-cultural patterns.[56]

Schneider and Schneider point at differences within Sicilian society. In their understanding, the Mafia is a promoter of certain values. Attitudes are the result of the presence of the Mafia and the daily operations of patronage that have been allowed to exaggerate and nourish those values.[57] Gambetta is also critical of cultural explanations and emphasises the *usefulness* of so-called Sicilian values. Rather than understanding *omertà* or violence as Sicilian cultural traits, these are considered skills and expectations that have been acquired through learning processes in the course of generations. Instead of analysing people as governed by causes, Gambetta suggests a rational perspective in which 'individuals are perceived as at least tentatively rational and responsible for their deeds', and where change and reform are conceivable.[58]

The argument is that the Mafia has produced and manipulated some cultural values. Rather than drawing a distinct line between Mafia culture and Sicilian culture, the former may be understood as a distortion of the latter, an exaggerated version of cultural traits that are diffused in Sicily. As Falcone pointed out, it is entirely possible to have a Mafia mentality without being criminal or a member of the Mafia.[59] While the anti-Mafia movement in Palermo has emphasised the distinction between Sicilian culture and Mafia culture, psychologists specialising in the testimonies of Mafia repentants, the *pentiti*, have pointed at some common characteristics.[60] So how, then, have Mafiosi used Sicilian culture?

Mafia leaders may use ideology, myths and symbols to maintain their territorial control. Ideology has been useful as an 'alibi', externally as well as internally. Mafia members have traditionally promoted the image of themselves as brave and generous men of honour, *uomini d'onore*, and supported the ideal of a self-made man who is dependent on nobody but his own capacity for his success. Mafia leaders have also used myths in order to render their criminal acts more legitimate, for example the old myth of a secret sect called Beati Paoli. The myth appeared in print in 1909 and 1910 in the regional newspaper *Giornale di Sicilia* but had its origins in early eighteenth-century Palermo. These men of honour were entrusted to intervene and punish social or private wrongs. They staged their operations from secret tunnels underneath central Palermo and were believed to act for the benefit of others, without any self-interested motives.[61] Another way in which Mafiosi like to present themselves is as humble – the simple man who speaks for everybody. Don Calogero Vizzini, a famous Mafia boss of the 'old school', described himself in the following way:

> A photograph of me? Whatever for? I'm no one. I'm just some citizen. It is strange.... People think that I don't talk much from modesty. No. I don't talk much because I don't know much. I live in a village, I only rarely go to Palermo, I know few people.... And besides, I've grown old, over seventy years old.[62]

Totò Riina presented himself in a similar way: as a simple, illiterate and rustic *viddanu* (peasant).[63] Many were surprised by the simple lifestyle of Riina's successor, Provenzano. Although he did not lack economic resources, he had the lifestyle and the appearance of a villager. One reason for adopting this lifestyle was probably strategic: to avoid capture (he spent 43 years on the run). It may also be seen as a way of promoting a specific image within the Mafia organisation itself and presenting an example of 'Mafia ethic' to other members. According to Mafia prosecutor Piero Grasso, 'Provenzano gave the image of a boss who sacrifices himself for others, like the captain who is the last to leave the ship'.[64] The simple lifestyle does not, however, correspond to the organisation and activities of the Mafia. The Mafia is utterly modern in its use of techniques to run its business, exemplified in the allocation of public contracts, money laundering, voting recommendations and support of candidates on crucial posts in the public administration.

Historically, religion has been used as one way of improving the Mafia's external image. Mafia symbols have been intermixed with religious symbols, for example in initiation rites, where the symbolism strengthens the internal cohesion of the Mafia members and enables Mafia members to distinguish themselves from ordinary people.[65] The small paper rolls Provenzano used to deliver information to his dependants, the so-called *pizzini*, ended with a quotation from the Bible with a reference to God and His will.[66] Mafia leaders have, in the past, sponsored religious processions in honour of various saints, and married, baptised their children and been buried by the Church. Gambetta describes the Mafia in terms of a trademark that uses advertisement to enhance the reputation of the Mafia firm. By parading through town beneath the banner of a saint, a Mafia leader is advertising. Gambetta suggests that the Mafioso is simply trying to 'rub off on the product and make it more attractive … to be seen associated with a powerful symbol enhances one's credibility'.[67] The Catholic Church has increasingly opposed the Mafia's use or abuse of its religious symbols and saints. Although the Catholic Church remained passive towards the Mafia for many years, its criticism of and open opposition to the Mafia have increased since the 1980s.[68] Another example from a different cultural context is the Japanese Yakuza, who have financed the production of movies as a way of spreading and promoting their own image of themselves.[69]

The Mafia's propaganda has a dark side, however, that may not be revealed by the examples above. Siebert describes the mental control the Mafia exerts as an attack on democracy at its very roots. The Mafia not only denies citizens their rights and freedom of speech, it also influences social interaction and leads to an acceptance of illegal behaviour. The effect on people's minds is sometimes unconscious, as people are unaware of the Mafia's influence on their personal life strategies.

> Sensational events aside, the mafia – in the many subtle and effective ways that are particular to it – attacks democracy at the roots, the entire democratic system, the 'natural' rights and

freedoms we enjoy. The mafia infiltrates the normal social fabric, the relations between people. Behind the façade of sensational events and exceptional facts lies, in a shroud of highly effective silence, the most dangerous aspect of mafia-related organized crime – that of becoming accustomed to tyranny and tolerating threats and blackmail. Living and conniving with mafia violence alters people's perception of their rights and transforms citizens into subjects.... The mafia's strict social control has a silent influence on everybody's minds. Personal life strategies are deeply influenced without people often being conscious of those limits.[70]

Siebert refers to the mayor of a small town in Calabria commenting on the mental control of the Mafia. The Mafia leads to a pessimistic perception of the future, since it hinders change:

such total control is a terrible thing, even more terrible than the criminal acts themselves or the fighting between different bands. It is like a door towards the future that has been shut in front of you, because there is no way out, you don't grow ... you're cut out.[71]

Distrust – cause or consequence of the Mafia?

The presence of the Mafia in an area breeds distrust. According to Gambetta's analysis, the principal market for Mafia services is to be found in unstable transactions in which the element of trust is fragile or absent. This is the case in illegal exchanges, where intervention by a legitimate agency to ensure that the rules are respected – in other words the state – cannot be invoked.[72] The existence of Mafia protection in an area increases mistrust, however, as persons who are 'protected' do not hesitate to swindle or misbehave against those who are unprotected and defenceless. The strategy used by the Mafia is also to nourish distrust and uncertainty, as 'protection' is offered not only to legal businesses but also to criminal activities in the area: 'When mafia protection is offered, mistrust and uncertainty consequently increase'.[73]

Conclusion

The relation between organised crime and the state may vary from a few contacts, to an exchange relation, to a full-scale penetration of major public institutions. Organised crime is sometimes analysed as a parallel institution to the state, but sometimes it engages in cooperation with actors at different political levels of the state. A more threatening scenario is when criminal groups or organised crime penetrates the state, to become present within the state.

The internal cohesion and consistency of the Mafia should not be overestimated. There are differences not only between the four Italian Mafia groups – the Cosa Nostra, the Camorra, the 'Ndrangheta and the Sacra Corona Unita – but also within each group. The notion of 'organised anarchy' characterises the Mafia's organisation.

The clientelistic pattern of political mobilisation at national, regional and local levels is an essential part of the Mafia's power. The influence of Cosa Nostra on politics seems more developed in Palermo and Sicily than in other regions in southern Italy. This may be explained by the stronger organisation of Cosa Nostra than the other Mafia groupings, but is also related to the fact that Sicily is an autonomous region.

The Mafia is not only a separate institution to the state, that acts against the state's interests, but it has also engaged in an exchange relationship with the state, where mutual favours are exchanged. The Mafia is also represented within the state, in its support of specific political candidates. The Mafia has in the past successfully managed to control the election of political representatives, even if this has been less clear since the fall of the First Republic. Some sectors of the economy are also penetrated by Mafia interests, for example the construction sector, where the procurement of public contracts represents an important source of income.

The different Italian Mafia groupings are distinguished by their capacity to control a specific geographical territory. Despite the increasing internationalisation of Mafia activities, Mafia groups still depend on local resources. Territorial control is important since it provides cheap labour, income and protection from law enforcement agencies, as well as popular support that may be mobilised in the form of political votes. Controlling the territory means imposing a certain way of behaviour and thinking on citizens in that very area. Mafia leaders have used ideology, myths and symbols to maintain their territorial control and to render their activities more legitimate. But the Mafia's mental control also seriously limits citizens' rights and freedoms in that area.

While the weakness of the state explains why citizens refer to the Mafia instead of the state in order to be protected, the Mafia strongly opposes any attempts to break its territorial power. The relation between the Mafia and the state may here be understood as a zero-sum game.

In the section on mental control, it was strongly argued that the Mafia should not solely be understood as a cultural phenomenon. Rather, it has actively exploited specific Sicilian values of use in its activities. Examples of such values are the values of distrust, *omertà*, individualism, fatalism, instrumental relations and a negative perception of the state.[74] It is today commonly asserted by those who research the Mafia that the mythology and ideology surrounding it operate as functional tools to increase its power.[75]

As discussed in the first two chapters, generalised trust is highly desirable in any society, as it enables people to cooperate and find solutions to problems of collective action. It is also desirable because it generates economic growth, democracy, income redistribution, political trust, personal happiness and health. Instead of generating generalised trust, the Mafia has – like authoritarian regimes – actively fostered a climate of distrust, where individualism and suspicion reign. To this end, some Sicilian values have been distorted and exaggerated to fit the Mafia's purposes.

The question of how far and in what ways the Mafia is inherent in Sicilian culture or external to Sicilian values is contested and political in nature. The discussion about Sicilian culture in relation to Mafia culture was taken to the political level by Leoluca Orlando when mayor of Palermo. The next chapter is dedicated to his fight against the Mafia during the 1990s, following the assassinations of Falcone and Borsellino. A critical review will be conducted of the political efforts in Palermo to break the territorial and mental control of the Mafia. This 'battle' had several dimensions, including mass mobilisation of the general public at the national and local level, political initiatives from the national level, and reinforcement of the army and law enforcement agencies. In the next chapter the focus will be on political efforts at the local level. Breaking the Mafia's territorial and mental control was a central theme of Orlando's new policy for Palermo.

Notes

1 P. Williams, 'Transnational crime and corruption', in B. White, R. Little and M. Smith (eds), *Issues in World Politics* (New York: Palgrave Macmillan, 2005), pp. 235–56. Williams gives North Korea as an example of full-scale penetration.

2 La Stidda consisted of Mafia leaders from Caltanisetta, Gela and Agrigento, but was eventually destroyed by Cosa Nostra. Groupings from Stidda are present in Germany. Prosecutor at the Palermo Court of Justice, interview, 15 March 2002.

3 M. Massari, 'Transnational organized crime between myth and reality. The social construction of a threat', in F. Allum and R. Siebert (eds), *Organized Crime and the Challenge to Democracy* (London: Routledge, 2003), p. 61.

4 Prosecutor at the Palermo Court of Justice, interview, 15 March 2002.

5 R. Sciarrone, 'Forza e persistenza delle mafie', in *La Mafia esiste ancora* (Turin: Alicubi SRI, 2004), pp. 2–4.

6 Prosecutor at the Palermo Court of Justice, interview, 15 March 2002.

7 A. Dino, 'Cosa Nostra si inabissa e cambia pelle', in *La Mafia esiste ancora*, Giorni di Storia 26 (Turin: Alicubi SRI, 2004), pp. 6–7.

8 Sciarrone, 'Forza e persistenza delle mafie', p. 4.

9 R. Sciarrone, 'The dark side of social capital: the case of mafia', paper presented at the Workshop on Social Capital and Civic Involvement, Cornell University, 13–14 September 2002, p. 9.

10 Sciarrone, 'Forza e persistenza delle mafie', pp. 3–4.

11 Calderone as quoted in R. Sciarrone, 'Le relazioni esterne: il capital sociale della mafia', in *La Mafia esiste ancora*, Giorni di Storia 26 (Turin: Alicubi SRI, 2004), p. 30.

12 J. Schneider and P. Schneider, 'Mafia, antimafia, and the question of Sicilian culture', *Politics and Society*, 22:2 (1994), p. 251; Sciarrone, 'Le relazioni esterne', p. 32.

13 D. Della Porta and A. Vannucci, *Corrupt Exchanges: Actors, Resources and Mechanisms of Political Corruption* (New York: Aldine de Gruyter, 1999), p. 217.

14 A. Vannucci, 'Politicians and godfathers: mafia and political corruption in Italy', in D. Della Porta and Y. Mény (eds), *Democracy and Corruption in Europe* (London, Pinter, 1997), p. 51.

15 M. Pantaleone, *Mafia e politica* (2nd edn) (Turin: Einaudi, 1972), pp. 227–32.

16 See L. Graziano, 'Center–periphery relations and the Italian crisis: the problem of clientelism', in S. Tarrow, P. Katzenstein and L. Graziano (eds), *Territorial Politics in Industrial Nations* (New York: Praeger, 1978), pp. 290–326.

17 Vannucci, 'Politicians and godfathers', p. 51.

18 U. Santino, *L'Alleanza e il compromesso. Mafia e politica dai tempi di Lima e Andreotti ai giorni nostri* (Soveria Mannelli: Rubbettino Editore, 1997), p. 8.

19 Sciarrone, 'The dark side of social capital', pp. 4, 7.

20 Public Prosecutor's Office, Palermo, as quoted in Vannucci, 'Politicians and godfathers', p. 57.

21 The regional parliament and regional council are in Palermo.

22 Vannucci, 'Politicians and godfathers', p. 57.

23 Vannucci, 'Politicians and godfathers', p. 56.

24 Pantaleone, *Mafia e politica*, pp. 206–7.

25 Pantaleone, *Mafia e politica*, ch. 19.

26 D. Gambetta, *The Sicilian Mafia: The Business of Private Protection* (London: Harvard University Press, 1993), pp. 8–9.

27 Vannucci, 'Politicians and godfathers', p. 56.

28 A. Bolzone, journalist at *La Repubblica*, personal communication, 1 March 2002.

29 Williams, 'Transnational crime and corruption', p. 250.

30 Massari, 'Transnational organized crime between myth and reality', p. 64.

31 H. Hess, *Mafia and Mafiosi: Origin, Power and Myth* (London: C. Hurst, 1998), p. 186.

32 L. Orlando, *Fighting the Mafia and Renewing Sicilian Culture* (San Francisco: Encounter Books, 2001), p. 174.

33 P. Arlacchi, *Mafia Business: The Mafia Ethic and the Spirit of Capitalism* (London: Verso, 1986), pp. 150–1; Orlando, *Fighting the Mafia and Renewing Sicilian Culture*, p. 142.

34 See Arlacchi, *Mafia Business*.

35 Gambetta, *The Sicilian Mafia*, pp. 199–200.

36 U. Santino, *La Mafia interpretata: Dilemmi, stereotipi, paradigmi* (Messina: Rubbettino, 1995).

37 Gambetta, *The Sicilian Mafia*, pp. 65–6.

38 Gambetta, *The Sicilian Mafia*, p. 37.

39 A. Jamieson, *The Antimafia: Italy's Fight Against Organized Crime* (London: Macmillan, 2000), pp. 232–4.

40 F. Armao, 'Why is organised crime so successful?', in F. Allum and R. Siebert (eds), *Organized Crime and the Challenge to Democracy* (London: Routledge, 2003), p. 33.

41 See Vannucci, 'Politicians and godfathers', p. 54.

42 Vannucci, 'Politicians and godfathers', p. 55.

43 Hess, *Mafia and Mafiosi*, p. 143.

44 G. Falcone and M. Padovani, *Men of Honour: The Truth About the Mafia* (London: Fourth Estate, 1992), p. 123.

45 Pantaleone, *Mafia e politica*, p. 237.

46 D. Della Porta and A. Vannucci, 'The "perverse effects" of political corruption', *Political Studies*, 45 (1997), p. 523.

47 Della Porta and Vannucci, 'The "perverse effects" of political corruption', pp. 527–37.

48 Vannucci, 'Politicians and godfathers', p. 55, quoting Weber.

49 Della Porta and Vannucci, 'The "perverse effects" of political corruption', p. 535.

50 See Arlacchi, *Mafia Business*; Hess, *Mafia and Mafiosi*.

51 Schneider and Schneider, 'Mafia, antimafia, and the question of Sicilian culture', p. 237.

52 See Hess, *Mafia and Mafiosi*.

53 Research at the Department of Psychology, University of Palermo, shows generational differences in the understanding of Sicilian proverbs. Personal communication, Gianluca Lo Coco, researcher at the Department of Psychology, May 2005.

54 F. Di Maria and G. Lo Verso, 'La donna nelle organizzazioni mafiose', in *Donne e mafie: Il ruolo delle donne nelle organizzazioni criminali* (Palermo: Università degli Studi di Palermo, Dipartimento di Scienze Penalistiche e Criminologiche, 2003), p. 91.

55 M. Santoro, 'Mafia, cultura e politica', *Rassegna Italiana di Sociologia*, 39:4 (1998), p. 457.

56 Santoro is particularly critical of Hess's work, arguing that Hess presents a culturalist interpretation of the Sicilian subculture. M. Santoro, 'Mafia, cultura e subculture', *Polis*, 14:1 (2000), pp. 100, 108.

57 J. Schneider and P. Schneider, *Reversible Destiny: Mafia, Antimafia and the Struggle for Palermo* (Berkeley: University of California Press, 2003), pp. 117–18.

58 Gambetta, *The Sicilian Mafia*, pp. 10–11.

59 See G. Lo Verso (ed.), *La Mafia dentro. Psicologia e psicopatologia di un fondamentalismo* (Milan: FrancAngeli, 2002), p. 33.

60 See, for example: I. Fiore, *Le radici inconsce dello psichismo mafioso* (Milan: FrancoAngeli, 1997); Lo Verso, *La Mafia dentro*; G. Lo Verso and G. Lo Coco (eds), *La psiche mafiosa. Storie di casi clinici e collaboratori di giustizia* (Milan: FrancoAngeli, 2003).

61 Schneider and Schneider, 'Mafia, antimafia, and the question of Sicilian culture', pp. 240–3, 246.

62 Hess, *Mafia and Mafiosi*, p. 73.

63 See Schneider and Schneider, 'Mafia, antimafia, and the question of Sicilian culture', p. 242.

64 See D. Martirano, 'Ecco perché il padrino viveva da povero', *Corriere della sera*, 15 April 2006. See also Pantaleone, *Mafia e politica*, p. 237, for a discussion on the importance of 'alibi'.

65 Sciarrone, 'The dark side of social capital', pp. 8–9.

66 A. Camilleri, 'When a Godfather becomes expendable', *New York Times*, 21 April 2006.

67 Gambetta, *The Sicilian Mafia*, pp. 48–51, quotation from p. 130.

68 For an analysis of the Catholic Church and its relation to the Mafia, see Jamieson, *The Antimafia*, pp. 135–44.

69 Gambetta, *The Sicilian Mafia*, p. 135.

70 Siebert, 'Mafia and anti-mafia', pp. 39–40.

71 Siebert, 'Mafia and anti-mafia', p. 40.

72 Gambetta, *The Sicilian Mafia*, p. 17.

73 Vannucci, 'Politicians and godfathers', p. 52.

74 These values will be briefly discussed in Chapters 6 and 7, when necessary for the presentation of descriptive statistics.

75 See Santoro, 'Mafia, cultura e subculture'; Gambetta, *The Sicilian Mafia*; Schneider and Schneider, *Reversible Destiny*.

5

Cultural warfare

While a great deal has been written on the Mafia in Sicily, there is less literature on the anti-Mafia movement. Santino's *Storia del movimento antimafia* is an indispensable source for readers interested in the history of that movement. Santino's contribution is a detailed description of more than 100 years of anti-Mafia efforts, starting with the Sicilian *Fasci* (a workers' movement) in the 1890s, continuing with the peasant protests during the post-war period, and concluding with the anti-Mafia movement during the last 40 years. Jamieson's *The Antimafia: Italy's Fight Against Organized Crime* focuses on more recent events in an analysis of the political response, the law enforcement response and the grass-roots response after the killings of judges Giovanni Falcone and Paolo Borsellino in 1992. Schneider and Schneider's *Reversible Destiny: Mafia, Antimafia and the Struggle for Palermo* provides an analysis of the Mafia's development after the Second World War. It also includes a more recent analysis of the civic movement in Palermo. A conclusion of these works is that 'As long as there has been mafia in Sicily, there have been antimafia intellectuals and officials seeking to analyse and contest its political and cultural power'.[1]

The first part of this chapter gives a general background to Leoluca Orlando's political programme during the 1990s, the so-called 'Palermitan renaissance', when he was mayor of Palermo. Thereafter the chapter focuses on national, regional and local initiatives to fight against the Mafia in public schools, with a particular emphasis on school policy during the 1990s. The chapter particularly emphasises cultural aspects of the anti-Mafia campaign.

Orlando's new policy for Palermo

During the 1980s, an anti-Mafia coordination movement emerged that cut across political parties and political cleavages. The growth of this movement was spurred by the increase in lawlessness and disorder and the severe judicial measures during this period. But it was also a result of changes within the Church and within the Christian Democratic Party itself. The local government in Palermo, led by Orlando after elections in 1985, was an important instigator of political renewal in Palermo. His government, which consisted of a coalition of members from the Christian Democratic Party, Communists, Greens and the Jesuit-inspired movement Città per l'Uomo (City for Humankind), was known as the 'Palermo spring'. Orlando's administration used a strong anti-Mafia rhetoric and his policy aimed to increase citizen participation, to impose transparency in local government and to cut the bonds between the Christian Democratic Party and the Mafia.[2]

That period also saw the emergence of anti-Mafia associations and organisations in Palermo, for example Centro Pedro Arrupe, Centro Borsellino, Libera, Arciragazzi, Scuola di Formazione Etico-Politica 'Giovanni Falcone' and Fondazione Falcone. A priority for many of these bodies was education for children in respect for the law, with the aim of preventing them from acquiring a 'Mafia mentality' of distrust and hostility towards public institutions. Those branches of the anti-Mafia movement that were trying to promote a change in Palermo were now increasingly considering cultural aspects of the Mafia's power.[3]

In 1990, Orlando turned his back on the Christian Democratic Party and formed a new party, La Rete (The Net). After the killings of Falcone and Borsellino in 1992, Orlando was re-elected mayor in 1993 on a strong anti-Mafia platform, with 75 per cent of the vote. He skilfully used the moment of emotion provoked by the assassinations of the two judges to launch a new programme for Palermo, focusing on three key sectors: culture, public schools and infrastructure. The major aims of Orlando's political programme were to restore the state's control of the city's territory and to promote a civic consciousness based on the rule of law.

Efforts were made to improve the city by renovating buildings and monuments and restoring green areas in central Palermo. Better public transport and illumination of the city were other examples. One of the architects at the Division for Urban Planning described the years under Orlando as a period of great expansion. One major achievement of Orlando's policy was the elaboration of a new urban plan for Palermo – the first since 1962. After years of uncontrolled urban expansion and abuse of construction licences – during the so-called years of 'Sacco di Palermo' – the plan represented a first step in the process of transforming Palermo from a 'non-city' into 'a normal town'.[4]

Orlando's programme was characterised by acts of symbolic significance and meaning, for example the opening of Palermo's main opera house, the Teatro Massimo, in 1997, after 23 years of mismanagement and speculation. The theatre had initially closed in order to upgrade its safety, but it had become a symbol administrative inefficiency, political corruption and the power of Mafia interests. The renovation of the church complex Lo Spasimo in the poor urban area La Kalsa was another example of Orlando's policy of improving the physical environment of the city. Lo Spasimo had previously been used as a church, a theatre, a warehouse, a leper colony, a hospital and a retirement home. It was damaged by bombs during the Second World War and then used as a dump for construction material for many years. Orlando transformed it into a beautiful and much frequented cultural centre. He also transformed the former industrial area of Zisa into a cultural space for meetings, expositions, theatre and so on. The change in Palermo was described – and promoted internationally – by Orlando as a 'Cultural Revolution' and a 'Palermitan renaissance'.

Orlando's policy in Palermo was paralleled by efforts made by the left-wing mayor of Naples, Antonio Bassolino. Both of them enjoyed increased power after the adoption of a new local government law in March 1993 that established the direct election of mayors at the same time as the power of the municipal council was reduced. From 1993 and onwards, Bassolino managed to govern what Ginsborg describes as 'one of the most chaotic and corrupt cities of Europe' and successfully made 'his own name the symbol of the city's resurrection'.[5] There were other similarities between Naples and Palermo. Bassolino revived the historic centre, transformed the former industrial area at Bagnoli into a park, and renovated Piazza del Plebiscito, making it one of the city's showpieces. Bassolino endeavoured to establish legality in a city ruled by the Camorra; local government was made more transparent, and the administration was made more efficient and responsible for its actions.[6] There were also some similarities in the school programme between Naples and Palermo during this period, which we will discuss later.

One of the underlying assumptions in Orlando's policy was to recapture the city from the Mafia, to give Palermo's territory back to its citizens. A central theme was 'love', to make citizens see the beauty of their city, to make them proud of it, to make them love it. Policy-makers believed that people would be ready to engage in the effort to change the city only after realising how much they cared about and appreciated their own community. Policy-makers to a large extent echoed Paolo Borsellino's own description of his love–hate relationship with Palermo: 'I didn't like Palermo, which is why I started to love her. Because true love consists of loving what you don't like in order to change it.'[7]

What the programme was all about was the reconstruction of the city and the reconstruction of the identity of its residents. The city administration expressed its policy in the review *Thema*:

> To construct a city: this is the most important challenge for local governments to handle.... The city [is] a community of persons, not an agglomeration of buildings. Constructing a city means supporting the development of networks between the persons who, by chance or by choice, live there: to realize and to reclaim the territory, to offer meeting places and conviviality.... In a city like Palermo, where until some years ago the Mafia's disruptive action and its dangerous relation to politics hindered the formation of a general feeling of citizenship ... the challenge today is to reconstruct a sense of 'ownership' among citizens for their own territory, to share the responsibility for the use of resources and for decisions that concern everybody.[8]

The discourse in Palermo is closely related to political efficacy, defined by Campbell, Gurin and Miller as the 'feeling that political and social change is possible, and that the individual citizen can play a part in bringing about this change'.[9] In the literature about political socialisation, the acquisition of political efficacy is often seen as crucial for future participation as an active citizen in a democracy and desirable for the stability of democracy.[10]

An important part of the political programme involved making a distinction between Sicilian culture and Mafia culture, and challenging cultural explanations for the Mafia.

Orlando's decline

Strong forces against Orlando's urban planning

Orlando's attempts to control the urban expansion and renovation of buildings in Palermo met with resistance from powerful interests. The construction sector had been one of the most influential in Palermo's urban economy since the Second World War. Opposition to urban planning was not new. Proposals for the reconstruction of Palermo's old centre had been initiated in the late 1970s and a plan was completed in 1982. Despite the adoption of the plan by the municipal administration in 1983, the political climate was hostile to change. According to Schneider and Schneider, the plan was also too general and directive in character, and not detailed enough to be operational. Orlando's first administration entered power in 1985 and wished to present a new, operational urban plan, and assigned the task to an interdepartmental team of university faculty members and students. Delays in the committee's work, however, made Orlando suspect corruption within the planning process. All of the commissioners in the team had been appointed by the previous administration, which had ruled during a construction boom. There was also reason to suspect that the university had stakes in the construction sector, being itself an important property owner in Palermo's historic centre. Orlando was increasingly impatient with the delays in the committee's work, and the city council decided to set up a new team of architects and planners. This time, only external actors were engaged – none of the members were Sicilian – as a way of avoiding clashes of interests. Announcements were also made that priority would go to northern Italian and continental firms in all contract bidding. More measures were eventually imposed in order to increase transparency in the construction sector, for example by controls over construction sites and by the inclusion in building contracts of commitments to transparency and legality.[11]

There were strong reactions to the decision to employ only non-Sicilians. The commissioner for the historic centre at this period, Emilio Arcuri, believed that, except for schoolteachers, the entire city was against the city council's decision. The team that had been dismissed also felt that Orlando's policy 'unnecessarily closed off avenues of alliance between a broad range of antimafia forces, tarring too many good-willed persons with the brush of collusion'.[12]

After Orlando's re-election in 1993, the most contested issue concerned the role of the construction sector in the new Palermo that Orlando was planning. The most important difference between the urban plan of 1962 and that of 1997 was between construction and reconstruction. While the former plan proposed new construction, the latter's assumption was that Palermo was overbuilt, that in fact the number of inhabitants would not increase, and so priority ought to be given to consolidation, by way of renovation of existing buildings. However, this new policy also meant shedding a substantial number of construction jobs.[13]

Interviews undertaken by Schneider and Schneider with 33 families in 1996, in some of Palermo's poorest areas, indicated that many perceived Orlando's strive for legality to be an economic threat to their families. Many linked the economic decline to Orlando's anti-Mafia programme, as it had slowed down construction, and expressed concern about their personal economic situation. One of the interviewees said there was a 'hysteria about legality', and several complained that the anti-Mafia programme had taken the work away. Several said they had voted for Orlando in the 1993 mayoral elections but did not support his candidates in the national elections of 1996, arguing that the legality programme and the urban planning represented a threat to them and their families.[14]

The return of small-scale clientelism

People's expectations of Orlando were enormous when he entered office in 1993. People were expecting a change, welfare, economic transfers, pensions and job opportunities. Orlando had set out to make important administrative, economic and social reforms, but he was facing budget cuts from the national level and his room for manoeuvre became more limited over time. People were expecting personal support according to the old clientelistic tradition, but Orlando failed to deliver.[15] On a more general level, the widening gap between northern and southern Italy and lack of economic progress in Palermo might have negatively affected Orlando's popularity, too.[16]

After the election of Silvio Berlusconi as prime minister in 1994, Orlando was himself increasingly resorting to clientelism –

he made nominations for posts within the public sector and was also criticised for having spent large sums on external consultants.[17] The political initiative that was launched in Palermo in 1997 in order to fight unemployment – the 'socially useful work' programme – was another example of this form of small-scale clientelism.[18] The purpose of the programme was to generate employment opportunities. All the parties supported the initiative, but it was eventually criticised for being both costly and flawed, as it did not favour those who were most in need. Many perceived the initiative as a clientelistic machine that only served to mobilise votes for the political class, as offers of employment were linked to recommendations.

Finding new arenas

Another explanation for Orlando's failure to appeal to the general public once in office was that he was not the team player required to mobilise support for his party. In an interview, he admitted that he was not particularly concerned about the declining support for his party, La Rete.[19] According to one of his municipal commissioners, he also seemed uninterested in the daily negotiations with the other parties. Further, although he was presenting himself in the elections for the regional presidency in 2001, he was not engaged in his succession at the local level and did not promote any specific candidate.[20]

In addition, Orlando had political ambitions at the national and international level. At the national level, there were rumours circulating in the late 1990s that a mayor's party would be formed after the 1997 municipal elections, including mayors from the most important Italian cities, among them Palermo. The 'image of stable, visible and powerful mayors was one of the most important factors in Italian politics during 1997'.[21] With time, Orlando became increasingly active on the international level. Two major international conferences were organised in Palermo within a short period: the CIVITAS Congress on civic education in 1999, visited by the US first lady, Hillary Clinton, and the United Nations conference on Transnational Organised Crime in 2000. The message presented to the international audience was clear: Palermo had successfully fought the Mafia – the fight against the Mafia was over. The image presented internationally was criticised at the local level. Orlando was reproached for promoting too idealised a picture of Palermo; the image offered did not correspond to the local reality many Palermitans were facing.

Fading interest in the anti-Mafia programme

At the national level, the intense political attention that followed the murders of Falcone and Borsellino was fading. It became increasingly clear that anti-Mafia policy was no longer the first priority and during the national electoral campaign in 1996 Mafia issues were hardly raised by any party. After the strong state response to the Falcone and Borsellino murders, many anti-Mafia associations experienced both a fading of political interest and a lack of engagement from the general public. Maria Falcone, the murdered judge's sister, described the situation in Palermo as 'a situation of stalemate, rather than renaissance', an opinion shared by many others.[22] Civil society returned to its normal (small) size and many associations ceased with their activities.[23] The mass mobilisations of the early 1990s ended; the general public was tired.[24] Despite the continued efforts of the anti-Mafia movement in Palermo, the general public was no longer actively engaged in it. The window of opportunity had closed.

Renaissance or failure?

In summary, several factors contributed to Orlando's decline. While continuous long-term efforts and reforms were necessary for economic development, the short-term priorities of the electorate and the political class took the upper hand in local Palermitan life. Orlando's personal ambitions for a national and international career seem to have distanced him from local political life. This was combined with a fading interest in, or fatigue with, his anti-Mafia policy. Moreover, strong forces opposed Orlando's plans for urban development and, through his policy of *spaccatura* (that is, to break the clientelistic networks with the Mafia), he also alienated his administration from broad parts of the anti-Mafia movement.

A conclusion more than 10 years after the peak of the so-called Palermitan renaissance would be that Palermo has changed to some extent, but not as fully as Orlando would suggest. Orlando mainly engaged in activities of symbolic and cultural importance, and did less to solve some of Palermo's most urgent problems, such as unemployment, housing, the traffic situation and the restoration of Palermo's historic centre. According to a Palermitan journalist, Orlando's politics was more about political imagination than political substance.[25] Less positive grass-roots assessments described his politics as 'nonsense' or 'just talk' (*chiacchiere*); Orlando was accused of window dressing.

Still, considering the cultural transformation of the city, many Palermitans would probably agree there is a somewhat stronger sense of Palermitan identity today than before, and an increased conscience about the need to fight the Mafia. The city is safer – certainly compared with the violent years of the 1980s – and the streets are visibly more crowded in the evenings (two decades ago the city centre was more or less empty after dark).

There is no doubt that Orlando was able to put Palermo on the right track during his years in power, particularly after the assassinations of Falcone and Borsellino, when he received massive political and public support. Many consider his school policy to be one of the most successful parts of Orlando's programme, largely thanks to Alessandra Siragusa, a dynamic municipal commissioner in Orlando's administration. During her years as commissioner, schools were constructed and 're-captured' from the Mafia, the 'School adopts a monument' project was launched and increased attention was given to education in good citizenship and the rule of law.

Increased interest in civic education

Civic education is not unique to Palermo but is a general aim of the Italian school system as a whole and includes teaching in several school subjects. During the 1990s, there was a growing concern in Italy about the role of school in the formation of responsible and informed citizens. Many rapid and fundamental changes occurred in the Italian political system during this decade: some of the major political parties disappeared, a new Republic was born and new political organisations emerged. The old cleavage between the north and the south was reinforced by the emergence of the separatist party Lega

Nord under the leadership of Umberto Bossi. The debate was fuelled by Bossi's racist declarations that targeted both foreigners and southern Italy. Discussions about a multiethnic and multicultural Italy were brought to the fore.

The term 'civic education' has a very broad meaning and refers to 'that area of values and problems that essentially concern the dimension of citizenship, without forgetting its connections with the ethical, civil, social and economic issues relating to the individual and to the worker'. Despite the broad sweep encompassed by civic education, the different components of the programme do have essences in common: they all refer to the Italian constitution and they express the fundamental rights and duties of all individuals and citizens.[26]

Civic education is organised under different subjects at various school levels. In primary schools, it is offered through lessons in history, geography and social studies. Lower secondary schools have a specific subject area called civic education that is taught in connection with history. Technical and vocational training schools offer civic education during lessons in law and economics. Education in the Catholic religion also contains relevant themes. At the extracurricular level, there are increasing numbers of courses, so-called cross-curricular education, that incorporate themes relevant to civic education, for example courses on peace, lawfulness, multicultural society and environmental protection.[27]

Anti-Mafia laws and school

The first law concerning anti-Mafia measures in schools was adopted a few months after the assassination of the president of the Sicilian region, Piersanti Mattarella, in January 1980. The regional law (no. 1980/51) – adopted in Palermo six months after the murder – was described as pioneering and was soon followed by similar regional laws in Campania and Calabria.[28] According to the Sicilian regional law:

> The Sicilian region will, in order to contribute to the fight against the Mafia on the educational level and to facilitate young people's education and knowledge of different aspects of the Mafia, promote in Sicilian schools … and at the university faculties … [a] series of initiatives that aims at developing a democratic civil consciousness, through research, individual and group work, studies, seminars, debates, cinema, photo exhibitions and every other kind of activity

necessary for a real consciousness of the problem and its historical, socio-economic, political and traditional implications.[29]

The law granted financial resources to schools for expenses related to the acquisition of bibliographic and didactic materials, the organisation of meetings with experts, research on the territory, exhibitions and the acquisition of other documents relevant to their educational work. Other laws, focusing on young citizens at risk, are also of relevance here; these relate to temporary separation from the family, support for families, activities in centres (*centri di incontro*), increased cooperation between social agencies and schools, and the presence of social workers in high-risk areas. A further piece of legislation from the Ministry of Justice focused on young criminals; it promoted school attendance and the diffusion of a lawful culture through sports and other activities.[30]

The anti-Mafia programme launched by regional law 1980/51 has been operational in Sicilian schools since 1980. But even if many schools manifested an interest in the programme, a large majority of them never applied for the financial support available. According to a survey conducted in 1988/89, only 12.5 per cent had done so. Moreover, schools' interest in the law followed the life cycle of the broader anti-Mafia movement during the 1980s: engagement at the start of the decade, after Mattarella's assassination in 1980, a peak during the years of the Maxi trial in 1986–87, and retreat by the end of the 1980s.[31] A number of factors are evident in the weak implementation of the law, such as its voluntary nature, coupled with time-consuming administrative procedures for requests for financial support. Furthermore, the legislation was further impeded by a lack of training for teachers.[32] Moreover, the initiatives often had a fragmentary and improvised character. The activities supported by the law were often things such as expert conferences followed by debates, the showing of films, and the acquisition and distribution of books to students. It was not until the late 1980s that more attention was given to the significance of 'Mafia values', through investigation by academics of what it means to be a Mafioso (*il sentire mafioso*), including analysis of behaviour, attitudes, activities, relations and linguistic codes.

With pressure from the Parliamentary Anti-Mafia Commission, education in good citizenship formally entered the national school curriculum in October 1993. Under the leadership of Luciano Violante, a former magistrate, the Commission devoted its second year in office to citizens' rights and the creation of socio-economic conditions favourable to education, economic development and employment. Priority was given to initiatives targeting youth: for example, prevention of truancy, improvement of educational and cultural facilities, and encouragement for young students to complete school. The Commission highlighted the correlation between low standards of schools and areas of Mafia infiltration. Calabria and Sicily had the lowest educational levels, the poorest sports facilities and few services for students with handicaps, compared with other Italian regions.[33]

The Parliamentary Anti-Mafia Commission revealed the link between low levels of education and poor quality of school facilities and crime in a report presented in 1993. It found that misallocation and abuse of educational resources were more widespread in Mafia-dominated areas. For example, the cost of educating one student was US$3,000 per annum in southern Italy, compared with US$1,380 in the north. The 1,500 full-time teachers employed in Calabria provided only a quarter of the number of courses offered by teachers in the region of Emilia Romagna (with fewer staff).[34] The organisation of education in morning and afternoon/evening 'shifts' – the use of so-called 'double turns' – was also more frequent in southern Italy than in other Italian regions, indicating the scarcity of available school structures. The infrastructure for students with handicaps was considerably weaker on the islands and in southern Italy than in the rest of Italy. The proportion of students who passed from the first to the second year in lower secondary school, as well as from the second year to the third year, was lower on both Sicily and Sardinia than in the rest of Italy (Table 5.1).[35]

The Parliamentary Anti-Mafia Commission pointed to the lack of adequate classrooms and school buildings in Mafia-dominated areas. The management of schools was costly, and the maintenance and repair of schools were kept to a minimum or ignored. Renovations were rarely completed on time. Students were subjected to unsanitary, inadequate and overcrowded conditions.[36] Violante's Commission expressed alarm at the poor conditions of school structures in Palermo and its provinces – they were 'dramatic' and 'alarming' – and felt that

Table 5.1 Educational standards at lower secondary level in public schools, 1996/97

	Number of classes with double turns	Number of students with double turns	Proportion of school buildings with lifts for students with handicaps (%)	Proportion of school buildings with escalators for students with handicaps (%)	Proportion of students passing to the second year (%)	Proportion of students passing to the third year (%)
Italy	237	4740	14.4	20.9	92.7	94.7
North-west	19	351	23.7	23.6	94.2	96.3
North-east	8	191	22.7	28.5	94.6	96.6
Central	–	–	13.2	20.7	93.4	95.4
South	160	3218	6.8	18.9	92.3	94.3
Islands	50	980	6.9	12.4	88.9	90.3

North-west: Piedmont, Valle d'Aosta, Lombardy, Liguria.
North-east: Trentino–Alto Adige, Veneto, Friuli–Venezia Giulia, Emilia-Romagna.
Central: Tuscany, Umbria, Marche, Lazio.
South: Abruzzo, Molise, Campania, Puglia, Basilicata, Calabria.
Islands: Sicily, Sardinia.

Source: Excerpt from Statistiche della scuola media inferiore. Anno scolastico 1996/97 (Rome: ISTAT, 1999), tables 3.7, 5.7 and 7.14.

'too often the gravity of the situation was underestimated by regional and local administrators'.[37]

Under pressure from the Commission, the national parliament approved increased funding for educational materials and improved school structures in southern Italy and in the central areas of cities in the north. Schools were also encouraged to introduce education in 'anti-Mafia awareness'. A few months after the assassinations of Falcone and Borsellino in 1992, the anti-Mafia awareness programme became part of the national school curriculum. A specific section was created by the Commission as a way of facilitating the schools' work and providing them with documents, information and advice. In 1995, anti-Mafia education eventually expanded to integrate Libera, a national anti-Mafia association, in its work.[38]

The central role of schools in the anti-Mafia campaign was clearly underlined in a circular from the Ministry of Public Education.[39] The Ministry underlined the importance of school, describing it as 'the first fundamental institution', after the family. The Ministry also claimed that students' impressions of school were often related to their perceptions of other public institutions, and so it was necessary that school represented 'a place where individual rights and freedoms were equal and a place for mutual respect'. The importance of class climate was also underlined. A classroom climate marked by transparency, coherence, equality and solidarity may sometimes be more efficient as a lesson in legality than a lot of words, the Ministry stated. According to the circular, the objectives of the legality programme (as the anti-Mafia programme became known) were to promote the values of freedom and the principles of legality. The education programme also aimed to establish a strong civic culture, correct juridical relations and a society based on the respect of individual rights; it refused 'any form of contamination between a rule-based society and a society based on the abuse of power'. The Ministry of Public Education described the fight against the Mafia and other forms of organised crime as 'a decisive occasion to defend the democratic institutions and to create life conditions that are equal and fair for all citizens'. Cooperation between institutions was encouraged as a way of presenting a broad and decisive response to all forms of criminality. The fight against organised crime could be conducted only with 'organic and continuous work' marked by determination, professionalism and 'educational passion', and efforts had to be made 'by everybody, on all fronts'.[40]

The Ministry of Public Education identified some areas of particular concern. A first priority was to reduce school drop-out rates. Experimental activities were mentioned as a way of avoiding social fragmentation. Relations between schools needed to be strengthened through mutual visits, exchange programmes or cultural programmes. The Ministry also underlined the need for adequate training of teachers for the anti-Mafia programme. Multimedia presentations and questionnaires could be used to test students' knowledge and perceptions of organised crime, the Ministry suggested, and it invited teachers to enrich the programmes according to their 'educational passions and professional skills'.

School policy in Palermo

The national anti-Mafia programme was adapted by the different regions. In Palermo, the programme concentrated primarily on civic education. The school policy also included improved management of school buildings, improved enrolment procedures and a reorientation of the educational content, with an increased focus on civic education and respect for the law. Particular efforts were initially made to make the anti-Mafia programme part of the curriculum in Palermitan schools. The programme eventually changed its name to the 'legality programme', based on the presumption that a pedagogic effort must be *for* something, and not *against* something. The programme started in primary school, that is, with students aged from 6 to 10 years, and continued in lower secondary school, with students between the ages of 10 and 14.[41]

One of the most urgent aspects of Orlando's school policy was construction of new schools. Already in 1971, the Anti-Mafia Commission had commented on the poor condition of Sicily's school buildings. In comparison with the rest of Italy, Sicilian classrooms were both overcrowded and in extremely bad condition. The use of 'double turns' was widespread and reflected the lack of available classrooms. Moreover, the classrooms used were often inadequate and designed for non-educational purposes. An important policy in Orlando's administration was to take over the ownership and control of public school buildings. In 1993 in the city of Palermo, as many as 70 per cent of schools rented buildings and spaces required for teaching and administration; this figure had been drastically reduced by 2000, to less than 30 per cent.[42]

Important efforts were also made to reduce school drop-out, a widespread phenomenon in Palermo. In the year 1987/88 – before Orlando came to power in 1993 – the Provincial Education Office of Palermo started an action research project in order to study the school drop-out rate and to fight its increase. Particular efforts were made to target socially and economically disadvantaged pupils and their families.[43] Statistics indicate that the efforts to keep students in school were promising. While the overall rate of school drop-out at lower secondary level in the city and province of Palermo reached 23 per cent during the scholastic year 1985/86, it continually decreased during the 1990s and was below 10 per cent in 2000/01. Nevertheless, differences within Palermo remained important. In some of the most deprived districts, for example the historic centre, Borgo Vecchio, Zen, Sperone and Danisinni, drop-out rates remained as high as 30 per cent.[44]

Enrolment procedures were improved as a way of fighting school drop-out. While the previous system was based on a model in which parents had the responsibility for enrolling their children, the City Department of Education became more actively engaged by sending out formal notices to families before school started. In 1985/86, almost 3 per cent of the children never showed up at the start of school at lower secondary level. In the mid-1990s, the proportion was less than 1 per cent. The number of students who started but later abandoned school decreased from 3 per cent in 1985/86 to less than 1 per cent by the end of the 1990s.[45]

The positive trend was later broken. As of March 2005, school drop-out at both lower and higher secondary level was on the increase in Palermo.[46] The proportion of children who *never* attended school was on the increase at all levels. The positive trend of the 1990s with continued reductions in the drop-out rate was therefore somewhat lost during the first years of the new millennium.

New didactic materials were developed that underlined the principles of citizenship, lawful behaviour, tolerance and co-operation between students. Some of the methods used involved sports, music, school journals, ceramics, stage plays and the organisation of students in cooperatives. Children were taught to behave in a 'sporting way', for example by shaking the hands of their opponents at the conclusion of a match. They were also instructed to solve conflicts by talking and not by using their fists, and to be tolerant of the views of others. Students learnt to help each other. Efforts were similarly made to encourage children to break the traditional *omertà* and to cooperate with law enforcement agencies when they had witnessed a crime. Police officers, judges and politicians were invited into schools as a way of improving the image of the state. Some schools engaged in exchange programmes with other schools in other Italian regions. Moreover, discussions of and research into criminal rackets, *pentitismo*, legal values, and the social and historic background of the Mafia were also organised by schools.[47]

Schools also encouraged students to produce drawings expressing the values of solidarity and cooperation. Many of these were later published in books. One example was a drawing representing an isolated Mafioso surrounded by students holding hands and declaring 'We are united'. Another drawing showed children playing together in a circle, saying 'We are all together', 'I am satisfied' and 'It is beautiful to play together'.[48] A further example of methods used was the video *The Brave Mayor Against Marco the Mafioso*, prepared by students in the primary school Borgo Nuovo 2. The video narrated the criminal career of a young drug addict, Marco, who manages in a short time to gain a position of power within the Mafia by murdering and being involved in other criminal activities. The mayor opposes him and is murdered by the young criminal. Citizens are enraged and testify against Marco and his accomplices. The video tackled themes such as *omertà* and solidarity, and condemned a culture based on fear, intimidation and passive consent to the Mafia's power.[49]

Generally, school policy in Palermo focused on education for citizenship, and control of the territory and of the city's collective memory.[50] One of the most visible and creative parts of the programme was a project launched by the city council in 1994: *Palermo apre le porte: la scuola adotta un monumento* ('Palermo opens its doors: school adopts a monument'). This was part of a national programme started by Fondazione Napoli '99 in 1992 under the auspices of the European Community. The programme was later implemented throughout Italy and, by 1994, 65 city councils, 100 schools and almost 100,000 students were actively involved in it. The project invited schoolchildren to adopt public or private monuments and to take over their physical care and maintenance. Many of these monuments had been abandoned, vandalised or closed to the public for decades, often as a result of political corruption. The project involved learning about and documenting the adopted monument's history, and students were encouraged to serve as guides for friends, families, neighbours and tourists. In memory of Falcone and Borsellino, the monuments opened every May to the general public and visitors had the possibility to choose between several different itineraries.[51]

During the three school years 1994/95, 1995/96 and 1996/97, 139 Palermitan schools joined the project and adopted 170 monuments. In the following two-year period (1997/98, 1998/99), 113 schools adopted a total of 140 monuments. In 1999, the City Department of Education estimated that more than 20,000 students from 150 elementary, lower secondary and higher secondary schools had participated.[52]

The ultimate aim of the project was to make students become more aware of and appreciate Palermo's cultural heritage, to increase their knowledge of the territory and to encourage their engagement with the city and its monuments. Quoting Orlando, the project 'planted the seed of awareness about the *res publica*, the "public thing" that belongs to everyone – an awareness what is not "yours" or "mine" is *ours* and must be jointly cared for'.[53] The adoption by a school of a monument was formally recognised in a municipal ceremony with the participation of the mayor, underlining the importance of the event.

The educational change was primarily about content and didactic methods, rather than increased budget resources.[54] It should be noted, however, that the city of Palermo paid for transport related to the programme, documentation and the printing of numerous reports and drawings done by schoolchildren. Several schools were also constructed during the Orlando regime in Palermo. Moreover, during this period the Parliamentary Anti-Mafia Commission and the national parliament prepared and financed additional resources related to the legality programme, including information, bibliographies and manuals for teachers.[55]

Nevertheless, more than 10 years after the introduction of an anti-Mafia curriculum, great need remains for further systematic evaluation of the Palermo school programme. Other than analyses of drop-out rates, there have been no qualitative or quantitative evaluations of Palermo's school policy.

Conclusion

In this chapter I have illustrated that Orlando's programme for Palermo was largely related to efforts within three sectors: infrastructure, culture and school. Many efforts were made to improve Palermo, to make it more attractive to its citizens, to take the control of the territory and to confront cultural stereotypes of the Sicilian character. Orlando's programme was characterised by acts of symbolic significance and meaning, such as the reopening of the opera house. Efforts were made to renovate buildings and monuments and to restore green areas in the city centre. Better public transport and illumination of the city centre were other examples of Orlando's policy.

The major aims of Orlando's political programme were to restore the state's control of the city's territory and to promote a civic consciousness based on the rule of law. A theme frequently developed was to 'recapture' the city from the Mafia and to give Palermo's territory back to its citizens. An important part of the political debate during these years concerned a redefinition of Sicilian culture by firmly distinguishing it from Mafia culture, and by challenging cultural explanations of the Mafia. Internationally, the new policy was launched as a 'Palermitan renaissance'.

Civic education and anti-Mafia education had already been stipulated in several laws. Under pressure from the Parliamentary Anti-Mafia Commission, education in good citizenship formally entered the national curriculum in October 1993.

School policy in Palermo during these years included improved management of school buildings, improved enrolment procedures, efforts to fight school drop-out, new educational material, and an increased focus on civic education and respect for the law. Other important aspects were education in citizenship, increasing students' knowledge of the territory and, in consequence, improving the city's collective memory.[56] One of the most visible and creative parts of the programme was the 'School adopts a monument' project, launched by the city council in 1994.

During Orlando's second term of office, criticism of his policies grew; these were characterised as superficial and inadequate to solve some of Palermo's most urgent problems, such as housing, urban planning and unemployment. Several factors contributed to Orlando's decline. His personal ambitions for a national and international career seemed to have distanced him from local political life, and his anti-Mafia policy was eventually met with fatigue on the part of much of the populace. Moreover, strong forces opposed Orlando's urban planning and through his policy of *spaccatura* he also alienated his administration from broad parts of the anti-Mafia movement. Nevertheless, school policy was considered one of Orlando's major achievements.

What happened after Orlando? In general, teachers and school leaders in Palermo complained about the weak political interest in school policy after the election of a right-wing local government in 2001.[57] They noted there was less financial support for handicapped children, economic cuts and no new initiatives at the local level in Palermo. While the preceding administration had launched several new programmes that affected schools, the new administration's school policy was less obvious and less visible. The 'School adopts a monument' project continued, although some schools decided to abandon it. Even if several members of the former administration continued in office, it was clear, when talking to school leaders and teachers, that the new administration was less visible on the ground. Contacts were fewer and many teachers and school leaders did not know the name of the new school assessor. In spite of the change of local government, schools continued their work on the legality programme.

In the next three chapters we will turn to an analysis of the results from the two surveys, starting with students' trust in political institutions.

Notes

1 Schneider and Schneider, 'Mafia, antimafia, and the question of Sicilian culture', p. 237. See References for other sources cited in this paragraph.

2 Jamieson, *The Antimafia*, pp. 68–9.

3 Schneider and Schneider, 'Mafia, antimafia, and the question of Sicilian culture', pp. 255–6.

4 Città di Palermo, *Relazione generale Palermo città di città* (Palermo: Città di Palermo, 1994), pp. 11–12; Comune di Palermo, *Abitare Palermo. Guida al nuovo piano regolatore* (Palermo: Assessorato al Territorio, 1998). For an analysis of Palermo's construction sector, see Chubb, *Patronage, Power and Poverty in Southern Italy*, chs 5, 6; Schneider and Schneider, *Reversible Destiny*, ch. 10.

5 Ginsborg, *Italy and Its Discontents 1980–2001*, pp. 315–16.

6 Ginsborg, *Italy and Its Discontents 1980–2001*, p. 316.

7 Quoted in Scuola Media Statale Giuseppe Piazzi, *Palermo è nostra* (Palermo: Città di Palermo, Assessorato Pubblica Istruzione, 1998), p. 5.

8 Author's translation. A. Siragusa, *Per una nuova identità cittadina. L'esperienza educativa di Palermo apre le porte la scuola adotta un monumento* (Palermo: Città di Palermo, 2001), p. 26.

9 A. Campbell, G. Gurin and W. E. Miller, *The Voter Decides* (Evanston: Row, Peterson, 1954), p. 187.

10 For a discussion of political efficacy and political participation, see: P. Adman, *Arbetslöshet, arbetsplatsdemokrati och politiskt deltagande* (Uppsala: Acta Universitatis Upsaliensis, 2004), ch. 2; and O. Petersson, A. Westholm and G. Blomberg, *Medborgarnas makt* (Stockholm: Carlssons, 1989), pp. 286–96.

11 Schneider and Schneider, *Reversible Destiny*, pp. 240–1, 256.

12 Schneider and Schneider, *Reversible Destiny*, pp. 242–3.

13 Schneider and Schneider, *Reversible Destiny*, pp. 252, 256.

14 Schneider and Schneider, *Reversible Destiny*, pp. 279–84.

15 A. Mastropaolo, municipal commissioner for citizens' rights in Orlando's municipal executive committee between 1992 and 1994, personal communication, 14 March 2006.

16 The gross domestic product (GDP) of southern Italy accounted for 25.3 per cent of the national GDP in 1991, and 24.2 per cent of the national GDP in 1997. Jamieson, *The Antimafia*, p. 153.

17 E. del Mercato, journalist, *La Repubblica*, 13 March 2002, personal communication; and M. Artale, director, Centro Padre Nostro, 22 February 2002, personal communication.

18 Del Mercato, personal communication.

19 Jamieson, *The Antimafia*, p. 70.

20 Mastropaolo, personal communication.

21 G. Baldini, 'The direct election of mayors: an assessment of the institutional reform following the Italian municipal elections of 2001', *Journal of Modern Italian Studies*, 7:3 (2002), p. 368.

22 M. Falcone, Fondazione Falcone, interview, 9 February 2000.

23 U. Santino, 'La Sicilia dopo la disfatta: Cu vinciù?', *La Rivista del Manifesto*, No. 20 (September 2001), p. 3.

24 A. Mastropaolo, 'Tra politica e cittadinanza', in *La Mafia esiste ancora* (Turin: Alicubi SRI, 2004), p. 47.

25 Del Mercato, personal communication.

26 B. Losito, 'Italy: educating for democracy in a changing democratic society', in J. Torney-Purta, J. Schwille and J.-A. Amadeo (eds), *Civic Education Across Countries: Twenty-Four National Case Studies from the IEA*

Civic Education Project (Amsterdam: International Association for the Evaluation of Educational Achievement, 1999), pp. 399–400.

27 Losito, 'Italy: educating for democracy in a changing democratic society', p. 399.

28 Regional laws underlining the importance of civic education in schools were adopted by the regional council in Campania on 6 May 1985; by the regional council in Calabria on 15 January 1986; and by the Tuscan regional council on 28 October 1994. For an account of the most important legislative acts, see G. Casarrubea, *Gabbie strette. L'educazione in terra di mafia: Identità nascoste e progettualità del cambiamento* (Palermo: Sellerio editore, 1996), pp. 155–69.

29 As quoted by Casarrubea, *Gabbie strette*, p. 155. Author's translation.

30 Ministry of Justice, circular no. 364764, 10 September 1991.

31 For a discussion of the different interpretations of the loss of interest, see: A. Cavadi, 'Sull'attuazione della legge 51/80', in A. Cavadi (ed), *A scuola di antimafia: Materiali di studio, criteri educativi, esperienze didattiche* (Palermo: Centro siciliano di documentazione Giuseppe Impastato, 1994), pp. 143–5; and A. Lorenzi, C. Morrocchi, M. Pezzini and A. Savoja, *Obiettivo: Coscienza civile* (Palermo: La Zisa, 1990), pp. 12–24.

32 Schneider and Schneider, *Reversible Destiny*, pp. 263–4.

33 Jamieson, *The Antimafia*, p. 58.

34 Jamieson, *The Antimafia*, p. 148.

35 Students in Italian schools can be required to repeat a school year.

36 J. Schneider, 'Educating against the Mafia – a report from Sicily', *Civnet's Journal for Civil Society*, 3:3 (1999), p. 4.

37 Lorenzi, Morrocchi, Pezzini, Savoja, *Obiettivo*, p. 26.

38 Jamieson, *The Antimafia*, pp. 58, 149. Libera is an association composed of 700 national and local groups, with branches in all Italian regions. Common to the associations which make up Libera is the belief that action by the police forces and by judges must be coupled with preventive measures in schools and neighbourhoods and by creating job prospects for young people.

39 All the quotations are from the same document: Ministry of Public Education, circular 302, prot. 23608/JR, 25 October 1993.

40 With the adoption of Letizia Moratti's reform in March 2003, law 53/2003, the involvement of all teachers in legal education was codified in national law.

41 G. Granata, school principal at Scuola Oberdan, interview, 12 February 2002.

42 A. Siragusa, municipal commissioner, City Department for Education, interview, 2 February 2000.

43 M. Gentile, 'The drop-out preventing project in Palermo', in M. Valkestijna and G. van de Burgwal (eds), *New Opportunities for Children and Youth: Good Practices and Research Regarding Community Schools*, a report on the European conference, EDE, The Netherlands, 2001, pp. 111–12.

44 Statistics provided by the Provveditorato agli studi di Palermo.

45 Statistics provided by the Provveditorato agli studi di Palermo.

46 In the Sicilian region as a whole, school drop-out was decreasing slightly, from 7.2 per cent in 2002/03 to 6.8 per cent in 2003/04. The regional

decrease masked an increase in Palermo, Siracusa and Enna. It also hid an increase in the proportion of students aged over 15 years who continued to attend lower secondary school in Palermo, Messina and Enna. School drop-out at higher secondary level also slightly increased, from 16.0 per cent to 16.2 per cent, particularly in Palermo, Trapani and Siracusa. See 'Dispersione scolastica, allarme in Sicilia', *Giornale di Sicilia*, 25 March 2005.

47 Leoluca Orlando, 'Preface', in *Darsi una mano: Educazione alla cittadinanza. riflessioni, percorsi, scelte di gemelaggi* (Firenze: Edizionie della Giunta Regionale, 2001), p. 10.

48 See Scuola Elementare G. Daita, *I colori della speranza* (Palermo: Comune di Palermo, Assessorato Pubblica Istruzione, 1996).

49 Circolo Didattico Borgo Nuovo 2, *The Brave Mayor Against Marco the Mafioso*, video (1994/95).

50 Circular, City Department of Education, City of Palermo.

51 See also Schneider and Schneider, *Reversible Destiny*, pp. 265–71.

52 City Department of Education, City of Palermo.

53 Orlando, *Fighting the Mafia and Renewing Sicilian Culture*, p. 196.

54 Siragusa, interview.

55 Schneider and Schneider, *Reversible Destiny*, p. 264.

56 Circular, City Department of Education, City of Palermo.

57 These conclusions are based on talks with school leaders and teachers in the schools that participated in the study in March 2005.

6

Students' trust in political institutions

Distrust of state institutions is frequently mentioned in the literature pertaining to the Mafia, as well as in the literature on southern Italy in general. The dominant explanation for this lack of trust is historical. It is argued that countries with histories of foreign domination by different colonial powers may exhibit a weakness of formal government structures and a perceived lack of legitimacy among citizens. Colonisers have come and gone and different models of governance have been brought to Sicily. Instead of relying on the benevolence of the state, citizens have withdrawn into informal systems of self-help, such as the family and various kin groups.[1] Still, Sciolla's research shows that, by the end of the 1990s, vertical trust in some institutions – the Church, the parliament and the courts – was stronger in southern Italy than in the north-west.[2]

In this chapter we will present descriptive statistics that focus on students' attitudes to the state and its agencies, that is, their vertical trust. We will focus on public institutions and political actors. As a point of comparison, we also asked about students' trust in the media, school and some professions. We will also present statistics about students' attitudes to the concept of *omertà*, here specifically willingness to report to the police after witnessing a crime, as this says something about students' attitudes towards law enforcement agencies. Differences and similarities between socio-economic areas in Palermo will be highlighted.

The descriptive statistics are based on the total samples from the two waves of sampling, in 2002 and 2005, described in Chapter 3, that is, students at the ages of 10–11 years and 13–14 years. Our primary interest is a descriptive analysis of students' trust in political institutions and not the analysis of explanations of individual change. What was the level of students' trust in different public institutions? Were there any differences between socio-economic areas? Was there any major change over time between 2002 and 2005 (at the aggregate level)? The last part of the chapter will compare the results from the Palermo study with results from the international and national studies of Italy conducted by the IEA. Are the students in this study more distrustful than students elsewhere?

Vertical trust

As discussed in Chapter 2, *vertical trust* or *political trust* is the trust citizens have in the political system and societal institutions. Political trust has several dimensions. It could, for example, refer to the political community, regime principles, regime performance, regime institutions or political actors.[3] It could also vary considerably between different public institutions (courts, parliament, police, government, school, etc.).[4]

In this study, students were asked whether they trusted representatives of the state, here defined as the president of the Republic, the Sicilian president and Palermo's mayor. Questions were also asked about students' trust in public institutions such as the national government, the local government, the courts, the police, the political parties, the national parliament and school. Questions about students' personal views on the political system, for example on the government's responsiveness to citizens' demands, were included in the questionnaire but will be excluded from the analysis, as students' comprehension of these questions was generally weak.[5]

Our main interest is therefore to see whether students' trust in various political institutions differs between socio-economic areas and whether there are any major changes at the aggregate level over time. The four possible answers – no trust at all, very little trust, a lot of trust and complete trust – were dichotomised in order to facilitate this analysis.[6]

Trust in political representatives

The first question concerned how much trust students had in political representatives, here specifically the president of the Italian Republic, the president of the Sicilian region and Palermo's mayor. Three other professions – doctors, athletes and lawyers – were added to the analysis as a point of comparison.

In 2002 (Table 6.1), students expressed most trust in Palermo's mayor (60 per cent of students reported trusting the mayor), followed by the president of the Sicilian region (53 per cent) and the Italian president (49 per cent). Differences between different socio-economic settings were marginal and significant only for trust in Palermo's mayor (students from the high-ranked area had less trust in the Palermitan mayor). Students expressed most trust in doctors (71 per cent).

Were there any changes between 2002 and 2005 (Table 6.2)? Averages show that students' trust in political representatives decreased over time. Students' trust in the Italian president, the president of the Sicilian region and Palermo's mayor were lower in 2005. The change was particularly important in relation to students' trust in Palermo's mayor (–12 per cent), followed by trust in the president of the Sicilian region (–9 per cent) and trust in the Italian president (–5 per cent). At the same time as students' trust in political representatives decreased, trust in the other professions increased. In 2005, students' trust in doctors (+5 per cent), athletes (+4 per cent) and lawyers (+2 per cent) exceeded their trust in political representatives.

Trust in political institutions

In general, students' trust in political institutions was low, however with important variations. In 2002 (Table 6.3), students expressed most trust in the local government (66 per cent), followed by trust in the national parliament (45 per cent), the national government (36 per cent) and political parties (23 per cent). Variations between the different socio-economic areas were small and not significant.

Were there any differences between the two waves? Our data show that trust in the political institutions followed the same pattern as trust in political representatives, that is, a decreasing trend. Students' trust in the political parties, already low in 2002, at 23 per cent, had fallen to only 14 per cent in the 2005 survey (Table 6.4).

It should be noted, however, that the rates of 'Don't know' answers for national political institutions were very high. About 20 per cent of the students marked the box indicating

Table 6.1 Trust in political representatives, 2002

Trust in…	Socio-economic level	Lack of trust (%)[a]	Trust (%)[a]	Don't know (%)	Mean[b]	SD[b]	N
The Italian	Low	38	51	11	2.61	0.837	249
president	Intermediate	48	40	12	2.44	0.850	83
	High	37	53	10	2.82	0.786	49
	Total	**40**	**49**	**11**	**2.60**	**0.838**	**381**
The president of	Low	31	53	15	2.68	0.799	249
the Sicilian region	Intermediate	33	57	10	2.58	0.717	84
	High	43	43	14	2.52	0.634	49
	Total	**33**	**53**	**14**	**2.64**	**0.762**	**382**
Palermo's mayor*	Low	27	63	10	2.84	0.848	248
	Intermediate	36	57	7	2.65	0.819	84
	High	39	49	12	2.58	0.823	49
	Total	**30**	**60**	**9**	**2.77**	**0.842**	**381**
Doctors	Low	23	69	8	2.98	0.848	246
	Intermediate	16	77	7	3.10	0.731	84
	High	31	69	0	2.96	0.771	48
	Total	**22**	**71**	**7**	**3.01**	**0.813**	**378**

					Mean[a]	SD	n
Athletes	Low	33	51	16	2.74	0.892	246
	Intermediate	36	46	18	2.72	0.906	84
	High	27	60	12	2.83	0.730	48
	Total	**33**	**51**	**16**	**2.75**	**0.874**	**378**
Lawyers	Low	37	48	15	2.64	0.896	243
	Intermediate	42	44	13	2.63	0.830	83
	High	35	53	12	2.74	0.875	49
	Total	**38**	**48**	**14**	**2.65**	**0.877**	**375**

Percentages based on valid responses, and rounded to the nearest whole number.

[a] Questionnaire responses were: 1 = no trust at all, 2 = very little trust, 3 = a lot of trust , 4 = complete trust, 0 = don't know. These were dichotomised as lack of trust (1, 2) and trust (3, 4).

[b] 'Don't know' answers were excluded from the calculation of means and standard deviations (SD).

*The correlation between socio-economic category and trust in the mayor was significant at the 0.05 level (two-tailed).

Table 6.2 Trust in political representatives, 2005

Trust in…	Socio-economic level	Lack of trust (%)[a]	Trust (%)[a]	Don't know (%)	Mean[b]	SD[b]	N
The Italian president	Low	40	41	19	2.47	0.80	197
	Intermediate	32	44	24	2.61	0.73	75
	High	28	57	14	2.69	0.86	42
	Total	**36**	**44**	**20**	**2.53**	**0.80**	**314**
The president of the Sicilian region	Low	40	44	16	2.50	0.74	196
	Intermediate	28	47	25	2.67	0.76	76
	High	38	38	24	2.47	0.57	42
	Total	**37**	**44**	**19**	**2.53**	**0.73**	**314**
Palermo's mayor	Low	40	50	10	2.61	0.84	196
	Intermediate	34	46	20	2.70	0.86	76
	High	43	43	14	2.50	0.84	42
	Total	**39**	**48**	**13**	**2.62**	**0.84**	**314**
Doctors	Low	22	75	4	3.04	0.78	196
	Intermediate	7	79	14	3.25	0.64	76
	High	24	76	0	3.05	0.74	41
	Total	**18**	**76**	**6**	**3.08**	**0.75**	**313**

Athletes							
	Low	28	58	14	2.88	0.87	196
	Intermediate	36	45	20	2.70	0.88	76
	High	24	64	12	2.89	0.81	42
	Total	**29**	**55**	**15**	**2.84**	**0.87**	**314**
Lawyers	Low	28	52	20	2.80	0.76	197
	Intermediate	28	47	25	2.79	0.88	76
	High	31	45	24	2.72	0.77	42
	Total	**29**	**50**	**22**	**2.79**	**0.78**	**315**

Percentages based on valid responses, and rounded to the nearest whole number.

[a] Questionnaire responses were: 1 = no trust at all, 2 = very little trust, 3 = a lot of trust , 4 = complete trust, 0 = don't know. These were dichotomised as lack of trust (1, 2) and trust (3, 4).

[b] 'Don't know' answers were excluded from the calculation of means and standard deviations (SD).

None of the correlations between socio-economic category and trust was statistically significant.

Table 6.3 Trust in institutions, 2002

Trust in…	Socio-economic level	Lack of trust (%)[a]	Trust (%)[a]	Don't know (%)	Mean[b]	SD[b]	N
National government	Low	42	37	21	2.38	0.85	244
	Intermediate	51	31	18	2.29	0.82	84
	High	46	40	15	2.41	0.74	48
	Total	**44**	**36**	**20**	**2.36**	**0.83**	**376**
Local government	Low	25	65	10	2.87	0.76	246
	Intermediate	20	74	6	2.89	0.71	85
	High	33	61	6	2.72	0.72	49
	Total	**25**	**66**	**9**	**2.85**	**0.74**	**380**
Political parties	Low	55	21	24	2.09	0.88	240
	Intermediate	60	26	14	2.18	0.95	85
	High	49	26	26	2.34	0.68	47
	Total	**55**	**23**	**22**	**2.14**	**0.88**	**372**
National parliament	Low	29	45	27	2.60	0.90	244
	Intermediate	32	49	19	2.68	0.89	84
	High	33	41	26	2.78	0.87	49
	Total	**30**	**45**	**25**	**2.64**	**0.89**	**377**
Courts	Low	44	43	13	2.46	0.90	244
	Intermediate	43	49	8	2.60	1.00	84
	High	27	62	10	2.63	0.76	48
	Total	**42**	**47**	**11**	**2.51**	**0.91**	**376**

Police*	Low	31	64	5	2.79	0.91	244
	Intermediate	27	70	2	2.85	0.92	84
	High	16	82	2	3.10	0.72	49
	Total	**28**	**67**	**4**	**2.84**	**0.89**	**377**
School	Low	10	86	5	3.21	0.73	241
	Intermediate	15	82	2	3.14	0.74	85
	High	17	81	2	3.17	0.76	48
	Total	**12**	**84**	**4**	**3.19**	**0.73**	**374**
Television	Low	34	59	7	2.74	0.90	244
	Intermediate	35	60	5	2.73	0.84	85
	High	40	58	2	2.64	0.70	48
	Total	**35**	**59**	**6**	**2.72**	**0.86**	**377**
Radio	Low	46	36	18	2.35	0.89	242
	Intermediate	49	41	9	2.47	0.74	85
	High	47	43	10	2.41	0.76	49
	Total	**47**	**38**	**15**	**2.39**	**0.84**	**376**
Newspapers*	Low	28	64	8	2.79	0.85	244
	Intermediate	12	82	6	3.05	0.67	85
	High	18	82	0	2.96	0.64	49
	Total	**23**	**70**	**7**	**2.88**	**0.80**	**378**

Percentages based on valid responses, and rounded to the nearest whole number.

[a] Questionnaire responses were: 1 = no trust at all, 2 = very little trust, 3 = a lot of trust , 4 = complete trust, 0 = don't know. These were dichotomised as lack of trust (1, 2) and trust (3, 4).

[b] 'Don't know' answers were excluded from the calculation of means and standard deviations (SD).

*The correlation between socio-economic category and trust was significant at the 0.05 level (two-tailed).

Table 6.4 Trust in institutions, 2005

Trust in…	Socio-economic level	Lack of trust (%)[a]	Trust (%)[a]	Don't know (%)	Mean[b]	SD[b]	N
National government	Low	48	29	24	2.30	0.71	195
	Intermediate	49	23	28	2.28	0.66	75
	High	38	31	31	2.38	0.62	42
	Total	**47**	**28**	**26**	**2.30**	**0.69**	**312**
Local government	Low	39	56	5	2.72	0.77	196
	Intermediate	34	57	9	2.67	0.74	76
	High	31	52	17	2.63	0.69	42
	Total	**37**	**56**	**7**	**2.70**	**0.76**	**314**
Political parties	Low	59	15	26	1.93	0.69	192
	Intermediate	63	10	26	1.84	0.71	76
	High	58	12	30	2.04	0.58	40
	Total	**60**	**14**	**27**	**1.92**	**0.68**	**308**
National parliament	Low	28	42	30	2.63	0.75	194
	Intermediate	29	34	37	2.60	0.74	76
	High	31	45	24	2.59	0.71	42
	Total	**29**	**40**	**31**	**2.62**	**0.74**	**312**
Courts	Low	34	47	19	2.64	0.82	195
	Intermediate	28	55	17	2.73	0.81	76
	High	31	55	14	2.78	0.90	42
	Total	**32**	**50**	**18**	**2.68**	**0.83**	**313**

Police	Low	17	77	6	3.09	0.76	195
	Intermediate	25	72	3	3.05	0.83	75
	High	21	74	5	2.98	0.73	42
	Total	**20**	**76**	**5**	**3.06**	**0.77**	**312**
School**	Low	14	82	4	3.13	0.69	195
	Intermediate	16	80	4	3.08	0.72	76
	High	31	67	2	2.78	0.69	42
	Total	**17**	**80**	**4**	**3.07**	**0.70**	**313**
Television	Low	39	54	8	2.68	0.85	196
	Intermediate	41	51	8	2.62	0.82	75
	High	52	40	7	2.44	0.68	42
	Total	**41**	**51**	**8**	**2.63**	**0.83**	**313**
Radio	Low	47	36	16	2.41	0.85	196
	Intermediate	49	36	16	2.38	0.77	76
	High	48	36	17	2.43	0.70	42
	Total	**48**	**36**	**16**	**2.41**	**0.81**	**314**
Newspapers	Low	35	59	6	2.77	0.84	196
	Intermediate	29	66	5	2.81	0.88	76
	High	31	67	2	2.88	0.84	42
	Total	**33**	**62**	**5**	**2.80**	**0.85**	**314**

Percentages based on valid responses, and rounded to the nearest whole number.

[a] Questionnaire responses were: 1 = no trust at all, 2 = very little trust, 3 = a lot of trust , 4 = complete trust, 0 = don't know. These were dichotomised as lack of trust (1, 2) and trust (3, 4).

[b] 'Don't know' answers were excluded from the calculation of means and standard deviations (SD).

**The correlation between socio-economic category and trust was significant at the 0.01 level (two-tailed).

that they were unsure or didn't know. This may indicate unfamiliarity with these institutions at this young age (10–11 and 13–14 years). Caution is therefore warranted when interpreting these results.

Trust in law enforcement institutions

There were important differences between students' trust in the police and the courts. While in 2002 an average of 67 per cent expressed their trust in the police, only 47 per cent said they trusted courts. Differences between socio-economic areas were significant for trust in the police: students in higher-ranked areas expressed more trust than those in lower-ranked areas: 64 per cent of the students in the low-ranked areas said they trusted the police compared with 82 per cent in the high-ranked area.

Did students' trust in the police and the courts change over time? Between the two measurements we observed some improvements. While there was a small increase of students' trust in the courts (+3 per cent), the increase was larger for trust in the police (+9 per cent). We also found some interesting differences between the three socio-economic areas. Trust in the police increased in the low-ranked and intermediate areas but decreased in the high-ranked area (–8 per cent). In 2005, trust in the police was higher in the low-ranked areas (77 per cent) than in either the intermediate (72 per cent) or the high-ranked area (74 per cent).

Trust in school and the media

Students expressed more trust in the Italian educational system (i.e. school) than in any other public institution. In 2002, 84 per cent of the students overall indicated they had trust in school. Differences between the socio-economic areas were small. Trust continued at a high level in 2005, at 80 per cent, but with differences between areas. Students in the high-ranked area actually lost some of their trust in the schooling system between 2002 and 2005. In 2005, only 67 per cent of the students in the high-ranked area said they trusted school, which was considerably lower than in the other areas.

With regard to the students' trust in television, radio and newspapers, students expressed most trust in the printed press

(70 per cent in 2002), followed by television (59 per cent) and radio (38 per cent). There was a small decrease of students' trust in these media between 2002 and 2005. The largest change was the loss of trust in television among students in the high-ranked area (–18 per cent).

Before turning to our comparative analysis of students' trust in Palermo and the rest of Italy, we would like to further discuss one of the concepts closely related to trust in law enforcement institutions.

Omertà

Omertà is one of the most important aspects of the Mafia. It means the capacity to maintain silence under difficult conditions. The term traditionally refers to the Mafioso and his capacity to remain silent in the face of public investigations of crime, but may also mirror a general reluctance on the part of witnesses to give testimony to law enforcement agencies. The concept, however, can also be related to the importance of being discreet, 'minding one's own business' and a general reluctance to talk openly about your private life and to interfere in other people's business.[7] In this regard Falcone identified a difference between Sicilians and the 'Mediterranean mentality' elsewhere:

> Here in Sicily it is totally unacceptable to reveal one's private thoughts in public. We are a million miles from the typical effusiveness of southern Italians. Emotions belong to the private sphere and there is no reason to display them.... This natural reserve encourages Sicilians not to become involved in *fatti altrui*, 'other people's business', which is both good and bad at the same time. It is a fact that meddling in other people's business often causes trouble.[8]

Omertà is manifest in an extreme form within the Mafia. An *uomo di onore* should always refuse any kind of cooperation with the law enforcement agencies, not only if he is directly involved in a case but also if he is indirectly involved.[9] It is often assumed that the importance of *omertà* is more widespread in areas marked by a Mafia presence.

To what extent did students agree with the statement 'You must always report to the police if you have witnessed a crime'? In the first survey in 2002 (Table 6.5), an average of 75 per cent

Table 6.5 Students' conception of *omertà*, 2002 and 2005[a]

	Strongly disagree/ disagree (%)	Agree/ strongly agree (%)	Mean	SD	N
*2002****					
Total	**25**	**75**	**2.94**	**0.92**	**382**
Low-ranked areas	30	70	2.85	0.96	248
Intermediate areas	22	78	2.95	0.88	85
High-ranked area	6	94	3.37	0.60	49
School A1	28	72	2.97	0.98	67
School A2	47	53	2.51	0.93	57
School A3	29	71	2.71	0.95	65
School A4	15	85	3.22	0.83	59
School B1	13	87	3.06	0.76	47
School B2	34	66	2.82	1.01	38
School C1	6	94	3.37	0.60	49
*2005****					
Total	**20**	**80**	**3.08**	**0.80**	**313**
Low-ranked areas	25	75	2.99	0.86	195
Intermediate areas	14	86	3.16	0.69	76
High-ranked area	10	90	3.33	0.65	42
School A1	24	76	3.00	0.96	57
School A2	30	70	2.85	0.86	40
School A3	12	88	3.24	0.66	42
School A4	29	70	2.89	0.85	56
School B1	20	80	3.00	0.72	44
School B2	6	94	3.38	0.61	32
School C1	10	90	3.33	0.65	42

[a] Students' conception of *omertà* was measured by their response to the statement 'Si deve sempre riferire alle forze dell'ordine di essere stato testimone di un reato (furto, rapina, agressione)' (You must always report to the police if you have witnessed a crime). Possible responses were 1 = strongly disagree, 2 = disagree, 3 = agree, 4 = strongly agree. (There was no 'Don't know' option for this question.)

[b] A1–A4 = schools in the low-ranked areas, B1–B2 = schools in the intermediate areas, C1 = school in the high-ranked area.

****Correlation between socio-economic area and willingness to report to the police was significant at the 0.01 level (two-tailed).

of the students agreed that this was true. Our results showed important differences between the socio-economic areas, however, with a higher propensity to report to the police in higher socio-economic areas. In the low-income areas in 2002, 70 per cent agreed it was important to report to the police, compared with 78 per cent in the intermediate areas and 94 per cent in the high-ranked area. Differences between schools in low-ranked areas were also striking, with variations between 53 and 85 per cent.

Was there any change over time? In 2005 (Table 6.5), there was a small move towards more agreement on the necessity of reporting to the police, up to 80 per cent compared with 75 per cent in 2002. Differences between socio-economic areas were smaller in 2005 than in 2002, but still statistically significant. While there was more agreement with the statement in the low-ranked and intermediate areas in 2005 than in 2002, there was less agreement over time in the high-ranked area. In summary, differences between the socio-economic areas decreased over time. While schools varied between 53 and 94 per cent in 2002, they varied between 70 and 94 per cent in 2005.

Are Palermitan students more distrustful than students elsewhere?

We will now turn to our comparison with the IEA Italian study,[10] and compare our results with those drawn from other 14-year-olds (Table 6.6). Did the 14-year-old students in this study express less trust than students in other parts of Italy? Unfortunately, we do not have points of comparisons on every item.

In general, the students had less trust in *political institutions* than the average Italian student. In 2005, only 28 per cent of students said they trusted the national government in our study, compared with 53 per cent in the IEA Italian study. Trust in the political parties was 14 per cent in 2005 in the Palermo study and 26 per cent in Italy as a whole. The students' trust in the national parliament was 40 per cent in 2005 in our study, compared with 62 per cent for Italian students. Trust in the local government was, however, on almost the same level in this study as in the IEA Italian study.

Table 6.6 Comparison of the results of the Palermo project and the IEA surveys

Trust in….	Palermo[b] 2002	Palermo[b] 2005	IEA Italy:[c] lower secondary	IEA Italy:[d] higher secondary	IEA international:[e] 14-year-olds
National government	36	28	53	50	48
Local government [a]	66	56	61	53	54
Political parties	23	14	26	20	28
National parliament	45	40	62	54	51
Courts	47	50	62	63	64
Police	67	76	75	72	65
News on television	59	51	42	39	62
News on the radio	38	36	37	33	59
News in the press	70	62	49	45	52

The table shows the percentages, based on valid responses and rounded to the nearest whole number, of students indicating trust in the various institutions. Note that the IEA study asked whether students had trust in political institutions 'always' or 'most of the time', whereas the Palermo study asked students whether they had no trust at all/very little trust/a lot of trust/complete trust.

[a] The IEA study used the term 'Il Comune', while the Palermo study used 'Il Comune di Palermo'.

[b] The first two columns report the results from the two surveys in the present study.

[c] The column refers to the IEA Italian survey distributed to students during their last year at lower secondary school.

[d] The column refers to the IEA Italian survey distributed to students at their first year of higher secondary school.

[e] The column refers to the IEA international survey of 14-year-olds.

Sources: J. Torney-Purta, R. Lehmann, H. Oswald and W. Schulz (eds), *Citizenship and Education in Twenty-Eight Countries: Civic Knowledge and Engagement at Age Fourteen* (Berlin: International Association for the Evaluation of Educational Achievement, 2001), table 5.1, p. 97, and Figure B.2e, p. 201; for the Italian IEA results on civic education, see 'IEA Civic Education – Documenti', section G, table G4 and G.14, http://archivio.invalsi.it/ricerche-internazionali/iea-civic/pagine/risultati.htm.

Regarding trust in *law enforcement agencies*, the students expressed less trust in the courts than the Italian average student did: 50 per cent in 2005, compared with 62 per cent for Italy. Trust in the police was at similar levels in the two studies.

Trust in *news* on television and the printed press was higher among the students in our sample than it was for the average Italian student. Trust in the radio was at almost the same level as in the IEA survey.

Conclusion

The general perception that citizens of Palermo are distrustful of the state is partially supported by these findings. There were some quite important differences in the degree of trust in the various public institutions.

In general, students' trust in political institutions was low, although again with important variations. In 2002, students expressed most trust in the local government (66 per cent), followed by the national parliament (45 per cent), national government (36 per cent) and political parties (23 per cent). Variations between areas were small and not significant.

In 2002, students expressed most trust in Palermo's mayor (60 per cent), followed by the president of the Sicilian region (53 per cent) and the Italian president (49 per cent). Differences across the socio-economic settings were marginal and significant only for trust in Palermo's mayor (students from the high-ranked area had less trust).

Another finding in our study was that students lost trust in the political representatives and the political institutions over time. In 2005, students' expressed less trust in their political representatives – the Italian president, the Sicilian president, and Palermo's mayor – than in doctors, athletes and lawyers. Our data show that trust in the political institutions followed the same pattern as trust in political representatives, that is, a decreasing trend.

In 2002, overall 67 per cent of students expressed their trust in the police, but only 47 per cent said they trusted the courts. Differences between socio-economic areas were significant for trust in the police: 64 per cent of the students in the low-ranked areas said they trusted the police compared with 82 per cent in the high-ranked area.

A majority of students agreed on the importance of reporting to the police after witnessing a crime, that is, to go against *omertà*. Differences were important, however, between both the three socio-economic areas and the schools. In 2002, in the low-income areas, 70 per cent agreed on the importance of reporting to the police, compared with 78 per cent in the intermediate areas and 94 per cent in the high-ranked area. Differences between schools in low-ranked areas varied between 53 and 85 per cent.

An interesting finding was that students expressed more trust in the Italian educational system than in any other public institution. In 2002, overall 84 per cent of the students indicated that they trusted school. Differences between the socio-economic areas were small. Students in the high-ranked area actually lost some of their trust in the schooling system over time: in 2005, only two-thirds of the students expressed their trust in school, compared with 81 per cent in 2002.

Were the students in this study more distrustful of the state than the average Italian student? In some instances, students were more distrustful, in others not. The Palermitan students had less trust in the political institutions than the Italian average student did. Trust in the national government was 28 per cent among the students in this study in 2005, compared with 53 per cent in the IEA Italian study. Trust in the political parties was 14 per cent in the Palermo study in 2005 and 26 per cent in the IEA international study on Italy as a whole, as referred to in Table 6.6. Students' trust in the national parliament was 40 per cent in the 2005 Palermo study, compared with 62 per cent for the average Italian student. Trust in the local government was, however, on almost an equal level as that of the Italian average student.

The low levels of trust in political institutions and the decreasing trend may of course be a reflection of students' parents and their values, which we have been unable to explore in this study. It may also be the result of students' maturation. Some further caution is warranted with regard to the reliability and validity of students' responses. We should recall that students were very young when they participated in this study, 10–11 years old at the first test and 13–14 at the second. It is natural that their conceptions of politics and public institutions were weak at this age. The high rates of 'Don't know' answers and students' reactions during the tests indicated that students sometimes had problems distinguishing the different state agencies and political actors.

It should be recalled that the sample in Palermo was not randomly selected, but strategically selected for an over-representation of schools in 'difficult' neighbourhoods, and so probably underestimates overall values of trust. Furthermore, this chapter has shown that distrust of the state was not general but varied between different public institutions. We also found some variation and different trends between socio-economic areas and, sometimes, between schools.

Notes

1 Hess, *Mafia and Mafiosi*, pp. 15–16.

2 L. Sciolla, *La sfida dei valori. Rispetto delle regole e rispetto dei diritti in Italia* (Bologna: Il Mulino, 2004), pp. 157–60.

3 Norris, *Critical Citizens*, pp. 9–10.

4 B. Rothstein, 'Social capital and institutional legitimacy', paper presented at the Annual Meeting of the American Political Science Association, Washington, DC, 31 August–3 September 2000, p. 21, table 1.

5 Examples of such questions were: 'It is only through personal favours that you receive what you want from the state', 'Politicians quickly forget their voters' request', 'When I vote I expect a personal favour from the politician', 'The government does its best to understand what people want' and 'Politicians are in general fair and respectful towards citizens'.

6 All four answers were used in the significance tests, however, after omitting 'Don't know' answers from the analysis.

7 E. Carlestål, *La Famiglia: The Ideology of Sicilian Family Networks* (Uppsala: DiCa, 2005), p. 142.

8 Falcone and Padovani, *Men of Honour*, p. 74.

9 Hess, *Mafia and Mafiosi*, p. 109.

10 B. Losito (ed.), *Educazione civica e scuola. La seconda indagine IEA sull'educazione civica: Studio di caso nazionale* (Milan: FrancoAngeli, 1999); B. Losito and A. D'Apice, 'Democracy, citizenship, participation. The results of the second IEA civic education study in Italy', *International Journal of Educational Research*, 39 (2003), pp. 609–20.

7

Students' perceptions of generalised trust

As described in Chapter 2, research has shown that generalised trust is important for personal happiness, safer neighbourhoods and cooperation between citizens. The presence of generalised trust is also related to better government, economic development, less corruption and more stable democratic institutions. It is believed to be necessary for the establishment of civil society, as it renders people more inclined to participate in political parties, trade unions or any other kind of organisation that is beneficial for democracy in general.[1]

In the literature on Italy, southern Italians are often described as less trustful than those in other parts of the country. The theme was presented by Banfield in the late 1950s, supported by Almond and Verba's comparison of five states, and later resumed in Putnam's study of Italy.[2] Trust is not, however, stable over time. Inglehart's research showed that levels of generalised trust increased in Italy during the 1990s.[3] Research by Italian sociologists has also found important changes *within* the different Italian regions over time, and more substantial variations between them have emerged.[4]

This chapter will describe students' trust in others. As in the previous chapter, the statistics are based on the two questionnaires distributed in 2002 and 2005 (see Chapter 3). Statistics will be presented for the total sample as well as broken down by socio-economic area. We will use different types of question in order to analyse students' perceptions of other people. First, we will use two questions on trust that are often used in surveys and that are closely related: 'Generally speaking, do you believe that most people can be trusted or that nobody can be trusted?', and 'Do you believe that most people try to help each other or that people generally only think about themselves?'

It seems reasonable to assume that students' level of trust may depend on their physical or psychological proximity to different people. Trust in people known to you or in those you frequently interact with, for example people living in your neighbourhood, may be very different from the trust you have in people you have never met before. Different mechanisms may explain why you trust your neighbours or classmates but not the inhabitants of your city or co-nationals. We therefore asked questions that related to trust in different categories of citizens. We will present data on students' trust in people they know well – family (*familiari*), relatives (*parenti*), neighbours and people living in their area (*quartiere*) – followed by a description of students' trust in persons in the school environment whom students are likely to meet daily or frequently – classmates, teachers, the school principal and the school staff. We also asked about students' trust in persons who are not personally known to them – Palermitans, Sicilians, Italians and foreigners.

What are the students' perceptions of other people? What is their perception of trust in other people and other people's willingness to cooperate? Were there any differences between the socio-economic areas? Was there any change over time between 2002 and 2005?

Generalised trust

In the questionnaire, trust was measured through several questions at different levels of abstraction. For their responses to the question 'Generally speaking, do you believe that most people can be trusted or that nobody can be trusted?' the students were asked to mark (with a cross) a scale of 0, most people can be trusted, to 4, nobody can be trusted, with the value that corresponded the most to their personal opinion. The results, though, are difficult to interpret, as most students marked the middle value (2), indicating that '50 per cent can be trusted'. The rest of the answers were more or less equally spread between the other four alternatives. The average indicated that students were somewhat more inclined to agree with the statement 'most people can be trusted' (i.e. the average was slightly to the left of the middle value).

By comparing the means we see that students were more distrustful in the low-income areas than in the intermediate and high-ranked areas. Students in the high-income category expressed most trust in other people. Differences between socio-economic areas were statistically significant in 2002, but not in 2005.

Did the level of generalised trust change over time? Comparisons of the averages indicate only small changes between the two waves. There was a small movement towards less trust in the intermediate and high-ranked areas. Despite this small loss of trust, students in the high-ranked area still expressed more trust in other people than did those in the lower-ranked areas. For example, none of the students in the high-ranked area had marked the extreme point 'nobody can be trusted', as compared with 9 per cent in the low-ranked areas, and 8 per cent in the intermediate areas. The results are shown in Table 7.1.

Are the 14-year-old students in the Palermo study less trustful than students elsewhere? Unfortunately, the IEA international study did not include questions on generalised trust, and so we have to refer instead to studies on adults' attitudes towards trust. Another difficulty is that these surveys use different scaling or measurement, which render comparisons more difficult. If we add the percentages of the two left-hand columns in Table 7.1, 'Most people can be trusted' and 'More than 50 per cent can be trusted', we may draw the tentative conclusion that quite small proportions of students in the Palermo study expressed trust in 'most people': 23 per cent in 2002 and 18 per cent in 2005.

According to Inglehart, Italians in the south were less trusting than those in the north in 1990, but the general trend in Italy at that time was towards increasing levels of trust. Inglehart refers to Almond and Verba's survey from 1959, in which only 8 per cent of the Italian public had agreed that 'most people can be trusted', whereas, in his own surveys, the proportion had risen to 27 per cent in 1981 and again to 30 per cent in 1986.[5] Another point of comparison is Putnam's study of Italy. Referring to two surveys commissioned throughout Italy in 1987 and 1988, he found that trust in other people varied between different regions. In regions ranking low on his civic community index, 17 per cent of the respondents agreed that you usually could trust other people, in comparison with 33 per cent in regions with a high civic community index (agreement

Table 7.1 Attitudes of generalised trust, 2002 and 2005[a]

	Most people can be trusted (%)	> 50% can be trusted (%)	50% can be trusted (%)	< 50% can be trusted (%)	Nobody can be trusted (%)	Mean	SD	N
*2002**								
Low-ranked areas	13	8	55	14	11	2.03	1.09	249
Intermediate areas	8	10	64	12	6	1.98	0.89	84
High-ranked area	12	31	39	14	4	1.67	1.01	49
Total	**12**	**11**	**55**	**13**	**9**	**1.97**	**1.04**	**382**
2005								
Low-ranked areas	9	8	65	10	9	2.02	0.93	197
Intermediate areas	10	7	62	13	8	2.01	0.97	76
High-ranked area	7	19	62	12	0	1.79	0.75	42
Total	**9**	**9**	**64**	**11**	**7**	**1.98**	**0.92**	**315**

Percentages based on valid responses, and rounded to the nearest whole number.

[a]Students' attitudes of generalised trust were measured by their response to the question 'Pensi che in generale ci si può fidare della maggior parte della gente oppure pensi che non ci si può fidare di nessuno?' (Do you believe that most people can be trusted or that nobody can be trusted?). The response was scaled: 0 = most people can be trusted, 2 = half of the people can be trusted, 4 = nobody can be trusted (a higher average indicates less trust). The two intermediate values (1 and 3) were marked only with numbers.

*The correlation between socio-economic area and trust was significant at the 0.05 level (two-tailed) in 2002 but insignificant in 2005.

rates of 32 per cent and 28 per cent were reported for regions ranking 'medium high' and 'medium low', respectively).[6]

Compared with these studies, we may draw the conclusion that the students in our study expressed less trust in other people than did citizens in other Italian areas. However, in the Palermo study there were some differences between the three socio-economic areas. Students in the high-ranked area were more trusting than students in the intermediate and low-ranked areas. It is worth noting that level of trust expressed by the students in the high-ranked area was not lower than that expressed (by adults) in other Italian regions.

Helpfulness

A general question that is closely related to the previous question is: 'Do you believe that most people try to help other people or that people generally only think about themselves?' The response to this question was scaled in the same way as the previous question. Most students in 2002, 44 per cent, answered that '50 per cent try to be helpful'. The average indicated a small inclination towards the statement 'people only think about themselves'. In 2002, higher proportions of students in the intermediate and the low-ranked socio-economic areas (15 per cent) than in the high-ranked area (2 per cent) agreed that 'people only think about themselves'. By comparing mean scores, however, between the socio-economic categories we see that students in the low-income category had a more positive perception of other people's helpfulness than those in the two higher-ranked areas. Students in the intermediate area had the most negative perception of people's willingness to help.

When comparing means between the 2002 and 2005 waves (Table 7.2), we found that students had moved even further towards the statement 'people only think about themselves'. The overall mean was 2.29 in 2005, as compared with 2.03 three years earlier. The change was most important for students in the high-ranked area.

Emerging from these two general questions is an interesting pattern we did not expect to find: students in the high-ranked area had lower average scores for generalised trust (indicating more trust in other people) at the same time as they had, in

Table 7.2 Perception of people's willingness to help, 2002 and 2005[a]

	Most people try to help other people (%)	> 50% try to help (%)	50% try to be helpful (%)	< 50% try to help (%)	People only think about themselves (%)	Mean	SD	N
2002								
Low-ranked areas	19	9	43	14	15	1.96	1.27	250
Intermediate areas	7	12	47	19	15	2.24	1.08	85
High-ranked area	6	19	42	31	2	2.04	0.92	48
Total	**15**	**11**	**44**	**17**	**14**	**2.03**	**1.19**	**383**
2005								
Low-ranked areas	11	6	50	14	19	2.23	1.16	197
Intermediate areas	4	11	52	12	21	2.36	1.06	75
High-ranked area	5	7	43	29	17	2.45	1.02	42
Total	**9**	**7**	**49**	**16**	**19**	**2.29**	**1.12**	**314**

Percentages based on valid responses, and rounded to the nearest whole number.

[a] Students' perceptions of people's willingness to help were measured by their response to the question 'Pensi che in generale la maggior parte della gente cerca di aiutare gli altri oppure che la gente, in generale, pensa soprattutto ai fatti propri?' (Do you believe that most people try to help other people or do you think that people only think about themselves?). The response was scaled: 0 = most people try to help other people, 2 = 50 per cent try to help, 4 = People only think about themselves. The two intermediate values (1) and (3) were marked only with numbers.

The correlations between socio-economic area and responses were not significant.

2005 at least, higher scores for people's willingness to help (indicating a perception that fewer people try to help). That is, there was no correlation between the questions on trust and helpfulness in the high-ranked area. Hence, students' trustful attitudes towards others were not coupled with a positive perception of other people's willingness to help. In the low-ranked and intermediate areas, however, the two were correlated: low levels of trust corresponded with low expectations of others' willingness to help, and vice versa.[7]

Still, the validity and reliability of the results are not entirely convincing. Despite the widespread use of these two questions in international surveys, the formulation of the questions appears too vague and too general to capture students' trust in other people or their perception of other people's willingness to engage. The questions do not, for example, specify who is to be included in 'people'. It is impossible to deduce whether students think 'people' in the question refers to their neighbours, people they meet in the street, local business people, inhabitants of the same city or their co-nationals. Moreover, the use of a five-point scale answer was not optimal, as around half the students used the middle value (2, '50 per cent can be trusted'), which renders the analysis difficult. The result may represent students' true values, but it may also indicate that students had difficulty answering the question and chose the least 'dangerous' answer, that is, the middle value. We will therefore turn to some other, more specific questions in our surveys and analyse whether students' degree of trust varied.

Trust in known people

We will now look at the levels of trust as regards people students meet regularly, or at least frequently, such as family members, relatives, neighbours, classmates, teachers, school principal and school staff. The response alternatives were 'No trust at all', 'Very little trust', 'A lot of trust' and 'Complete trust'. The four categories were dichotomised in order to facilitate the analysis.

Unsurprisingly, the level of trust was very high for family (*familiari*) and relatives (*parenti*) in all socio-economic areas. In both cases and in both surveys (2002 and 2005), more than 90 per cent of the students said they had 'a lot of trust' or 'complete trust' in their families and relatives (Tables 7.3 and 7.4). In comparison with Sciolla's study of six Italian cities, situated in northern, central and southern Italy, the students in the Palermo study expressed more trust in both families and relatives, which is probably because of our students' young age.[8]

An interesting finding was that students expressed a high level of trust in their teachers: in 2002, almost 90 per cent said they had a lot of trust or complete trust in their teachers. Trust in school principals was also high, at 78 per cent. The proportions of students indicating a lot of trust or complete trust in neighbours (52 per cent), school staff (63 per cent) and classmates (66 per cent) were, however, considerably lower.

Generally, students expressed high levels of trust in their families, relatives and teachers in all of the socio-economic settings. Differences between areas were significant on only three items in 2002: trust in relatives, trust in neighbours and trust in classmates. Students in higher-ranked socio-economic areas expressed more trust in these instances. Only 46 per cent of students in the low-ranked areas trusted their neighbours, compared with 55 per cent in the intermediate areas and 72 per cent in the highest-ranked area. The most important difference concerned trust in classmates in 2002 (although by 2005 there was no longer a significant difference on this measure): only 60 per cent of the students in the low-ranked areas trusted their classmates, compared with 71 per cent in the intermediate areas and 90 per cent in the high-ranked area. Differences between socio-economic areas were small on all other items.

Between the two waves, the most remarkable loss of trust was found in the high-income area. In 2002, 90 per cent of the students said they trusted their classmates, compared with only 66 per cent in 2005. The loss of trust in the school staff was also remarkable in the high-ranked socio-economic category. In 2002, 63 per cent of the students said they trusted the school staff, in comparison with 38 per cent in 2005, which was lower than in the other socio-economic areas.

Trust in unknown people

If trust in neighbours varied with the socio-economic status of the locality, what did students say about their trust in people

Table 7.3 Students' trust in people they know, 2002[a]

	Socio-economic level	Lack of trust (%)	Trust (%)	Mean	SD	N
Family	Low	3	97	3.64	0.57	250
	Intermediate	6	94	3.58	0.60	85
	High	4	96	3.84	0.47	49
	Total	**4**	**96**	**3.65**	**0.57**	**384**
Relatives**	Low	8	92	3.40	0.64	246
	Intermediate	6	94	3.40	0.64	83
	High	2	98	3.71	0.50	49
	Total	**7**	**93**	**3.44**	**0.63**	**378**
Neighbours**	Low	54	46	2.42	0.85	248
	Intermediate	45	55	2.70	0.78	83
	High	28	72	2.83	0.68	46
	Total	**49**	**52**	**2.53**	**0.83**	**377**
Classmates**	Low	40	60	2.69	0.82	247
	Intermediate	29	71	2.73	0.70	85
	High	10	90	3.06	0.52	49
	Total	**34**	**66**	**2.75**	**0.77**	**381**

Teachers	Low	12	88	3.15	0.70	248
	Intermediate	14	86	3.14	0.64	84
	High	12	88	3.18	0.64	49
	Total	**12**	**88**	**3.15**	**0.68**	**381**
School principal	Low	20	80	3.07	0.76	247
	Intermediate	25	75	2.95	0.78	84
	High	28	71	2.88	0.83	49
	Total	**22**	**78**	**3.02**	**0.78**	**380**
School staff	Low	35	65	2.76	0.85	244
	Intermediate	42	58	2.66	0.83	83
	High	37	63	2.63	0.70	49
	Total	**37**	**63**	**2.72**	**0.82**	**376**

Percentages based on valid responses, and rounded to the nearest whole number.

[a] Students' trust in people they know was measured by their response to the question 'Quanta fiducia hai nelle sequenti persone?' (How much do you trust the following persons?). The response was scaled: 1 = no trust at all, 2 = very little trust, 3 = a lot of trust, 4 = complete trust.

** Correlation between socio-economic area and item was significant at the 0.01 level (two-tailed).

Table 7.4 Students' trust in people they know, 2005[a]

	Socio-economic level	Lack of trust (%)	Trust (%)	Mean	SD	N
Family	Low	2	98	3.76	0.51	196
	Intermediate	0	100	3.83	0.38	76
	High	0	100	3.88	0.33	42
	Total	**2**	**98**	**3.79**	**0.46**	**314**
Relatives**	Low	5	95	3.49	0.64	194
	Intermediate	9	91	3.53	0.70	76
	High	0	100	3.81	0.40	42
	Total	**5**	**95**	**3.54**	**0.64**	**312**
Neighbours**	Low	48	52	2.52	0.81	194
	Intermediate	28	72	2.86	0.81	76
	High	31	69	2.88	0.77	42
	Total	**41**	**59**	**2.65**	**0.82**	**312**
Classmates	Low	35	65	2.86	0.87	196
	Intermediate	36	64	2.83	0.79	76
	High	34	66	2.80	0.75	41
	Total	**35**	**65**	**2.84**	**0.84**	**313**

Schoolmates	Low	59	41	2.38	0.84	194
(new item)	Intermediate	63	37	2.32	0.73	76
	High	59	41	2.39	0.77	41
	Total	**60**	**40**	**2.37**	**0.80**	**311**
Teachers	Low	19	81	3.14	0.81	196
	Intermediate	16	84	3.14	0.78	76
	High	17	83	3.12	0.67	42
	Total	**18**	**82**	**3.14**	**0.78**	**314**
School principal	Low	27	73	2.90	0.85	195
	Intermediate	37	63	2.75	0.93	76
	High	21	79	3.07	0.78	42
	Total	**29**	**71**	**2.89**	**0.86**	**313**
School staff	Low	39	61	2.64	0.89	196
	Intermediate	46	54	2.57	0.91	76
	High	62	38	2.45	0.77	42
	Total	**44**	**56**	**2.60**	**0.88**	**314**

Percentages based on valid responses, and rounded to the nearest whole number.

[a] Students' trust in people they know was measured by their response to the question 'Quanta fiducia hai nelle sequenti persone?' (How much do you trust the following persons?). The response was scaled: 1 = no trust at all, 2 = very little trust, 3 = a lot of trust, 4 = complete trust.

**Correlation between socio-economic area and item was significant at the 0.01 level (two-tailed).

living in their area? Moreover, what did they say about their trust in Palermitans, Sicilians, Italians and in foreigners? Here we seek to evaluate students' trust in people whom they do not know personally.

Results from the 2002 and 2005 surveys (Tables 7.5 and 7.6) showed that a majority of students in the low-income areas had 'no trust at all' or 'very little trust' in citizens living in their own area (*quartiere*). In 2002, 58 per cent said they did not trust people in their area, compared with 39 per cent in the intermediate areas and 45 per cent in the highest-ranked area. In response to a separate open question in the surveys, many students described people in their area as either honest, civilised and educated, or as dishonest, uncivilised and bad mannered.

Although many students complained about the uncivilised behaviour of people in their own area, results from the quantitative study showed they had an even more negative perception of the trustworthiness of Palermitans in general. About two-thirds of the students in all socio-economic categories said they had no trust or very little trust in Palermitans. Differences were small between the three socio-economic categories and not statistically significant.

Students also had a negative perception of Sicilians in general: about 60 per cent in all socio-economic categories said they had no trust or very little trust in Sicilians. Differences between categories were small and not statistically significant.

An interesting finding was that students expressed more trust in Italians than in either Palermitans or Sicilians. Differences between the socio-economic areas were small and not significant.

The lowest levels of trust were found for foreigners. An average of 26 per cent in 2002 said they had a lot of trust or complete trust in foreigners. While trust in foreigners was lowest in the lowest socio-economic category, it should be stressed that the students' trust in foreigners was very low in all of the areas.

Are our results high or low? Unfortunately, we are unable to compare these results with those of the IEA study, as that survey did not include questions related to interpersonal trust. However, comparison with Sciolla's study of adults' generalised trust in six Italian cities is of some help when comparing students' trust in Palermitans and Italians. Students' trust in Palermitans, at 36 per cent in 2005, was relatively high compared with Sciolla's results. In northern Italy, Sciolla found that respondents' trust in inhabitants from the same city was 11 per cent in Milan and 10 per cent in Turin. In the two cities in southern Italy, Teramo and Caltanisetta, trust in inhabitants was 16 per cent and 24 per cent, respectively. In central Italy, trust reached 22 per cent in Modena and 20 per cent in Vicenza.[9]

With regard to Italians in general, 50 per cent of the Palermo students in 2005 indicated they would place a lot or complete trust in them; in the six cities in Sciolla's study, the proportions were much smaller, between 10 and 15 per cent.[10]

Conclusion

In this chapter we analysed students' level of generalised trust by asking questions at different levels of abstraction. Starting with the most abstract question, 'Generally speaking, do you believe that most people can be trusted or that nobody can be trusted?', we found that students leaned somewhat towards the statement 'most people can be trusted'. Students in the low-income areas were more distrustful than those in the intermediate and high-ranked areas. The change between the two waves was small, but there was a small movement towards less trust in the intermediate and high-ranked areas. Although different scales render comparisons with other studies difficult, the results seem to support the perception that the level of generalised trust is low in southern Italy.

We thereafter analysed students' responses to another question that is often used in international and national surveys: 'Do you believe that most people try to help other people or that people generally only think about themselves?' We here found a small inclination towards the statement 'People only think about themselves'. An interesting finding was that students in the low-ranked areas had a more positive perception of other people's willingness to help than those in the two higher-ranked areas. When studying change over time, we found a small move towards the statement 'People only think about themselves'. We will have reason to return to this finding in Chapter 9, where we analyse students' letters.

Another interesting finding was that the results from these two abstract questions seemed to be correlated with each

Table 7.5 Students' trust in people they do not know, 2002[a]

	Socio-economic level	Lack of trust (%)	Trust (%)	Mean	SD	N
People in your area (*quartiere*)**	Low	58	42	2.33	0.78	249
	Intermediate	39	61	2.56	0.80	84
	High	45	55	2.57	0.79	49
	Total	**52**	**48**	**2.41**	**0.79**	**382**
Palermitans	Low	65	35	2.27	0.79	250
	Intermediate	70	30	2.24	0.77	85
	High	69	31	2.25	0.70	48
	Total	**67**	**33**	**2.26**	**0.77**	**383**
Sicilians	Low	57	43	2.40	0.84	246
	Intermediate	62	38	2.36	0.79	84
	High	61	39	2.27	0.78	49
	Total	**58**	**41**	**2.37**	**0.82**	**379**

Italians	Low	47	53	2.56	0.83	245
	Intermediate	44	56	2.60	0.83	85
	High	41	59	2.53	0.79	49
	Total	**46**	**54**	**2.56**	**0.82**	**379**
Foreigners	Low	75	25	1.98	0.90	249
	Intermediate	73	27	2.06	0.86	84
	High	73	27	2.06	0.86	48
	Total	**74**	**26**	**2.01**	**0.88**	**381**

Percentages based on valid responses, and rounded to the nearest whole number.

[a] Students' trust in people they did not know was measured by their response to the question 'Quanta fiducia hai nelle seguenti persone?' (How much do you trust the following persons?). The response was scaled: 1 = no trust at all, 2 = very little trust, 3 = a lot of trust, 4 = complete trust.

**Correlation between socio-economic area and item was significant at the 0.01 level (two-tailed).

Table 7.6 Students' trust in people they do not know, 2005[a]

	Socio-economic level	Lack of trust (%)	Trust (%)	Mean	SD	*N*
People in your area	Low	59	41	2.33	0.85	196
(*quartiere*)**	Intermediate	35	65	2.69	0.75	75
	High	33	66	2.69	0.68	42
	Total	**50**	**50**	**2.47**	**0.82**	**313**
Palermitans	Low	62	38	2.42	0.71	197
	Intermediate	68	32	2.17	0.77	76
	High	62	38	2.36	0.62	42
	Total	**64**	**36**	**2.35**	**0.72**	**315**
Sicilians	Low	59	41	2.40	0.68	196
	Intermediate	56	43	2.34	0.72	76
	High	71	29	2.26	0.66	42
	Total	**60**	**40**	**2.37**	**0.69**	**314**

Italians	Low	51	49	2.50	0.74	197
	Intermediate	45	55	2.61	0.66	75
	High	50	50	2.52	0.63	42
	Total	**50**	**50**	**2.53**	**0.71**	**314**
Foreigners	Low	71	29	2.07	0.87	197
	Intermediate	68	32	2.17	0.84	76
	High	64	36	2.26	0.77	42
	Total	**70**	**30**	**2.12**	**0.85**	**315**

Percentages based on valid responses, and rounded to the nearest whole number.

[a] Students' trust in people they did not know was measured by their response to the question 'Quanta fiducia hai nelle seguenti persone?' (How much do you trust the following persons?). The response was scaled: 1 = no trust at all, 2 = very little trust, 3 = a lot of trust, 4 = complete trust.

**Correlation between socio-economic area and item was significant at the 0.01 level (two-tailed).

other only in the low-ranked and intermediate areas (where high levels of generalised trust were associated with positive expectations of other people's willingness to offer help). In the high-ranked area, this correlation was non-existent.

Looking at people who were not personally known to the students, we found that they made quite important distinctions between different categories of citizens. The lowest levels of trust were expressed for foreigners, followed by Palermitans and Sicilians. Italians enjoyed the most trust. In the 2005 survey, 30 per cent said they had a lot of trust or complete trust in foreigners, 36 per cent expressed trust in Palermitans, 40 per cent trusted Sicilians and 50 per cent had trust in Italians. Differences between the socio-economic areas were small and not statistically significant.

This finding is interesting. If Putnam is right in his conclusions, Sicilians should not trust anyone they do not know personally. They should not trust Palermitans, Sicilians, Italians or foreigners. In this study, we found interesting variations between students' trust in different categories of citizens. Moreover, in the comparison with Sciolla's survey of six Italian cities, we also found that students expressed more trust in inhabitants from the same city and in Italians than did the respondents in other cities: 36 per cent of the students in the 2005 Palermo survey expressed trust in their co-inhabitants, in comparison with 10–24 per cent in the six cities. Some caution is warranted in interpreting these results. As already mentioned, Sciolla's study is based on a representative sample of adults. It is possible that trust disappears with age or that these young Palermitans belong to a new generation of Italians who are more trusting. The observed differences may be explained by both differences between generations and the effects of maturation.

Differences between socio-economic areas were important on only four items in 2002: trust in relatives, neighbours and classmates, and people in the area. The differences were striking for trust in neighbours and trust in classmates. Only 46 per cent of the students in the low-ranked areas trusted their neighbours, compared with 55 per cent in the intermediate areas and 72 per cent in the high-ranked area. Only 60 per cent of the students in the low-ranked areas trusted their classmates, compared with 71 per cent in the intermediate areas and 90 per cent in the high-ranked area. Another interesting finding was that students in the high-ranked area lost a lot of trust between the two surveys. In 2002, 90 per cent of the students said they trusted their classmates, compared with 66 per cent in 2005. In 2002, 63 per cent of the students in the high-ranked area said they trusted the school staff, in comparison with 38 per cent in 2005, which was considerably lower than in the other socio-economic areas. The change was not due to any particular changes in the classes in the high-ranked area.

These differences (and changes) indicate that students' trust might be conditioned by the situation in their immediate surroundings. If the area they live in is problematic and marked by crime, this also affects their degree of trust in people living there. We will have reason to return to this finding, too, in Chapter 9, where we will analyse students' own accounts in the Letter Project.

With regard to trust in people who are personally known to them, the students generally expressed high levels of trust in their families, relatives and teachers. We are not surprised by the high levels of trust in families and relatives, but an interesting finding was that teachers enjoyed very high levels of trust in all socio-economic areas. Statistics presented in Chapter 6 showed that students had a lot of faith in school in general: 84 per cent expressed 'a lot of trust' or 'complete trust' in their school in 2002. Schools enjoyed more trust than any other public institution. These findings suggest that schools and teachers have an important potential to influence students' values. This conclusion leads us to the next chapter. By using our panel data, we will explore which factors support students' development of trust or, perhaps, loss of trust.

Notes

1 Mishler and Rose, 'Trust, distrust and scepticism', p. 419.

2 Banfield, *The Moral Basis of a Backward Society*; Almond and Verba, *The Civic Culture*; Putnam, *Making Democracy Work*.

3 R. Inglehart, *Modernization and Postmodernization: Cultural, Economic and Political Change in 43 Societies* (Princeton: Princeton University Press, 1997).

4 See Sciolla, *La sfida dei valori*.

5 Inglehart, *Modernization and Postmodernization*, p. 173.

6 Putnam, *Making Democracy Work*, pp. 111–12, table 4.5, and p. 189.

Putnam's actual phrasing of the question was 'Some people say that you usually can trust people. Others say that you must be very wary in relations with people. Which is your view?'

7 Pearson's correlation coefficients (r) for trust in other people and other people's helpfulness in 2005 were 0.42 in the low-ranked areas and 0.33 in the intermediate areas. Both correlations were statistically significant at the 0.01 level (two-tailed).

8 In Sciolla's study of *adults*, trust in families varied between 83 and 92 per cent, while trust in relatives was lower, between 40 and 49 per cent. The results from this study and Sciolla's are similar to those from other national or international studies. Sciolla, *La sfida dei valori*, p. 196, table 7.1. See also L. Sciolla, *Italiani. Stereotipi di Casa Nostra* (Bologna: Il Mulino, 1997), pp. 45–9.

9 Sciolla, *La sfida dei valori*, p. 196, table 7.1.

10 The proportions trusting Italians were as follows: in the north, 10 per cent in Milan and 12 per cent in Turin; in the centre, 15 per cent in Modena and 13 per cent in Vicenza; in the south, 14 per cent in both Caltanisetta and Teramo.

8

Explaining generalised trust

Hanna Bäck, Carina Gunnarson and Magdalena Inkinen

In the previous chapter, we saw that students had most trust in Italians, followed by trust in Sicilians, Palermitans and foreigners. Results from the 2002 survey showed that 54 per cent of the students had trust in Italians, 41 per cent in Sicilians and 33 per cent in Palermitans. The lowest levels of trust were shown towards foreigners: only 26 per cent expressed trust in foreigners. There were no significant differences between the three socio-economic areas and changes between 2002 and 2005 were small.[1]

The descriptive statistics presented in the previous chapter did not permit an analysis of change on an individual level, nor of the causes of individual change. In this chapter we will turn to our panel data (see Chapter 3, and below) and use regression analysis in order to explore possible change at the individual level between the two waves. Before that, we will briefly reiterate the major point of departure for this work.

Institutions and school

One important focus of theories on social capital has been on the significance of organisations when explaining different levels of generalised trust. This study analyses the importance of *institutions*. Is it possible to enhance trust by state action? Is it possible to change students' values through civic education at a grass-roots level?

Research shows that generalised trust is transferred across generations; it is established early in life, is stable over time, and is dependent on education and socio-economic status. The importance of institutions for the development of generalised trust has been analysed in several studies on social capital. Theories have focused on factors such as the design of public institutions, for example the government and administration, or on the universality of welfare systems.[2] The relevance of education for trust is generally acknowledged in the literature.[3] Education is by far the most important predictor to civic engagement; as Putnam argues, 'highly educated people are much more likely to be joiners and trusters'.[4] Still, there has been little research on school as a builder of generalised trust. It is highly plausible that schools do have a significant impact on students' values, owing to the central role of schools in citizens' early lives. As mentioned previously, school represents the first personal experience of young citizens with public institutions and they spend a considerable amount of time in school during their formative years. Research on trust has, though, traditionally targeted adult citizens and often entirely ignored the early formation of values.

Academic investigations of the potential of school as an agent of change are not new, however. Numerous studies of civic education have sought to analyse the influence of schools in the development of political knowledge, values of good citizenship, trust in public institutions, political efficacy and future participatory behaviour, and so on. However, previous investigations of civic education have not examined its impact on interpersonal trust. It should also be noted that there has been strong disagreement within the literature regarding precisely which aspects of civic education have an impact on students' values. Is it school climate, classroom climate, students' participation in internal democracy, formal education, timing of civic education, extra-curricular activities, student interaction, teacher experience, school leadership or size of the school that matters?

There seems to be an important bridge to build between the discourses on social capital, on the one hand, and civic education, on the other. Whereas theories of social capital have acknowledged the importance of institutions and education for the development of trust in general, there is less research on school and the early formation of values. Whereas research on civic education has studied young citizens and identified several possible explanations for children's knowledge, civic attitudes and behaviour, little attention has been paid to the effects of school on generalised trust.

Formative years

The years spent in school represent a formative period of children's lives. Many describe the years in lower secondary school as crucial for future choices and life paths; some students drop out, others quit school for good, and yet others continue their studies to higher secondary level and university. Between the ages of 10 and 14 years, students grow from children to adolescents and take their first steps as young and independent citizens.

There is little doubt that school plays an important role in students' lives. Empirical evidence from this study shows that no other public institution enjoyed more trust than schools (see Tables 6.3 and 6.4). In our study, 84 per cent of the students said they trusted school (Table 6.3) and 88 per cent expressed trust in their teachers (Table 7.3) when they started lower secondary school in 2002. Only family and relatives enjoyed more trust than teachers did, which makes school a very interesting object of study.

Moreover, it is highly warranted to study young citizens' attitudes when analysing the origins of generalised trust, since there is strong empirical evidence that generalised trust is established early in life. Generalised trust is also considered to be fairly stable over time. Even if changes may occur during adulthood, as an effect of job experiences, family events, social experiences or changes in society, it has been found that these changes do not in general interfere with the basic pattern established early in life. A significant foundation for political life is already well established by the time young people reach adulthood.[5]

Theory and major hypotheses

Previous research on civic education has pointed at different aspects of school that may have an impact on students' political knowledge and awareness. These include school programmes, school climate, classroom climate, the 'hidden' curriculum (i.e. teachers' private values), formal activities at school, extracurricular activities, students' active involvement in various kinds of community projects, interaction between students, the school's interaction with parents, leadership and teachers' didactic skills. In our panel study we particularly focus on variables at the school and classroom level. The five variables used to analyse school effects are 'openness of school structures', 'fairness of institutions', 'caring school environment', 'peer interaction', 'openness of classroom climate', as well as the different school programmes.

Personal experiences of participation in formal decision-making procedures at school, for example on student councils, could also have an impact on attitudes such as civic commitment. Political efficacy is usually defined in terms of citizens being able to make a difference to government decisions. At school, the equivalent would be that students perceive that they can influence decisions regarding their school.[6] They could, for example, influence the teaching methods used, the content of their education, the books used or how the school should be decorated. This aspect is interesting but could not be tested in this study since student councils are not present in Italian lower secondary schools (they are introduced only at higher secondary level). However, we did ask students about their perception of the *openness of school structures*, by which we meant whether they considered it easy or not to confide problems in the school staff.

Rothstein highlights the importance of *impartial, just and fair social and political institutions* for the development of generalised trust. The character of service delivery, the impartiality of street-level bureaucrats, as well as the perceived opportunities to cheat the system, create differences in regional or national institutional trust, which in turn influence generalised trust. Citizens who have directly or indirectly experienced unfairness, dishonesty, unresponsiveness, lack of respect or corruption in their contacts with public institutions transfer these experiences and views to people in general. Thus, the institutionalisation of generalised values such as trust and reciprocity depends on the character of political institutions.[7] In an experimental study, Eek and Rothstein found that increased vertical trust had positive effects on horizontal trust, while decreased trust in institutions had only small negative effects on horizontal trust. Horizontal trust did not have any effect on vertical trust. Thus, their results support the view that the causal effect runs from institutions to generalised trust, and not the other way around. The logic is as follows. If a person observes that public servants do not follow the law, why should he or she believe that anyone else does? On the other hand, if the same person sees a person in the street behaving badly, it does not necessarily imply that the public authorities are corrupt.[8]

Emotional engagement, flexibility and adaptation to the situation are other factors that may affect generalised trust. Stenesöta argues that we expect public sector workers (e.g. medical professionals, social workers, teachers) to be not only fair or impartial, but also to be engaged and to show compassion. This 'logic of care' adds an important dimension to discussions about the fairness of institutions, since it emphasises the emotional value of caring and adapting to the circumstances. The logic of care is relevant where there is a physical encounter between civil servants and citizens, where the civil servant makes judgements and decisions, and where the situation is dynamic.[9] The logic of care does not imply that care is fairly distributed to everyone, however; rather, it applies to those in need in a particular situation. At the emergency unit in a hospital, for example, we would expect doctors and nurses to treat the most seriously injured persons first. In relation to immigration, we would expect civil servants to act with more compassion if refugees are suicidal or have suffered from torture or other abuses. In a school environment, students would expect teachers to help and care for children who have been bullied. Students would further expect teachers not only to be fair about their grades and to behave correctly in the classroom, but also to be emotionally engaged and compassionate.[10]

Social interaction in general, particularly outside the narrow circle of the family, may contribute to the development of less selfish and more socially engaged attitudes and values. Various types of informal interaction between friends and peer groups may have an impact on students' degrees of trust. Hooghe and Kavadias note that different forms of informal interaction probably have increased in importance as a socialising agent during the past decades, with the development of an increasingly autonomous youth culture in most Western societies.[11] School may be understood as a social arena constructed by teachers and students, where *peer interaction* between students comprises a relevant variable to consider.

The importance of the implicit or hidden curriculum is a factor widely recognised in the literature on civic education. Analyses by Torney-Purta *et al*. also support the impact of the *classroom climate* on students' values. In their first IEA study, they found that students participating in classroom discussions had higher scores on anti-authoritarian and knowledge measures than students who were only memorising dates or facts about politics. Does it matter for the development of trust whether teachers permit or encourage an open dialogue in the classroom?[12]

Another factor that may have an effect is the *school programme* at each school. Niemi and Junn observed in their 1998 study that participation in civics courses, the timing of the courses, the number of topics brought up and the discussion of political events had significant effects on political knowledge.[13] Furthermore, participation in extracurricular activities has sometimes been understood as a contributor to students' self-esteem, academic achievement, educational ambitions and attainment.[14]

During discussions with school staff for the present study, it became increasingly clear that many schools organised excursions to the city as a way of increasing students' knowledge of and engagement with the city of Palermo. It was believed that such activities would enhance the students' willingness to engage in change (see Chapter 5). Even if such programmes generally aim to increase students' political efficacy, it may be interesting to analyse whether they can also affect levels of interpersonal trust. How far and in what ways does isolation from other parts of Palermo foster values of distrust, particularly towards other citizens? And do excursions and visits to other areas in Palermo increase trust?

Data and method

The schools

The focus of the analysis performed here is on the educational programme at the lower secondary level in seven Palermitan schools. Four schools are situated in difficult neighbourhoods marked by high unemployment, micro-criminality and a strong presence of the Mafia. Two schools are located in mixed areas. The other school is in a wealthy residential area in central Palermo.

The research is conducted through a panel study (i.e. a survey repeated over time). Panel designs are rare in the literature on social capital and civic education, as they are both time-consuming and resource-demanding enterprises.[15] The panel design increases the opportunity to deal with issues of selection bias, as we know the students' level of trust when they started lower secondary school. The panel design also permits a better assessment of the direction of causality between different forms of activities and the dependent variable, in this case generalised trust. The panel of the present study consists of two waves. Questionnaires were distributed to students in October–November 2002, during their first semester at lower secondary school, and in February–March 2005, during their last term of compulsory schooling. A total of 246 students participated in both tests, which represents 64 per cent of the original sample of 386 students (see Chapter 3).[16]

An explicit ambition of all of the schools participating in this study was to stimulate increased cooperation between students, to increase trust, and to promote values of solidarity, tolerance and the respect for diversity. These objectives were expressed both in school programmes and by school principals. Emotional and relational values were emphasised as objectives by all schools. One school explicitly declared that its programme aimed to 'increase social capital', although without further definition of social capital.[17] A common feature of the schools was their emphasis on legality, civil rights and respect for the law. Another point in common was the goal to increase the students' knowledge about their own area: Palermo, Sicily, Italy and Europe in general. All of the schools participated in the programme 'School adopts a monument' (see Chapter 5). Most schools had invited public officials to give talks to the children, for example judges, police officers and politicians, or organised visits to public institutions in Palermo. Sports and artistic activities were integrated into the programme at all schools. Efforts to decrease school drop-out and to actively engage parents were also emphasised. A total of one to two hours per week were dedicated to civic education in all the schools.

The selected schools are public institutions. Three of them are so-called comprehensive institutes that include education at both elementary and lower secondary levels, which may improve coordination between the two levels. All these schools are situated in the low-ranked socio-economic area.[18]

The other four schools offer education only at lower secondary level. The schools varied in size: from 268 to 1,008 students, with an average of 530 students per school.[19]

Operationalisation of the variables

We will here describe the operationalisation of all the variables included in the analyses performed in this chapter. In both waves of the panel survey, questions were asked about both the dependent variable of interest, generalised trust, and about the independent variables, measuring different aspects of the school context.

There are a number of different ways in which we can measure trust. The survey included several questions to gauge the level of trust among the students. These questions have been summarised as five different indexes of students' trust in different categories of people. Factor analysis confirmed a common dimension between the variables in each index.[20]

- Index 1, *Trust in known people*, is an additive index based on questions about the level of trust in family, relatives, neighbours and people from the area (*il quartiere*).[21]
- Index 2, *Trust in the school environment*, is an additive index based on questions about the level of trust in classmates, teachers, the school principal and school staff.[22]
- Index 3, *Trust in unknown people*, has been created by adding items about the level of trust in Palermitans, Sicilians, Italians and foreigners.[23]
- Index 4, *Trust in people in general*, is an additive index based on three general questions on trust: 'Do you believe that most people can be trusted or that nobody can be trusted?'; 'Do you believe that most people try to be helpful or do you think that people only think about themselves?'; and 'Do you believe that most people try to be honest, or do you think that most people are not honest?'[24]
- Index 5, *Sicilian sayings*, is an additive index based on proverbs about trust, sincerity or cooperation: 'To live well it's better to mind your own business'; 'If you need something, it's better to rely on yourself'; 'When people cooperate they never achieve positive results'; 'Real friendship does not exist'; and 'Nobody does anything for free'.[25]

Index 1 is an example of so-called bonding social capital, illustrating trust in people already known to students. Index 2 measures the students' trust in persons in the school environment, which may be a mix of both known and unknown persons. Index 3 represents generalised trust, which is trust in people who are not personally known to the students. Index 4 analyses generalised trust and is based on three questions that are frequently used in national and international surveys. Index 5 is based on Sicilian sayings that in different ways express views on trust. In the regression analyses performed in this chapter, we have chosen to use index 3, measuring generalised trust, as our main dependent variable. The reason why we chose index 3 instead of index 4 (or 5) is that it is more precise and distinguishes trust in various categories of citizens. Few surveys ask about trust in specific groups. In an attempt to bridge comprehension issues due to the young age of our participants, we decided to use the more precise index 3 instead of the more abstract wording of questions in index 4. Furthermore, the general questions comprising index 4 have been criticised in the literature. It has been argued that respondents may understand them differently, and more specifically that the questions are sensitive to wording, life experiences and context.[26]

As mentioned above, we are interested in the effects of a number of school variables on students' generalised trust. First, one hypothesis suggests a positive correlation between open school structures and the levels of trust. *Openness of school structures* was measured by asking students about the ease with which they felt they could confide problems in teachers, the school psychologist or the school principal. A second hypothesis is that the higher the fairness of the school institutions, the higher the level of trust will be. *Fairness of institutions* was measured by asking students whether they estimated their teachers to be 'fair', whether teachers were 'only interested in the best and most intelligent students' and whether they felt 'badly treated by teachers'. Another theory is that a caring environment should foster trust. *Caring school environment* is here measured by using two indicators: 'Teachers pay attention to my situation' and 'Teachers make me feel at ease'. The nature of social interaction between students is also expected to affect their level of trust. *Peer interaction* was measured by asking students about their school environment: was swearing frequent among students, were there often quarrels between students, or did they feel badly treated by other students? An open classroom climate is also expected to increase the level of trust. *Openness of classroom climate* is here measured by using questions from the IEA international study. The questions asked to what extent teachers encouraged students to express their opinions; to what extent students felt encouraged to develop personal ideas and opinions on various topics; and whether they felt free to express their thoughts openly in class, or to propose discussions on current problems. In all these cases, the different items were included in a simple additive index.[27]

In this study, we also endeavoured to include variables that covered each *school's particular curriculum*. These questions were constructed in discussion with schools when the project was first started and by studying the different educational programmes established by the institutional council (*consiglio di istituto*) of each school. Activities included both individual activities and activities based on teamwork. They included activities that are part of the formal curriculum as well as extracurricular activities. Examples of activities belonging to the formal curriculum were the production of a school journal, engagement in sports, cooperatives or environmental groups, or an artistic group of any kind (music or theatre). Examples of extracurricular activities were visits to the gym, photography, ceramics, computers, games, dancing, painting, music, theatre or woodwork.

The *control variables* that will be included in the regression analyses are family-related variables, such as the parents' educational level, the families' socio-cultural level (measured as number of books at home), the parents' involvement in school-work (participation in meetings at school and engagement in homework) and the families' interaction with neighbours (help, visits, discussions). Various individual features of the student will also be included as control variables, such as participation in organisations, personal ambitions in school (degree of interest in studies), interest in society (reading news articles, watching news on television, listening to news on the radio), and gender.[28]

Methodological considerations

Some methodological issues should be discussed before we present our results. First, we have here chosen to perform several multivariate regression analyses. This is the standard approach when measuring the effects of a number of independent variables (for each of which the others are controlled for) on a dependent variable of a continuous (or close to continuous) nature. There are, of course, alternatives to this approach. In the education literature, many researchers use so-called multi-level or hierarchical regression models.[29] This is predominantly because this type of research often deals with data of a hierarchical nature, where students are nested within schools that are in turn nested within communities or regions, and so on. This research project is dealing with such data, and we are certainly interested in the effect that the context exerts on the students' level of trust, rendering a multi-level approach highly appropriate. The problem that we face here, and the reason why we have not used a multi-level model, is the small number of contextual (higher-level) units. The survey data were, as mentioned above, gathered from only seven schools, all within the same city and within the same region, which either gives us too little variation in interesting features at any level higher than the individual, or leaves us with too few units at such levels (using random-effects models for seven units is not feasible).[30]

As previously indicated, the panel data offer several advantages over cross-sectional information in the investigation of causal relationships.[31] In general, the main advantage is that we can measure our dependent variable of interest – generalised trust – at a later point in time than our measures of the independent variables. This gives us a check on the direction of causality. We have therefore measured the level of generalised trust in the second wave of the survey (i.e. in 2005). Ideally, we would have liked, accordingly, to have measured our independent variables in the first wave of the survey. The problem with doing so in this particular case is that the questions are about the students' experiences of school, and for the first wave these would largely refer to the situation in primary school, as the survey was in the first semester of lower secondary school. In this instance we are interested in the importance of the educational programme at the secondary level, and we have therefore chosen to use the school variables measured in the second wave. All of the control variables were, however, measured in the first wave of the survey. Furthermore, this allows us to take full advantage of the fact that the survey was performed in two waves.

Another advantage with panel data is that we can include a lagged version of the dependent variable; that is, we can include the level of trust recorded in 2002 as a variable. In general, the inclusion of the lagged dependent variable enables us to avoid potential bias from omitted variables.[32] By including the lagged dependent variable, we can be sure that it is in fact some feature of the school environment and not a feature of the student that he or she had before entering school that explains the student's level of generalised trust. The inclusion of this lagged dependent variable allows us to study the effects of our independent variables on the *change* in the level of generalised trust between 2002 and 2005.

Levels of trust in 2002 and 2005

The following introduction to our analysis presents a summary of the results and indexes used. What were the average scores for generalised trust in 2002 and in 2005? Were there any changes in any particular direction?

The average scores on our five indexes present a mixed pattern. Whereas students' trust in people personally known to them (family, relatives, neighbours, people from the area) increased between 2002 and 2005 (from 3.06 to 3.12), students' trust in people that they meet on a daily basis decreased somewhat, from 2.96 in 2002 to 2.88 in 2005 (see Table 8.1). Students' degree of trust in unknown people (Palermitans, Sicilians, Italians and foreigners) remained more or less at the same level. The fourth index of generalised trust showed a small increase of students' distrust of unknown people. The fifth index was based on a selection of Sicilian sayings expressing individualism and negative attitudes towards cooperation. The students agreed to a lesser extent with the sayings in 2005 than in 2002.

Scores on the third index of generalised trust were almost exactly the same in 2002 and 2005. Were there any differences between socio-economic areas and schools? In a comparison of the three categories of area, we saw that trust decreased slightly in the low-ranked category, but increased in the higher-ranked areas (Table 8.2). We saw, however, relatively large differences between schools. While trust was lost in three schools (A1, A4

Table 8.1 Mean scores on five indexes of trust, 2002 and 2005

	2002	2005
Index 1	3.06	3.12
Index 2	2.96	2.88
Index 3	2.32	2.33
Index 4	2.03	2.05
Index 5	2.23	2.12

Index 1: Trust in family, relatives, neighbours, and people in the area (*il quartiere*).

Index 2: Trust in classmates, teachers, school principal and school staff. (The 2005 survey also included a question on students' trust in schoolmates. As this question was not part of the 2002 survey, the item was not included in the index.)

Index 3: Trust in Palermitans, Sicilians, Italians and foreigners.

Index 4: 'Do you believe that most people can be trusted or that nobody can be trusted', 'Do you believe that most people try to be helpful or do you think that people only think about themselves?', 'Do you believe that most people try to be honest, or do you think that most people are not honest?' Values vary between 1 and 4. NB. Lower scores indicate more trust, higher scores more distrust in others.

Index 5: 'To live well it's better to mind your own business', 'If you need something, it's better to rely on yourself', 'When people cooperate they never achieve positive results', 'Real friendship does not exist', 'Nobody does anything for free'. Values vary between 1 and 4. Lower scores indicate less agreement, higher scores more agreement.

Table 8.2 Index 3[a] by area and school, 2002 and 2005 (means)

	2002	2005
Total	**2.32**	**2.33**
Area		
Low (A)	2.37	2.34
Intermediate (B)	2.25	2.29
High (C)	2.24	2.32
School		
A1	2.36	2.30
A2	2.20	2.33
A3	2.38	2.43
A4	2.51	2.33
B1	2.30	2.20
B2	2.18	2.43
C1	2.24	2.32

[a]Trust in Palermitans, Sicilians, Italians and foreigners.

and B1), it increased in the other four schools (A2, A3, B2 and C1). We are particularly intrigued to see that trust increased in two of the schools in the low-ranked area, A2 and A3, as these are situated in particularly difficult surroundings that are renowned even within Palermo.

When looking at all five indexes (Table 8.3), we notice that these two schools, A2 and A3, performed better than the other schools on almost every item. In these schools, students increased their trust in people they knew, in people within the school environment and in unknown people, and their levels of agreement with the Sicilian sayings were lower in the second wave. In contrast, there was one school (A1) where students seem to have lost trust on almost every index. It should be highlighted, however, that changes in either direction were small in many cases. However, we believe that Table 8.3 highlights some general trends and differences between schools.

How do we explain the different patterns between schools? How do we explain the loss of trust in school A1? And how do we explain the positive trends in schools A2 and A3? What factors enhance the development of trust? In the following section we analyse changes in generalised trust between the two waves.

Testing the hypotheses

The previous section showed that the level of trust among students in different schools changed over time. This section examines what impact various school factors have on the inclination of students to trust others. More specifically, we want to find out whether students are more inclined to trust other people if the school structures are open, fair and caring. Moreover, are students more likely to trust other people if relations between students are friendly, if the classroom climate is open and if the school is engaged in various programmes aimed at enhancing the students' civic engagement? The analysis in this section is divided into two parts. First, we will investigate the effect of each school factor separately. Thereafter, we will analyse the impact of all the school factors simultaneously, in order to find out which characteristics of the school are most important in generating trust.

Table 8.3 Changes between 2002 and 2005, by school

School	Index 1 Bonding	Index 2 School	Index 3 General	Index 4 General	Index 5 Sicilian sayings
A1	Lower	Lower	Lower	Lower	Less agreement
A2	Higher	Same	Higher	Higher	Less agreement
A3	Higher	Higher	Higher	Higher	Less agreement
A4	Higher	Lower	Lower	Higher	More agreement
B1	Higher	Lower	Lower	Lower	Less agreement
B2	Higher	Lower	Higher	Lower	Less agreement
C1	Higher	Lower	Higher	Lower	Less agreement

Index 1: Trust in family, relatives, neighbours, and people in the area (*il quartiere*).
Index 2: Trust in classmates, teachers, school principal and school staff. (The 2005 survey also included a question on students' trust in schoolmates. As this question was not part of the 2002 survey, the item was not included in the index.)
Index 3: Trust in Palermitans, Sicilians, Italians and foreigners.
Index 4: 'Do you believe that most people can be trusted or that nobody can be trusted', 'Do you believe that most people try to be helpful or do you think that people only think about themselves?', 'Do you believe that most people try to be honest, or do you think that most people are not honest?' Values vary between 1 and 4. NB. Lower scores indicate more trust; higher scores more distrust in others.
Index 5: 'To live well it's better to mind your own business', 'If you need something, it's better to rely on yourself', 'When people cooperate they never achieve positive results', 'Real friendship does not exist', 'Nobody does anything for free'. Values vary between 1 and 4. Lower scores indicate less agreement, higher scores more agreement.

Let us begin by analysing the effect of each school factor separately. As discussed in the methodology section, we have chosen to use index 3 as our dependent variable. A number of background factors will be used as control variables and in order to capture change over time we have included the lagged dependent variable in the analysis.[33] The results of this analysis are presented in Table 8.4. It is interesting to note that several school factors affect the students' inclination to trust others. In line with our hypotheses, openness of school structures, fairness of institutions, caring school environment and openness of the classroom climate all have positive and statistically significant effects on trust. The negative and significant effect of peer conflict is also in accordance with our hypothesis. The results are, however, more mixed in relation to school activities aimed at increasing the students' civil engagement. While school visits to the city of Palermo increase students' inclination to trust others, participation in other school activities and extracurricular activities do not. One reason for this difference may be that school excursions, as opposed to the other school activities examined here, take place outside school and therefore allow students to develop more generalised feelings of trust. We will have reason to return to the 'school visits' variable in Chapter 9, on students' letters. Since the other forms of school activities do not seem to matter for the level of generalised trust, they will not be included in the regressions that follow.

For the sake of simplicity, Table 8.4 shows only the effects of the school factors on trust. However, it is also worth commenting briefly on the control variables, since these can be linked to important theories within scholarly work on generalised trust. An interesting result, which is consistent in all the regressions discussed here, is that the control variables did not have statistically significant effects on the students' inclination to trust others. The parents' educational level, the families' socio-cultural level, the parents' involvement in schoolwork, the families' interaction with neighbours, and the students' personal ambitions in school and interest in society did not affect students' generalised trust. Even more interestingly, the students' participation in voluntary organisations had a significant but *negative* effect on trust in all the regression models. The effects of all these variables remain more or less the same even if we exclude the school factors from the analysis altogether or conduct bivariate regressions.

Table 8.4 Effects of school factors on generalised trust

School factors[a]	Effect (b)	Standard error	Adjusted R^2	Number of responses for analysis
Openness of school structures	0.09**	0.04	0.10	200
Fairness of institutions	0.13***	0.04	0.12	205
Caring school environment	0.09**	0.04	0.11	207
Peer conflict	−0.07**	0.03	0.12	205
Openness of classroom climate	0.14**	0.06	0.10	210
School excursions to the city	0.08**	0.04	0.10	211
Participation in school activities	0.01	0.01	0.08	211
Participation in extracurricular activities	0.01	0.01	0.08	211

b = regression slope coefficient, significant at * the 0.10 level, ** the 0.05 level, *** the 0.01 level. Entries are unstandardised regression coefficients.
[a] Each model includes the following control variables: the parents' educational level, the family's socio-cultural level, the parents' involvement in schoolwork, the family's interaction with neighbours, the students' participation in organisations, personal ambition in school, interest in society, and gender.

Contrary to the civil society argument, our analysis shows that students are *less* inclined to trust others if they are active in voluntary associations.[34] Even when conducting bivariate regressions, the negative impact of participation in associations is systematically negative. Possible explanations for this interesting finding will be discussed in the conclusion of this chapter.

Finally, all the regressions demonstrate a significant effect of gender, with boys being more inclined than girls to trust other people. An explanation for this difference may be that girls are more often told than boys are to be careful in their relations with strangers. Another explanation may be that patterns of informal interaction differ between boys and girls.

We have so far concluded that various school characteristics, as opposed to family conditions, personal ambitions and organisational activities, affect the students' inclination to trust other people. This conclusion raises the question of *which aspects* of the school climate are most important in generating trust. Are fair institutions more important than caring ones, and does friendly interaction between students matter more than formal school programmes? In order to provide a tentative answer to this question, we will now analyse the effects of various school factors in the same regression model. Factors that remain significant despite controlling for the impact of the other school factors are likely to be particularly important.

The results of this analysis are presented in Table 8.5. It can be noted here that only three of the school factors continue to have statistically significant effects on the level of trust: openness of school structures, fairness of institutions and peer conflict. This suggests that having open and fair school structures and friendly relations between students may be especially important for the students' tendency to trust others. In comparison, having a caring school environment, an open classroom climate and programmes aimed at enhancing the students' civic engagement seem to be less important. The same pattern is observable as above with regard to the control variables. While the students' family conditions, personal ambitions and civic engagement did not have significant effects on the inclination to trust others, participation in voluntary associations had a weakly negative effect and (male) gender a positive effect, with boys being more inclined than girls to trust other people.

Table 8.5 Effects of school factors tested in the same model

School factors	Effect (b)	Standard error
Openness of school structures	0.08**	0.04
Fairness of institutions	0.09*	0.05
Caring school environment	−0.00	0.05
Peer conflict	−0.08**	0.04
Openness of classroom climate	0.03	0.08
School excursions to the city	0.04	0.05
Participation in voluntary associations	−0.02*	0.01
Parents' education	−0.06	0.05
Parents' interaction with neighbours	−0.01	0.02
Parents' involvement in schoolwork	0.22	0.19
Family's socio-cultural level	0.04	0.05
Student's ambition in school	0.03	0.06
Student's interest in society	0.01	0.09
Gender	0.20*	0.09
Adjusted R^2	0.14	
Number of observations	192	

b = regression slope coefficient, significant at * the 0.10 level, ** the 0.05 level, *** the 0.01 level. Entries are unstandardised regression coefficients.

To conclude, the empirical analysis in this section gives strong and consistent support to our school hypotheses. The analysis clearly shows that students are more inclined to trust other people if the school structures are open, fair and caring, if relations between students are friendly, if the classroom climate is open, and if the school organises activities to increase the students' civic engagement (school excursions to the city). In addition, an analysis of all the school factors in the same regression model suggests that having open and fair school structures and friendly peer interaction may be particularly important for the increased tendency to trust people in general.

In contrast to the school factors, the students' family conditions, personal ambitions and involvement in voluntary associations do not seem to affect their changing tendency to trust others.

Of further interest to this project is whether various school factors affect children differently, depending on their socio-economic status. Empirical research on the impact of schooling suggests that it may have a particularly strong effect on socio-economically deprived students. In contrast, relatively well-off students seem to be more affected by their families and other socialising agents. Based on the work of Hess and Torney as well as Almond and Verba, Ehman argues that 'it appears that schooling may be relatively more important than home or other socializing agents for lower socio-economic groups than for higher status groups'.[35] However, when we analysed the effect of the school factors on students in socio-economically disadvantaged and wealthy areas, separately, we could not establish any substantial differences in this regard.[36]

We are also interested in examining the gendered nature of the impact of various school factors. This question is interesting, since women in Palermo were said to be more active and more open to change than men. For instance, the experiences of social agencies indicate that women are more inclined to visit social centres and to participate in the activities offered there.[37]

We used two separate models – one including only the control variables and one including both the control variables and the school variables – in order to examine the explanatory power of the school factors on boys' and girls' generalised trust, respectively. We found that the explained variance for the control variables did not differ between boys and girls, while the variation explained by the school variables was higher for girls than for boys. This indicates that school has more impact on girls' level of trust than is the case for boys.[38] This finding is thus in line with practitioners' experience, suggesting that women are more inclined to be influenced by government institutions.[39]

Conclusion

Previous research on trust has shown that the behaviour of street-level bureaucrats toward clients can influence citizens' values.[40] An important theoretical conclusion is that it is possible to stimulate the development of generalised trust by state action at the grass-roots level, for example by schools giving classes in civic education. The results thus support institutional explanations for the development of trust. It has also been shown that it may be possible to encourage the development of trust within a shorter time frame than Putnam suggests: trust may not need centuries to develop; it may take only two or three years.

Although those who research social capital generally acknowledge the importance of education and are increasingly recognising the impact of institutions, surprisingly few studies have investigated the role of school as a socialising agent and generator of trust. This study has identified several school factors that have an effect on students' generalised trust: openness of structures, fairness of institutions, caring teachers, friendly peer interaction, openness of classroom climate and excursions to the city. The most influential factors were openness of structures, fairness of institutions and degree of peer conflict at school.

The importance of openness of school structures and classroom climate has generally been acknowledged in the literature on civic education. In addition to these, we found two factors – fairness of institutions and 'logic of care' – that also have an impact on students' values. These factors are not entirely new. Tyler, Levi and Rothstein have all emphasised the importance of fairness of institutions, and the importance of logic of care is supported by Stenesöta's research.[41] Another interesting finding was that school excursions had an effect on students' generalised trust as well.

Economists analysing gender differences in game theory have found that men exhibit greater trust, while women show higher levels of reciprocity.[42] All the regressions in this study demonstrate a significant effect of gender, with boys being more inclined than girls to trust other people. As it is still rare to highlight gender differences regarding trust in the literature on social capital, these findings will be interesting to follow up in future studies.[43] An analysis of variance showed that school factors explained more of the variance in generalised trust for girls than for boys.

Previous research has shown that schooling may have a more important impact on students in lower socio-economic settings. When analysing the effect of the school factors on students in socio-economically disadvantaged and wealthy areas, we could not establish any substantial differences in this regard.

An important conclusion is that we did not see any positive effect on trust of the students' engagement in voluntary associations. Indeed, the link we saw was slightly negative:

engagement in associations seemed to lead to less trust. This finding contradicts theories that emphasise the importance of membership of associations.[44] How should we understand this negative effect? A first reflection is that the study analysed young people, not adults. Young people do not necessarily react in the same way as adults to organisational engagement. Selection bias may be a problem, too, since their engagement may be a result of the influence of parents' choices or desires. Unwilling students may be forced or convinced by their parents to join an organisation for whatever reason.[45] We suggest that the explanation may lie in the character of the 'inner life' of the organisations. The impact of social interaction found in this study – that peer conflict negatively affects generalised trust – is an aspect that may also be considered when studying different interaction patterns *within* groups or associations. If the social interaction within a particular group is aggressive, these factors will probably negatively influence a person's inclination to trust people in general. Moreover, leadership within these associations may also have an important impact on students' attitudes. A story told by one of the boys participating in the Letter Project suggests that participation in an organisation was not always linked to positive experiences:

> I practise water polo. Unfortunately my trainer is not the best one. Instead of encouraging us if we make mistakes, he takes us out from the pool and swears at us.... Often I have to play with boys who are 3–4 years older than me, i.e. much bigger than I am. Yesterday, we went to Messina to play.... I found myself in front of a boy, triple my size, and whom I didn't manage to hold. At my first mistake my trainer took me out from the play, and instead of encouraging me he teased me … my trainer … said I was a woman and that I should stop playing water polo.[46]

In this specific case, we were unable to see whether this boy developed or lost generalised trust. However, he did seem to manage quite well, sharing the hardships with the comrades in his team:

> It doesn't really matter … I continued to play and didn't care about what he said. In my team, we have got used to it and it doesn't matter to us. We also said to each other that we shouldn't have continued to play and that from tomorrow we will only swim. He has not yet understood that without explaining what we are doing wrong, we do not understand our errors.[47]

It should be recalled that this study was conducted in poor areas where the presence of the Mafia was often strongly felt. Despite the difficult circumstances that these schools are facing in their daily work, we found that several school factors had an impact on students' generalised trust even if these effects were rather small. The research design chosen for this study was to encompass the 'worst case scenario'. If change is possible in these critical areas, where conditions are less favourable to change, it is also likely, or more likely, to occur in places where conditions are more favourable. The changes we found were therefore not expected. It may also be argued that without the school programme, we would most likely have seen a general loss of generalised trust, instead of small gains.

It may be argued that age explains the positive development of generalised trust, that is, students become more trustful as they grow older. However, this seems unlikely, as we observed different patterns between schools. Students in one school, A1, seemed to have lost trust on almost every index, while students in another school, A3, increased their trust. If only age or maturity explained gains or losses of trust, we would expect to see a similar pattern in all schools, which we did not.

We were not able to discern whether gains or losses of trust were related to changes in families' economic situations. Is it possible that a general positive development in the Italian economy explains increases in trust? In fact, the Italian economy during the years of this study did not perform well. Italy's economic ranking in the world and in Europe was eroded, and public finances deteriorated. The Italian economy's backbone – family-owned companies, which were successful during the 1970s and 1980s – are now facing increasing difficulties to adapt to a global economy. In 2005, Italy's share of global trade fell to 2.7 per cent, from 4.6 per cent in 1995. In 2005, the Italian budget deficit reached 4.1 per cent of its gross domestic product.[48] Thus, economic improvement cannot explain the increase in students' level of generalised trust. However, more information is needed about the income of individual families in order to dismiss economic explanations for students' levels of trust.

In summary, the empirical analysis in this chapter showed that the inclination of students to trust other people changed somewhat over time. The development also varied between schools. The extent to which students trusted others was affected by the school climate. Therefore, we argue that the importance of institutions in general, and school in particular, is a factor that needs to be increasingly addressed in future research on generalised trust.

Effects were small, however, and we will now turn to students' own stories, as revealed to us in the Letter Project.

Notes

1 The panel data (the subject of this chapter) showed the same pattern.

2 B. Rothstein and D. Stolle, 'Social capital, impartiality and the welfare state: an institutional approach', in M. Hooghe and D. Stolle (eds), *Generating Social Capital: Civil Society and Institutions in Comparative Perspective* (New York: Palgrave Macmillan, 2003), pp. 191–209.

3 Uslaner, *The Moral Foundations of Trust*.

4 Putnam, 'Tuning in, tuning out', p. 667.

5 Uslaner, *The Moral Foundations of Trust*, pp. 162–5.

6 Torney-Purta *et al.*, *Citizenship and Education in Twenty-Eight Countries*, pp. 131–2.

7 Rothstein, *Just Institutions Matter*, pp. 140–3. See also Rothstein and Stolle, 'Social capital, impartiality and the welfare state', pp. 191–209.

8 Eek and Rothstein, 'Exploring a causal relationship between vertical and horizontal trust', pp. 2, 6.

9 Stenesöta, *Den empatiska staten*, pp. 49–50.

10 B. Rothstein and J. Teorell, 'What is quality of government? Impartiality in the exercise of political power', QoG Working Paper Series No. 6 (Quality of Government Institute, Göteborg University, 2005).

11 Hooghe and Kavadias, 'Determinants of future willingness to vote', p. 4.

12 Torney-Purta *et al.*, *Civic Education Across Countries*, p. 14.

13 Niemi and Junn, *Civic Education*.

14 Holland and André, 'Participation in extracurricular activities in secondary school'.

15 An exception is John and Morris's two-wave study of student attitudes among 15–17-year-olds in 25 schools in the UK. See P. John and Z. Morris, 'What are the origins of social capital? Results from a panel survey of young people', *British Elections and Parties Review*, 14 (2004), pp. 94–112.

16 According to the program GEESIZE, a sample size of 100 observations would have been required as a minimum for this study: 65 for the low-ranked category, 22 for the medium-ranked and 13 for the high-ranked socio-economic category. The program (developed by James Rochon) performs sample size calculations for repeated-measures experiments.

17 School A2, *Piano della offerta formativa*, 2001/02, 17.

18 Comprehensive institutes: A1, A2 and A3.

19 The numbers of students in all schools are based on information provided by those schools in March 2005, except for school A1, for which the available information related to February 2002: A1, 460 students; A2, 268

students; A3, 491 students; A4, 664 students; B1, 487 students; B2, 335 students; and C1, 1,008 students.

20 Analysis of Cronbach's alpha for each index was based on the total sample from 2005.

21 Cronbach's alpha = 0.634.

22 Cronbach's alpha = 0.795.

23 Cronbach's alpha = 0.748.

24 Cronbach's alpha = 0.522.

25 Cronbach's alpha = 0.634.

26 For a discussion of this issue, see T. W. Smith, 'Factors relating to misanthropy in contemporary American society', *Social Science Research*, 26 (1997), pp. 170–96; E. Uslaner, 'Trust as a moral value', paper presented at the conference Social Capital: Interdisciplinary Perspectives, University of Exeter, 15–20 September 2001.

27 All of these variables are the students' perceptions of the school context, rather than objective measures of these features. It is difficult to find such objective measures and we therefore opted to rely on the students' subjective evaluations. Note also that for the fairness index, two of the variables (interest in intelligent students, badly treated) were recoded before they were included in the index.

28 For a fuller discussion of these variables, see Chapter 3.

29 See S. W. Raudenbush and A. S. Bryk, *Hierarchical Linear Models: Applications and Data Analysis Methods* (2nd edn) (Newbury Park: Sage, 2002).

30 This is also why we have chosen to measure all school variables at the individual level, instead of aggregating them up to a school level, which would be the straightforward alternative when we are interested in the effects of the school context. It is of course possible to study classes as level-2 (contextual) units, which would give us 20 such units. This would, however, then leave us with quite a small number of level-1 units (students) within each level-2 unit, which is one of the reasons why we have not opted for this approach.

31 For an overview of the advantages of using panel data, see for example S. E. Finkel, *Casual Analysis with Panel Data* (London: Sage, 1995).

32 See Finkel, *Causal Analysis with Panel Data*.

33 To make sure that the results are not affected by how we define our dependent variable, we conducted additional analyses with the dependent variable measured both as index 4 and as the change in trust. All these analyses yielded similar results.

34 Most students were engaged in sport clubs; nearly 50 per cent of them engaged in sport activities on a weekly basis. Girls participated less frequently in organised activities on every item, except participation in religious groups.

35 L. H. Ehman, 'The American school in the political socialization process', *Review of Educational Research*, 50:1 (1980), p. 103.

36 In order to answer this question, we divided the students into two major groups based on the overall socio-economic conditions of their respective residential areas. Since we are mainly interested in comparing the poor areas with the non-poor ones, we collapsed the intermediate and high-ranked areas into one category, thereby making a distinction between

low-ranked and wealthier areas. We thereafter conducted separate regression analyses for the low-ranked and the wealthier areas.

37 Based on discussions with Nino Rocca, Centro Sociale di San Severio, Albergheria, 26 January 2000; Ivana Manone, Centro Padre Nostro, 2 February 2002.

38 The explained variance (R^2) was 0.085 for boys and 0.139 for girls.

39 In order to discern whether characteristics of the school have different effects on boys and girls, we analysed the effect of the school variables on boys and girls in separate regression models. The analysis showed that girls and boys react differently to different school variables. The most important factor affecting the inclination of girls to trust others was peer conflict, while boys were more dependent on having open school structures.

40 Levi refers to a study of the Australian community of Elisabeth which showed that 'a neighborhood that is badly treated by government comes to resent and distrust all agents of government'. Levi, 'A state of trust', p. 93. For a general discussion on how street-level bureaucrats might organise and structure their encounters with citizens, see M. Lipsky, *Street-Level Bureaucracy: Dilemmas of the Individual in Public Services* (New York: Russell Sage Foundation, 1980).

41 Tyler, *Why People Obey the Law*; Levi, 'A state of trust'; Rothstein, *Just Institutions Matter*; Stenesöta, *Den empatiska staten*.

42 Chaudhuri and Gangadharan, 'Gender differences in trust and reciprocity'.

43 As mentioned in Chapter 2, studies of gender differences and social capital have largely focused on differences between the types of association preferred by men and women.

44 Putnam, *Making Democracy Work*.

45 We could not see any correlations between socio-economic area and participation in organised activities, however, nor any statistically significant correlation between the parents' educational level and students' participation in voluntary associations.

46 'Io pratico lo sport della pallanuoto. Purtroppo il mio allenatore non è dei migliori. Invece di corragerci se sbagliamo ci fa uscire dalla piscina e ci urla contro parolacce.... Spesso devo giocare con dei ragazzi di 3–4 anni più di me, quindi molto più grandi di statura. Proprio ieri … siamo andati a Messina a giocare.... Mi ritrovai davanti un ragazzo di triplo di me che non riuscivo a tenere. Al primo errore il mio allenatore mi ha fatto uscire e, invece di corregarmi mi ha sgridato prendendomi in giro … il mio allenatore … mi disse che ero una femminuccia e che dovevo ritirarmi dalla pallanuoto.' No. 71, C1, 3rd letter. (See Chapter 9 on the Letter Project.)

47 'Poco mi importa … ho continuato a giocare fregandomene di quello che diceva. Ormai nella mia squadra ci siamo abituati e non ci importa. Ci anche detto che non avremmo più giocato e che da domani avremmo solo nuotato. Non ha ancora capito che, senza spiegarci quello che sbagliamo non capiremo i nostri errori.' No. 71, C1, 3rd letter.

48 'Italy's once-plucky little factories now complicate its battle with "Made in China"', *New York Times*, 14 May 2006.

9

The Letter Project – students' own stories

This chapter is based on letters from students in which they describe their life inside and outside school. What are their stories about school and how do they evaluate their experiences of school?

In this chapter we will explore students' letters in order to improve our understanding of the school variables discussed in the last chapter. In this way the letters will be used as a complement to the questionnaires.[1] We will also endeavour to see whether students' letters from schools A1 and A3 differ. As Table 8.3 showed, the schools performed quite differently on our trust indexes. While students in school A1 lost trust on all indexes but one, the development in school A3 was the opposite: students gained trust on every item.

The analysis in the last chapter identified several school factors that had positive and significant effects on students' generalised trust. The variables identified were openness of school structures, fairness of institutions and the degree of peer conflict (the less conflict, the more generalised trust). The analysis also showed that caring teachers, openness of classroom climate and school excursions were related to higher degrees of generalised trust. Unfortunately, we were unaware of these results when we formulated and distributed the letters, which is why students' answers were not always very elaborate with regard to every variable. However, their letters gave important clues to their major concerns in life, both inside and outside school.[2]

The analysis of students' letters will be organised according to three themes. The first consists of students' descriptions of *school life*. This theme is broad in character and encompasses: students' general perception of school, their views on school structures as exemplified by school breaks, and their perceptions of their interactions both with teachers and with their peers at school. How do students describe their interactions with their classmates? This variable is closely related to the variable identified in the previous chapter. The first theme also encompasses students' narratives about school excursions, which is again close to the analysis in the regression analysis in the last chapter. Why are excursions important for the development of generalised trust? This chapter will provide us with clues. The second theme is students' narratives about *trust in other persons*. How do these young people reason around trust? Do they believe that people in general can be trusted, or are they cautious when dealing with other people? Finally, the third theme relates to students' narratives about *their neighbourhoods*.

The letters were made anonymous by the use of numbers for students. In the text we will refer only to these numbers, followed by a reference to the school (for example student no. 64, school B2). Some students seemed quite proud of their 'secret numbers', referring to themselves in letters by their personal code; one boy said out loud in his class that he was 'number one'. Letters were personal and as a way of protecting the integrity of students, classmates and teachers, single-letter abbreviations will be used where the names of teachers and other students appeared in their letters. These abbreviations do not correspond with the persons' real names.

Before looking at the students' narratives, however, we will briefly describe the Letter Project and how it was organised.

Description of the Letter Project

The Letter Project started in February 2003 and ended in May 2005.[3] The project was inspired by a similar study organised by the Swedish National Agency for Education in 1995–97.[4] The Swedish study received a lot of attention and gave new and important information about young people's thoughts and lives. It was also interesting from a methodological point of view, since it proved it was possible to receive open and extensive texts even from very young individuals. Students from different classes were identified and selected for the Swedish study. In our case, we chose a different methodology. Instead of identifying students in different classes, we invited all students in one class at each of four schools to participate in the project: two schools in low-ranked socio-economic areas (A1 and A3), one from an intermediate area (B2) and the school in the high-ranked area (C1). All four classes also participated in the two surveys.

We asked students to write letters on different themes.
- Letter 1: A normal day in my life, at school and after school
- Letter 2: My district and its inhabitants
- Letter 3: Relations with other people
- Letter 4: Reflections on important events during recent years at school and reflections about the future.

We received between 50 and 60 letters on every theme, which means that about two-thirds of the students participated in the project. The response rate varied between 55 and 77 per cent between the different letters, and some variation was evident between boys and girls. An equal number of boys and girls wrote the first letter, more girls wrote the second letter, while boys were in the majority for the third and fourth letters. The response rate varied considerably between schools, with the highest participation rate in the high-ranked category. Details of the responses rate are given in Tables 9.1 to 9.3.

Table 9.1 The Letter Project: numbers of letters received, by gender (percentage of total in parentheses)

Gender	Letter 1	Letter 2	Letter 3	Letter 4	Total
Boys	30 (50)	23 (43)	36 (61)	31 (62)	120 (54)
Girls	30 (50)	30 (57)	23 (39)	19 (38)	102 (46)
Total	60 (100)	53 (100)	59 (100)	50 (100)	222 (100)

Table 9.2 The Letter Project: numbers of letters received from each school (total number of students in each class in parentheses)

School	First letter	Second letter	Third letter	Fourth letter	Total/ school
A1	12 (19)	9 (19)	13 (16)	10 (16)	44
A3	11 (24)	12 (26)	13 (20)	15 (20)	51
B2	18 (24)	7 (26)	14 (17)	10 (17)	49
C1	19 (23)	25 (25)	19 (24)	15 (24)	78
Total	60 (90)	53 (96)	59 (77)	50 (77)	222

Table 9.3 The Letter Project: percentage response rate by school

School	First letter	Second letter	Third letter	Fourth letter	Mean/ school
A1	63	47	81	62	63
A3	46	46	65	75	58
B2	75	27	82	59	61
C1	83	100	79	62	81
Mean	67	55	77	65	66

Percentages rounded to the nearest whole number.

Students' motivation

The project started as an experiment; we had no idea whether students would be suspicious or interested, motivated or unwilling to write something substantially interesting in their letters. However, the experiment turned out extremely well. A majority of the students who participated seemed to enjoy writing the letters and were remarkably frank about their lives and thoughts. We received many cheerful and personal greetings from students throughout the duration of the project, and many indicated that they were highly enthusiastic about being involved: 'Thanks for everything. I hope to see you again soon! Bye bye, a lot of greetings from 59.'[5] 'A big hello from your friend number 78.'[6] 'Bye, until the next letter, I will happily write to you.'[7] 'Bye, write to us soon.'[8] 'Big kisses, I really hope to hear from you. We'll meet next year.'[9] 'Carina, even if you come from Sweden I would like to meet you, I am asking you, please come and see us again.'[10]

Some students expressed their gratitude and enthusiasm for the project more explicitly, making comments on the Letter Project and/or the questionnaire: 'I … say hello to all those who have organised this project and a big hello to Carina and Pasqualino.'[11] 'A kiss from 59, I can hardly wait to do the questionnaire.'[12] 'Continue with this project, according to me it's very good!'[13] 'I hope that I will be able to participate in the Letter Project once again next year, and – most of all – see the book that will be published … I am happy to have written this letter, I am very happy that even Sicilians (particularly Palermitans) are considered for research.'[14] 'Thank you for having given us another opportunity to mature by talking about our feelings and other emotions. I will miss your letters because I now consider you a "pen-friend".'[15]

Except for the class from the high-ranked socio-economic area, classes from the other areas were not exceptional. The classes in the low-ranked areas were lively and we had some difficulties in maintaining calm during the completion of surveys in class. There were several students in both classes who were restless and required more attention from teachers. There were more drop-outs from two classes, A3 and B2, than from the two other classes.[16] As Table 8.3 showed, the schools performed quite differently on our indexes of trust. While students in school A1 lost trust on all indexes but one, the development in school A3 was the opposite: students gained trust on every item. The pattern was more mixed in schools B2 and C1. In the last chapter, the sample size did not permit a quantitative analysis of the results on the classroom or school level. In this chapter we will explore students' letters in order to identify differences between the schools in more detail.

Distribution of assignments

The assignment for each letter was distributed directly and personally to the students. An effort was made to motivate their participation, particularly when presenting the project to students for the first time. They were informed that their participation was voluntary, but at the same time we underlined the importance of their contribution. Students appreciated the anonymity of the letters and expressed concern that their identity would not be revealed to anybody. Our impression was that students' motivation increased over time as they won confidence, felt more secure and became better acquainted with the project.

The first two letters were given as assignments to write at home, as we believed it would make them feel more confident and at ease with the project. We also asked them to reflect on the assignment for several days before writing the letter. Students had about two weeks at their disposal for the write-up before returning the letters in a sealed envelope. Eventually we changed *modus operandi* and asked students to write the letters in class. The reason was mainly administrative: it was time-consuming to go back and forth to schools to distribute the assignment and then return later on to collect the letters. Students forgot to bring the letters back on the scheduled day, they said they had not had time to write the letters, or that their assignments had been torn apart by pets or younger sisters and brothers. For the letters written during class time, around one hour was dedicated to the write-up of the third letter, and two hours to the fourth letter. These letters were collected directly from the students.

The change of *modus operandi* increased the response rate to some extent. Students themselves said that it did not matter whether they had to write the letter at school or at home. However, some students preferred to write their letters at school, albeit not always for the noblest of reasons: 'Thanks for giving me the possibility to skip the class in Italian';[17] 'the next time take more hours from the teacher so that we will study less, come particularly during the class in mathematics'.[18] Another student described a welcome interruption to the daily school routines: 'Another day was really good, we had 2 hours of assessments and then, unexpectedly, you came Carina and we were all very calm because there were no more assessments … I say to you with all my heart: thank you Carina.'[19]

Students were also told that we were interested in their thoughts and that they should not worry too much about spelling and grammar and so on. We endeavoured to give students feedback on their letters, by writing a follow-up letter with a short general summary on what students had put in their letters. Another way of encouraging their motivation and participation in the project was to send personal photographs from Sweden and from other trips abroad.[20]

The third letter was written shortly after the distribution of the second questionnaire; it was clear that students, particularly from the low-ranked and intermediate areas, appreciated the continuity of the project and our personal visits to their school:

- 'I am very pleased that you came back to this school, as you said you would two years ago.'[21]
- 'We are very pleased that you finally came to our school … this visit has pleased us all a lot and we would like to wish you welcome.'[22]
- 'How are you? I hope well. I am well; in fact I'm very happy to find you in our class this year for the third time. For me next year will be very bad because we will not meet again.'[23]

- 'I have finished my story, and now I am greeting everybody … thank you for having selected our class.'[24]
- 'Thanks for giving me the opportunity to write all this.'[25]
- 'I am very happy to write this letter, and to confide in you my relations with other people.'[26]
- 'I am very happy to have written this letter to you.'[27]
- 'P.S. I will always remember you as if you were a dear friend.'[28]

School life

The first and fourth letters gave important information about students' perceptions of school. In their first letter, we asked students to describe a normal day in their life and to write about their feelings: how did they *feel* when they went to school, what did they *think* during the lessons, what did they do and how did they *feel* during the breaks? Did they like or dislike something particular at school? How did they *feel* when the school day was over? What were their interests and what kind of games did they play?

In the fourth and last letter, students were asked to write about an event or events that had meant a lot to them during their years in school. They were asked to write about something that had affected them in a particular way, something that had made them stop and think. Students were asked to reflect on events at school, their friends or any situation at school. Students were also invited to write about events that had happened outside school. Finally, because the fourth letter coincided with the students' last few weeks at lower secondary school (and with the end of their compulsory education), we asked them to write about their feelings regarding leaving school: what were their plans or thoughts for the future?

General comments on school

In their letters, some students expressed satisfaction with school and schoolwork, while others wrote that they disliked school and were not very interested in their studies. Some mentioned school structures in positive terms: their school was 'magnificent and beautiful',[29] or there were a lot of activities and facilities, such as a library, computers, gym and so on.[30] Some of those who said they disliked their studies nonetheless acknowledged the importance or usefulness of going to school:

- 'school … is something that I like so so … I understand that it's good to study, but not too much, otherwise you get stupid.'[31]
- 'I think that the lessons are very important, because they can serve you in your future work or in your daily life.'[32]
- 'I don't like to study but it's important to complete at least lower secondary level.'[33]
- 'for me, school is useful … I like to study in order to follow my desire to become policeman … I have to work a lot to take the diploma.'[34]

Generally, students had few comments on specific lessons or subjects at school. They enumerated their favourite subjects without commenting particularly on *why* they liked them: some subjects were simply boring, others were interesting. There was a tendency for students in the low-ranked and intermediate areas to prefer or request more creative or physical activities at school, while students in the high-ranked area also expressed their interest in theoretical school subjects.

Breaks and recreation

Several students wrote passionately about their school breaks. The importance accorded to breaks was striking in all classes in all schools. One student described break time as 'the "holy" break' that all the students were 'so much waiting for'.[35] Another student wrote: 'The most beautiful moment that we all are waiting for is the break, what a pity that it is so short, only 10 minutes, and therefore we eat in a hurry to be able to talk, play and trade cards [swap picture cards being collected].'[36] Another boy, who seemed to dislike school, particularly enjoyed the breaks: 'the best moment is the break, because we can eat and stand up … and talk with friends without getting reproached. At this moment I am very happy and I try to enjoy it to the full.'[37]

The students' longing for breaks is understandable, at least from a Swedish perspective. During a normal school day, starting at 8.15 and ending at about 13.10, students had only a 10-minute break, sometimes less. Several students lamented its shortness: 'the breaks, I think that they should last longer because we hardly have the time to put something to eat in our mouths and the bell rings'.[38] Sometimes breaks were circumscribed with restrictions: 'during the break we don't do anything because the teachers do not allow us to go out in the corridor, besides … a ten-minute break is not enough, they pass immediately.'[39] 'I don't like the break because they have put them at different hours … we have to adapt to the clock and I don't like it … when we have the breaks, we have to have them in the classroom … when we go to the toilets we must walk and not talk'.[40] 'For me the break is a moment of relaxation but since last week it is no longer like before because we can no longer go out of the classroom because of some serious incidents that happened to students…. I am pleased anyway because it is important as a break from 5 hours of study.'[41]

Several students wrote about the relief that they felt when the school day was over. A girl made herself the spokesperson for her classmates: 'We all like school when we watch a film or when we go out, the things we don't like is that they are giving us rules and we have to respect them. When school is over we feel relieved.'[42] A boy described his feelings while waiting for the final bell to ring: 'the sound of the last bell is the most beautiful one, for me it's so beautiful because it brings me home and I'm waiting for it all the time, because it signals the end of the lessons.'[43]

Interactions with teachers

Few letters mentioned any particular interaction between teachers and students. It was evident that students were attentive to variations in teachers' characters and styles. There were a few examples of students who described their own participation or active involvement in discussions. Students were 'following' classes and they were 'listening' to teachers' explanations, or else they complained about assessments and the existing rules. 'During the lessons I attentively *follow* [emphasis added] teachers' explanations.'[44] 'I don't particularly like to go to school because they are always explaining things and that bores me.'[45] '[T]he things that I dislike with school are: too much homework and when the teachers yell and write reports.'[46]

In their letters, students described different strategies to escape authoritarianism, such as daydreaming, frequenting the bathrooms and delaying their return to the classroom or by talking with friends between classes: 'When the teachers bore me I start dreaming with my eyes open, without ever getting caught. If the lesson interests me, I participate and follow.'[47] 'When the bell rings we return to the classroom and we immediately ask for permission to go to the bathroom, to take a small walk and to relax a little bit.'[48] 'One of the most beautiful moments is between lessons, because we can relax while we wait for the teacher to come; in this recreational moment we often ask for permission to go to the toilet, often because we want to skip the first minutes of the next lesson, but also because in the toilet there is a radiator and when it's cold we lean against it and warm ourselves.'[49]

Students' letters revealed that different teachers used different types of behaviour towards students, and that the *degree of authoritarianism* varied considerably. A general impression from the letters was that students in the high-ranked area paid more attention to their teachers' capacity, skills, character or personality. One student described her teachers' different characters during a normal day at school:

> The first lesson on Mondays, we have … with Professoressa L: she is not mean; on the contrary she is very gentle and good at explaining things. The second and third lesson we have … with Professoressa M: she is very severe and we are not even allowed to go to the toilet, and if we don't behave she doesn't even allow us to have a break…. After the break we have … Professoressa C: she is very kind and with her we are having a lot of good and interesting discussions. After that we have … Professoressa G: I think she is the best of the whole school and she is very kind and never gives us notes and she makes us do a lot of things.[50]

Sometimes even the daily mood of the teacher was accounted for: 'as soon as the teacher enters I observe her carefully in order to see if she has got out of bed on the right side'.[51]

The nature of the interaction between students and teacher, what we called the classroom climate, thus varied significantly between different teachers. Different teachers also had different degrees of toleration. In one case, a boy from the high-ranked area described how he was 'rescued' from suspension by a teacher's intervention: 'this morning at school I misbehaved a little bit and the art teacher wanted to suspend me, but thanks to the music professor … the nicest of them all, the suspension was avoided…. I am very thankful to her for this.'[52]

Students who had participated in musicals, recitals and so on expressed gratitude for the *attention* received. A boy who had participated in a musical at the request of one of his teachers described his emotions after the performance: 'After so many months of rehearsals … the day of the performance finally arrived at a theatre in Palermo, the Metropolitan. I was very excited and in the end the spectators gave me a lot of compliments. For me it was like a dream and I thought that finally somebody gave me some attention, and I was very happy.'[53]

We will now turn to our comparison of the two schools from the low-ranked areas, A1 and A3. As previously discussed, school A1 had a negative development of trust, while trust increased in school A3. By comparing narratives from students' letters, particularly their fourth letter, we get a clue about the difference between the schools.

One of the male students at school A1 admitted that students had been quite hard on their teachers over the years. The situation in this class had deteriorated during the three years at lower secondary school, he wrote, and he feared that they would face problems at higher levels:

> One thing that is wrong is that we during these three years haven't respected the teacher and we have joked with them all the time from the first year … now that we have arrived to the third year, things are getting worse. If we continue like this, that is, not studying like we should, we will have a lot of problems in the upper [secondary school].[54]

Another boy in the same class wrote that the first day at school had been 'the most strange and the most normal' at the same time, because 'there were no fights and no confusion. But we made acquaintance with the professors and the other students.'[55] His letter may indicate that fights and 'confusion' were otherwise part of the daily routine of this class. A girl from the same class dedicated her entire fourth letter to an incident at school in which other students had attacked her. She was furious, because neither her friends nor the teacher, who had witnessed the whole scene, had intervened:

> I got angry and managed to push back the group using all my force … it felt like pushing a fleet with sailors each weighing 80 kg. M.T. quickly ran away and I started to cry and ran to the toilet. The thing that irritated me the most was that neither the Prof. (who had seen the whole scene) nor my friends (particularly R) did

> anything. So I called my father, who came to school at 13.35, with
> my mother.[56]

Another student in this class expressed his sadness after having been separated from the class: 'I thought I would resist but instead, in the beginning of the separation from the class, I felt sad … when I saw my friends go down to have gymnastic lessons I wanted to do that at any cost, too, but for the moment I'm not always alone because sometimes they put me in a class with my friends.'[57]

This kind of account was almost absent from the last letter in the other school, A3. In their fourth and last letter, many students wrote about the positive social interaction not only between students but also between students and teachers. Despite general problems with order and discipline in this class, as narrated in previous letters, several students in their final letter described the support received from classmates. Students' comments on teachers were general but positive: '[T]he most important thought at this moment, really, is to leave the teachers and all my friends.'[58] 'This year I have spent so many good moments with my friends or with the teachers, but I already dislike the thought of passing the exams, because I will never find teachers or friends who are like them.'[59] There were also complaints, however, about teachers from this class. One of the students wrote that teachers often punished the whole class if other students had misbehaved: 'The thing I dislike is that the teachers give us a lot of homework and most of all, if my classmates have misbehaved the professors let us all pay for it.'[60] Nevertheless, the overall impression was that the students were pleased with their school. A boy declared that A3 was 'one of the best in Palermo' and that he would recommend it to anyone because 'this school is really GREAT'.[61]

Peer interaction

In the previous chapter, we found that the degree of peer conflict had effects on students' development of generalised trust: the more peer conflict, the less trust. Peer conflict or peer interaction was a theme frequently discussed in students' letters. Their narratives included numerous accounts of conflict but they often wrote about their interaction with friends during breaks, of the joy of being with their classmates, playing with them, laughing and joking, or receiving their support. Or, as one student put it: 'what I think about school is that it's not only a place where you learn things but also a place for amusement'.[62] Students expressed an interest in the success of their fellow students, evident in the admissions of helping each other during tests or individual challenges: 'we help each other; even at the tests we are passing small notes ... when there is a problem we discuss it ... we feel self-confident about ourselves ... during the lessons and the gymnastics, when we are dancing in class, when we are singing.'[63] Many students enjoyed the time before and after school, when they had time and the possibility to talk and play with their friends.

There were also examples of peer interactions causing turbulence and anxiety in class:

> I normally talk with my friends; I am very happy because I can confide in my friends and them in me. We also talk about how things are in the class, about rascals, talking about rascals there is one called X, he has psychological problems and is very dangerous. Every time he quarrels with my friends I suffer because I don't want them to fight. Another day he was fighting with my friend A, and they gave each other kicks, shoves and fists; then my friend A said that he would throw him out from the window and then X ran to the window and sat down on the window-sill and said that now I will through myself out. The teachers ran towards him and drew him towards the interior [of the room] and at this moment I asked: X. why are you doing this. We were all upset and my friend A cried because if X had fallen out he would never have forgiven himself. The story ended and they became friends again and started to talk to each other.... I was very proud of them.[64]

Relations between students changed over time, as they grew older. In their last letter, many students wrote extensively about their first experiences of love, or about their girlfriends or boyfriends.

Were there any differences between the two schools in the low-ranked areas? There were fewer stories about peer interaction in school A1. There were two letters describing quarrels with friends, but in both cases students had managed to solve their problems and had become friends again.[65] Accounts about friendship and peer interaction were more frequent in the other school, A3. One student admitted that his class was making the teachers despair, but friendship ties appeared stronger than in the other classes:

> we are a very lively class and we make the professors despair because of our behaviour. We are all risking not passing the exams

and if so I will be able to spend more time with them but then I want to realise my dream, I want to be big and to know how to talk with other people and that people appreciate me for the way I am, I am very confused, I'm afraid of leaving school and to leave my friends, they make me feel good and we are all helping each other even during the tests we are passing small notes, and they like me and I like them a lot.[66]

A girl wrote that the class had been calmer during the first year, because at that time students did not know each other. During the second and third year they had changed, however, apparently for the worse. She further explained that she did not want to leave her class and her friends 'because I trust them'.[67] In previous letters, however, there had been accounts about hard attitudes, violence and the use of deprecating nicknames between students: 'there is a comrade who is sitting behind me who always disturbs me and calls me the wash-up sink … I hate him … next to me there is one who we all call the monkey. The other day we were strapping each other's hair because she had given a fist to my friend and I pulled her hair and she went away crying.'[68]

> My comrades made fun of me calling me Nino d'Angelo [a popular singer from Naples], because I had long hair just like him and they were always singing his songs. One day I cut my hair and all of them were disappointed because they didn't know whom to make fun of. After two hours' silence we were making fun of one of our comrades who has much bigger ears than us and we called him 'Jumbo ears', 'satellite receiver', and that he could go to space and serve as a satellite receiver…. After these insults he told the teachers and they reported the whole class. As we could no longer make fun of him we were starting with another comrade who always brought sandwiches with marmalade and we said 'prisoner, today bread and water' … and he always became angry, we are still saying it, but he's not paying attention to it any more, because he is good and we all like him very much even though we are sometimes making fun of him, we know each other from the first day at lower secondary school and we all like each other a lot, he is also very small and we are also calling him dwarf and he gets angry. Then there is another comrade who has long whiskers and we call her Lupatelli like the football player who has long whiskers and no hair. She pretends not to hear but after a while she starts to cry. All of us are sometimes making fun of each other but we like each other a lot.[69]

A general reflection from their letters is that students did not particularly reflect on the effects their nicknames had on their classmates. It was evident from the letters, however, that the nicknames caused confusion and despair among some of the 'victims'.

> they are joking with me because every time I go to school my mother makes me a sandwich with Nutella and from that moment they call me 'prisoner'. When they are teasing me I try to forgive them but I can't, I don't know why they are making so much fun of me, maybe they do it, I understand that maybe they like me a lot.[70]

Nevertheless, several of the students' final letters were littered with descriptions of their affection for their friends and referred to their experiences together: 'I don't want to leave my friends, I am very attached to them because with them I have had fun, I have laughed, cried, made a lot of jokes … the simple thought of leaving them makes me feel bad.'[71] 'I don't want to leave my friends, particularly some of them that I am very close to and that I have known for a long time.'[72] A girl who was new in the class wrote about negative experiences in another class, but said she had instantly made friends with her new classmates. Moreover, they had chosen her as the head of the class, a new experience for her. She described her strong feelings for them, saying that they made her feel 'important'.[73]

In the questionnaire, students were asked for their opinion on the statement 'real friendship does not exist'.[74] The questionnaires showed that most students valued friendship a lot. On average in 2002, 76 per cent of the students disagreed with the statement, while 24 per cent agreed that 'real friendship does not exist'. There were, however, some important differences between the different socio-economic areas. About 75 per cent of the students in low and intermediate areas disagreed with the statement, compared with 96 per cent in the high-income area. Differences between socio-economic areas were significant in both surveys (2002 and 2005 – see Table 9.4).

Results from the two surveys indicated that students valued friendship even more in 2005 than in 2002. Despite the general improvement in students' perceptions of friendship, about a fifth of students in the low-income category remained adamant that true friendship did not exist. There were also important variations within the low-ranked areas.[75] Considering the importance students attached to friendship, it seems a logical conclusion that the degree of peer conflict has an impact on students' values.

Table 9.4 Perception of friendship, 2002 and 2005[a]

	Socio-economic level	Strongly disagree/ disagree (%)	Agree/ strongly agree (%)	Mean	SD	N
2002**	**Total**	**76**	**24**	**1.91**	**0.90**	**378**
	Low	73	27	1.98	0.94	245
	Intermediate	75	25	2.00	0.86	85
	High	96	4	1.42	0.58	48
2005**	**Total**	**84**	**16**	**1.68**	**0.85**	**311**
	Low	79	21	1.81	0.92	193
	Intermediate	92	8	1.43	0.68	76
	High	90	10	1.48	0.67	42

Percentages based on valid responses, and rounded to the nearest whole number.
[a]Students' perceptions of friendship were measured by their response to the statement 'L'amicizia sincera non esiste' (Real friendship does not exist). The response was scaled: 1 = strongly disagree, 2 = disagree, 3 = agree, 4 = strongly agree.
**The correlation between socio-economic area and friendship was significant at the 0.01 level (two-tailed).

Excursions

In Chapter 8, we found that school visits had a positive effect on students' development of generalised trust (see Table 8.4). In their letters, several students wrote about school excursions. One student particularly lamented the lack of excursions: 'the thing that I dislike with this school is that we never go on excursions, which I disapprove of a lot!'[76] Students' positive experiences of excursions were vividly described in the fourth letter, for which students were asked to write about important events during their years of schooling. One school from a low-ranked area had made a six-day trip to Tuscany, and the school in the high-ranked area had made a three-day excursion to Noto in eastern Sicily. Apart from these journeys, some students enthusiastically described private trips in Italy or abroad with their families or clubs they belonged to. Many students described the places they had visited and their emotions in relation to these visits: 'Sculptures, paintings and art made by illustrious artists were surrounding us, an unforgettable and unique feeling.'[77] But most of all, students were enthusiastic about their interaction with friends and teachers during these trips. Considering students' lamentation about the shortness of school breaks and the limited possibilities for interacting with their friends during schooltime, it is not surprising that these excursions represented important breaks to the daily routine and an opportunity to get to know each other better.

Both schools in the low-ranked areas had made excursions to other areas. While students at school A1 had made an excursion during their first year, those at A3 had made a more recent trip, to Tuscany during students' final year at lower secondary level, which seemed to increase the frequency of its mention within their letters. In school A1, only one student mentioned the trip as a particular event during the years at school: 'the best year was the first year because we went to Ragusa and Caltagirone etc. and I had a lot of fun'.[78] Several students in school A3 wrote about their excursion in their fourth and final letter.

> During the 3 years in this school a lot of events have marked my life, one of them is recent and that was the school trip to Tuscany. For the first time we were away from home for 6 days without my family and in a way this gave me a sense of responsibility, to pass these days with my friends gave me the possibility to talk and live beautiful moments with them.... Everything was

changing, our daily routines were lost and all of us revealed different personalities.[79]

'It was a beautiful experience', exclaimed one of her classmates, 'because I had the chance to know my friends better and to establish true friendship…. Even the professors seemed changed, they seemed better.'[80]

A girl who had gone on this school trip reflected on the trustworthiness of Italians and Palermitans. In her letter she described an incident in Florence, where she and her classmates had paid 10 euros to a person who said he was collecting money for HIV victims. She and her classmates eventually learned they had been fooled and she concluded: 'from this experience we understood that there are cheaters not only in Palermo, but also in a well-to-do area such as Florence.'[81]

What other factors have an effect on students' generalised trust? We will now turn to another explanation that we were unable to explore in the quantitative analysis. Is it possible to see whether the students' generalised trust is based on personal commitment or experiences of life?

Students' own stories about trust and faith in other people

The third letter bore directly on the central theme of this research study – students' view on trust and cooperation. Students were asked to write about their experiences of relations with other people. We asked whether they had ever experienced being fooled by anybody. If so, who fooled them – somebody they knew or somebody they did not know so well? In what way were they fooled? What did they think and feel when it happened? Were they able to solve the problem afterwards and become friends again? The assignment ended with the following general question (also used in the questionnaires): 'Do you think that in general one can trust other people or do you think that one has to be very careful when having contacts with others?'

If students had never had the experience of being fooled by someone, they were asked to write about an occasion when they had received help from other people. Did they get help from someone they knew or from someone they did not know so well? In what way were they helped? Students were asked to write about the thoughts and feelings they had when they received help. Here the general question at the end was: 'Do you think that people are helpful, in general, or do you think that people mainly think about themselves?'

Many students told us they had appreciated the theme of the third letter the most, saying it was more personal than the previous letters. Many of them wrote about disappointments and disillusion caused by people they considered 'best friends'. Most had experienced being fooled or teased by friends or class-mates. Sometimes students managed to become friends again, in other cases not. A girl living in a well-off area wrote about the betrayal of a friend, whom she thought sincere: 'from this experience I have come to the conclusion that you can never trust your friends, not even those who are most sincere.'[82] Another girl, who lived in a poor area, wrote that, in spite of her optimistic and positive character, she believed it difficult to trust friends: 'I think that when you have friends you have to be very careful because it's very improbable that they are really sincere, there is always something beneath! I don't want to be presumptuous but I think that I'm quite a good and positive person … I believe that today it's very difficult to trust anybody in general, sometimes impossible, there is always a side of the personality that one can never reveal.'[83]

Yet negative personal experiences did not always lead to a negative perception of other people. One of the girls participating in the Letter Project (from the high-ranked socio-economic area) came to the opposite conclusion. She argued that people in general should be trusted, because they 'deserve' it. As she put it:

> I don't believe very much in the saying: 'to trust is good, to not trust is better' because I am convinced that people deserve trust. I have had disappointments in my life but I believe that this is normal and is part of life.[84]

This girl's reflection is thus very close to Uslaner's moralistic trust (i.e. a general belief in other people's faithfulness). Accord-ing to Uslaner moralistic trust is robust over time, despite the negative experiences one may have had in life.[85]

In their stories, many students wrote about occasions when friends, or people unknown to them, had offered unexpected help or support. One example was a girl who had lost her nephew on the beach but was helped to find him again with the help of a boy she did not know.[86] A boy told a story about being lost in the forest and helped to find his family by a person he did not know.[87] Another wrote about how he had received consolation from his friends when his mother had died. He had not expected their support as he did not consider them close friends; he only used to hang out with them. However, they tried to encourage and support him at a very difficult moment in his life.[88] A girl estimated people to be both available and ready to engage, since she had once received help herself from unknown people:

> I was helped by two ladies when I fainted in the street and they called my mother to come and get me; I felt very happy when they helped me, because I didn't expect anybody to offer help. You asked me whether I believe that most people are ready to give me help and I really think they are, thanks to this experience I have had.[89]

Other students were not as lucky as the students mentioned above. A boy in the high-ranked area referred to personal observations when coming to the opposite conclusion: 'I think that most people only think about themselves and they rarely help other people. I have seen this on numerous occasions.'[90] A boy living in a low-ranked area wrote about other people's lack of availability and willingness to help. He said that he had never received any help from anybody outside his own family. When people offered help, it was only because they foresaw receiving something in return:

> Every day, they are joking with me. They are doing it for fun but it's exhausting. They make fun of me with bad words and offences … when I make friends I am always careful with whom I'm doing it. The only occasions I have been helped are when my family has helped me with my studies, with electrical things and other small things. I have *never* received any help from friends or acquaintances…. In the end you can only fully trust your family members and never friends or acquaintances. Because the persons (friends or acquaintances) are never available, they are only available if they receive something in return, otherwise nothing.[91]

The letters gave a very varied picture; some students had had bad experiences with their friends, others not. Some students trusted other people, others did not. Some students believed in other people's helpfulness, others had a more pessimistic view. Some students had lost their faith in others after personal experiences, others had not.

Students' stories about their neighbourhood

In the second letter of the Letter Project, students were asked to write about their neighbourhood. The assignment was given in January 2004, during the second year of lower secondary school. Students were asked to reflect on and respond to the following issues: What is good in your neighbourhood? Is there anything you do not like? Do you feel safe and secure in your area? If you were Palermo's mayor for a day, what would you do to improve the area you live in?

Students were also asked to write about the people living in their area. Was it easy or difficult to make new friends? Were people friendly and helpful? Students were asked to write about concrete events or incidents that they had experienced in their area and to write about situations that had made them happy or incidents that had made them sad or angry.

The letters we received were very interesting and told us a lot about students' perceptions of people living in their area. Quite strong words were used to describe the people: they were kind, available, civilised, vulgar, uncivilised, ignorant and sometimes even dangerous. It was evident that students were very conscious of which people to stay away from in their area, people who were considered 'not approachable'. Students were generally very aware of problems with pollution, drugs, traffic and lack of green areas. A theme that was almost universal was concern about the lack of parks, gardens and open spaces where children could gather and play together. Many said there was space for younger or older children than themselves, but few activities for children of their age. Many suggested the construction of gardens, parks, playgrounds and other areas for children. Many expressed concern about pollution, lack of cleaning in their area, traffic fumes and the poor state of the buildings.

Students' perception of security in the area varied considerably between the high-ranked and low-ranked areas. Many said they felt secure in their area, while others expressed deep concern about the lack of safety. Those living in more difficult areas were more worried than students in other areas: 'I don't feel safe at all in the area. I don't like the people in C., most of them are ignorant and vulgar.'[92] 'I don't feel very safe in my area because a lot of bad people are living there; there is nothing that is good.'[93] 'To live in my area is really not optimal, because you're not very safe there.'[94] 'I don't feel safe in my area because there is no police station in the zone … but if you know somebody you're safe and nothing happens to you.'[95] Another student complained: 'My area is ugly and when you go out you always hear people swear.'[96]

Some students living in difficult neighbourhoods expressed fears of both earthquakes and criminals. '[I] do not feel safe because all the things are old and if there was an earthquake like the one on 6 September 2002 everything would collapse.' The same student added, 'when one goes out from the door of the staircase one doesn't know if they will shoot you'.[97] Another student wrote that 'my area is not one of the most secure ones and I don't feel safe at all, often you hear about people who have been arrested for drug dealing, nothing more needs to be said to understand that dangerous people live there'.[98]

Nevertheless, many students had quite a balanced view and were able to distinguish between good and bad people: 'some persons are available and social, but others are aggressive and it's better to stay away from them'.[99] Another student wrote that 'The persons who aren't mean are kind and available and good persons are coming to live here'.[100] One of the students complained about the prejudice many people had regarding his area: 'in an area like mine, which has a bad reputation, it's not that everyone is evil, uneducated or unkind, but it's a small part (I am saying this to you because even a lot of professors at my school believe that we are all the same!)'.[101] Another student appreciated the area she lived in but not its citizens: 'My area is very elegant and exquisite but unfortunately the clothes do not make a monk! That is, there are some persons that have bad manners and they are destroying it.'[102]

The class of 26 students in the intermediate area returned only seven letters on this second theme.[103] This school was situated close to a big market in Palermo. Even according to Palermitan standards, the area is busy and crowded, particularly so during big events and fairs. Even if some students appreciated the activities available in the area, several complained about the traffic situation and the abundance of rubbish: 'every morning when I wake up and walk to school I see how ugly everything is: it stinks! People scream, there's traffic and I can't even smell the odours of spring.'[104] Another student had a more balanced view: 'Even if there's a lot of garbage cans, the area I live in is very dirty, 50% is caused by the Friday market, however a positive thing is that it's full of colours and life.'[105] Some students felt safe where they lived, others did not.

Students in the high-income area were generally aware of their privileged status, living in an area considered safe and secure: 'there are all kind of services ... it is not a risky area',[106] 'there are no dangers whatsoever ... the persons living in this building are good people',[107] 'the persons live normally without problems',[108] 'it's a peaceful area that is inhabited by calm people'.[109] One can read between the lines, however, that students were not entirely confident about society: 'I don't feel very safe because there is no door-keeper and therefore nobody to protect us if strangers or people with bad intentions would approach',[110] or 'I feel safe because my entrance is provided with an automatic gate and watch-dogs'.[111]

Generally, people were described as civilised, nice, available and honest. However, some students wrote about the distance between people, even if these comments were exceptions to the rule. One girl wrote that people in the area 'are very kind but they are never available because they work all the time'.[112] Another student, a boy, complained that people in his area were too busy living their frenetic lives:

> People in my area live in the stressful turbine of daily work, school, hobby, and the other normal activities in average life, children to take care of, dogs to walk etc ... the majority are like lonely wolves drowned in their own problems and their own frenetic lives.[113]

He described people as hypocritical, cold, indifferent and bad-mannered. In consequence, they 'were not interested in having friends, apart from a quick hello on the staircase'.[114]

Relating letters to statistics

The narratives above give some clues to a finding reported in Chapter 7. That is, in the responses to two general questions in the main surveys, 'Do you believe that most people can be trusted or that nobody can be trusted?' and 'Do you believe that most people try to be helpful, or do you think that people only think about themselves?', we found an interesting pattern we did not expect to find: students in the high-ranked area expressed most trust in other people at the same time as they agreed to a greater extent than students in the other areas that 'people think only about themselves'. There was no correlation between these two questions on trust and helpfulness in the high-ranked area. Hence, students' trustful attitudes towards others were not coupled to a positive perception of other people's willingness to help. In the low-ranked and intermediate areas, however, perceptions of generalised trust and people's willingness to help were correlated: low levels of trust were associated with low expectations of others' willingness to help, and vice versa – high levels of trust were associated with high expectations of people's willingness to help. This finding reflects that although life could be quite harsh in poor neighbourhoods, there were positive expectations about other people's willingness to offer help.

How do these accounts relate to results from the questionnaires? What does the quantitative study tell us about students' perceptions of the area where they live? As the letters indicated, differences between the three socio-economic areas were important. In the low-ranked areas, only 58 per cent described their area with positive formulations, compared with 78 and 76 per cent in the intermediate and high-income areas, respectively (Table 9.5). In the low-ranked areas, 26 per cent of the students used negative words and phrases in their descriptions of their neighbourhood, compared with 9 per cent in the intermediate area and 16 per cent in the high-ranked area.

Differences between schools in the low-ranked areas were also important. Between 16 and 33 per cent of students in different schools described their area in negative terms. The most negative comments were found on the questionnaire (in open responses) in school A2 (which did not participate in the Letter Project), where one-third of the students said they disliked their neighbourhood, for different reasons. Examples of their descriptions were 'it is very ugly',[115] 'it's too chaotic',[116] 'I feel very bad there, because a lot of people quarrel all the time',[117] and 'they should do something about it, because a lot of people get ill'.[118]

Considering students' evaluation of their immediate neighbourhood, the results presented in Chapter 7 were understandable. We found significant differences with regard to trust in neighbours between socio-economic areas. The higher-ranked a socio-economic area was, the more trust there was in neighbours. There were also significant differences with regard to

Table 9.5 Perception of home area, 2002: overall percentage classifications of students' responses to an open questionnaire item[a]

	Positive	Positive and negative	Negative	Neutral
Total	65	12	20	2
Area [b]				
Low (A)	58	13	26	3
Intermediate (B)	78	11	9	2
High (C)	76	9	16	0
School [b]				
A1	61	18	16	5
A2	48	13	33	6
A3	64	11	25	0
A4	60	9	28	2
B1	71	18	9	2
B2	86	3	9	3
C1	76	9	16	0

Percentages based on valid responses, and rounded to the nearest whole number.

[a] Responses to the open question 'Cosa pensi del tuo quartiere?' ('What do you think about your neighbourhood?'). Results based on the total sample.

[b] A1–A4 = low-ranked areas, B1–B2 = intermediary areas, C1 = high-ranked area.

trust in classmates in the first wave: students in higher-ranked areas had more trust in their classmates than those in lower-ranked areas. This difference may be explained by the fact that many students did not yet know each other during the first semester at lower secondary school, and therefore did not trust each other, indicating an experienced-based level of trust.

Despite the different contexts students were experiencing, this did not seem to have an impact on their generalised trust. As we recall from Chapter 7, students' trust in Palermitans, Sicilians, Italians or foreigners did not differ between the three socio-economic areas. The situation in students' areas had an impact only on their trust in people living in their neighbourhood, not on their trust in people they did not know. It thus appears as if students' perceptions of people living in their neighbourhood is based more on experience (i.e. strategic trust), but that this did not affect their trust in other categories of citizens.

Conclusion

In this chapter we have attempted to explore the mechanism between the variables reported to be significant in Chapter 8 and generalised trust. In Chapter 8 we identified six school factors that had an impact on students' generalised trust: openness of structures, fairness of institutions, caring teachers, friendly peer interaction, openness of classroom climate, and excursions to the city. The most influential factors were openness of structures, fairness of institutions and the degree of peer conflict at school. As already stated, we were unaware of the results when formulating and distributing the letters. The project started in February 2003, during the students' second term at lower secondary school, and ended in May 2005, during their last term.

Four classes participated in the project: two schools in low-ranked socio-economic areas, one class from an intermediate area and one class in a school from the high-ranked area. Students wrote letters on different themes: 'a normal day in my life', 'my district and its inhabitants', 'relations with other people' and 'reflections on important events during the last years at school and reflections about the future'. We received between 50 and 60 letters on every theme, which means that about two-thirds of the students participated in the project. The response rate varied between 55 and 77 per cent for the different letters, and some variation was evident between boys and girls.

In the previous chapter we measured *openness of school structures* by asking students about the availability of teachers. Openness of school structures was not a theme that students spontaneously wrote about in their letters. However, many indirectly referred to authoritarian structures at school, particularly in relation to school breaks. Several students wrote passionately about their school breaks. This theme may be related to the factor 'openness of school structures'. The importance accorded to breaks was striking in all classes in all schools. One student described it as 'the "holy" break' that all the students were 'so much waiting for'.[119] Several students lamented the short duration of breaks and that the accorded 10 minutes passed too quickly. Sometimes breaks had restrictions, such as the students not being allowed to leave the classroom; sometimes breaks were timed differently from those of other classes; and sometimes breaks were even cancelled altogether by teachers. In their letters, students described different strategies to escape authoritarianism, such as daydreaming, frequenting the bathrooms and delaying their return to the classroom or by talking with friends between classes. Some students also wrote about their dislike of homework, rules or teachers shouting. At the same time, some students were also aware, by the end of the third year at lower secondary school, that they had not always respected their teachers: 'If we continue like this, that is, not studying like we should, we will have a lot of problems in the upper [secondary school]. '[120]

Caring teachers was another factor that proved important for students' development of generalised trust. There were a few examples in the letters on this aspect of their schooling. Some letters told how specific teachers had cared for them. In one case, a boy from the high-ranked area described how he was 'rescued' from suspension by an intervening teacher. Another boy, who had participated in a musical at the request of one of his teachers, wrote about his excitement over the attention he received.

Only a few students described the *classroom climate* or their own participation in class, or their active involvement in discussions. Generally, students had few comments on specific lessons or subjects at school. They enumerated their favourite subjects without commenting particularly on *why* they liked them: some subjects were simply boring, others were interesting. Students' letters revealed that different teachers had different standards. There were sometimes important variations between teachers' degrees of authoritarianism in relation to students. The interaction between students and teacher, that is, the classroom climate, thus varied significantly between teachers. But, as we saw above, the different standards could sometimes be helpful for students, for example if a student was helped in relations with a severe teacher.

The school effects found in Chapter 8 were small. In this chapter we have been able to explore students' perceptions of their teachers in a little bit more detail. Students' letters suggest that their interactions with teachers varied according to the teachers' character and mood. As the questions on classroom climate were not specified to any particular teacher or topic, it is likely that we would have found stronger regressions had we been able to control for the effect of different teachers.

As analysed in Chapter 8, however, we saw that *peer conflict* negatively affected students' levels of generalised trust. Peer conflict or peer interaction was a theme frequently discussed in students' letters. They often wrote about their interaction with friends during breaks, the joy of being with their class-mates, playing with them, laughing and joking, or receiving their support. Students expressed an interest in the success of their fellow students, evident in the admissions of helping each other during tests or individual challenges. There were also examples of incidents with peer interaction causing anxiety among students. Considering the importance students attach to friendship, it seems logical to conclude that the degree of peer conflict will have an impact on students' values.

Students' positive experiences of excursions were vividly des-cribed in their fourth letters, in which they were asked to write important events during their years of schooling. In Chapter 8, we found that school visits had a positive effect on students' development of generalised trust. In their fourth and last letter, several students wrote about school excursions. Their letters revealed that the importance of excursions was to some extent related to both peer interaction and interaction with teachers. Excursions represented important events, where students were allowed to interact informally with both friends and teachers. Considering students' lamentations about the brevity of school breaks and the limited possibilities of interacting with their friends during schooltime, it is not surprising that these excur-sions represented important departures from the daily routine.

There were some differences between the least success-ful and the most successful school regarding school factors. Students in school A1 seemed less enthusiastic about their school and more often reported negative experiences at school. In school A3 students wrote about social interactions with peers or teachers in more positive terms. They also had strong memories related to a recent school trip to Tuscany (many described the trip as an important life experience). However, their accounts also revealed tough attitudes between students, for example the use of nicknames, and lack of discipline in the class. Furthermore, ties between students seemed stronger, as indicated by their formulations when writing about their school, peers and teachers. We also saw some differences between students' narratives from the least successful school and those from the most successful school. While students in the former reported some negative experiences at school and were less positive in their narratives, students in the latter school wrote enthusiastically about their peers and teachers.

The number of letters was small, however, and more in-depth studies of the two schools are necessary in order to depict other possible school factors that affect students' generalised trust. It should also be taken into consideration that school A3 was both newly built and recently established in the area. Its establishment had been strongly desired and the school was one of the few establishments in the area with a playground for children. In addition, the school had also enjoyed strong leadership and a stable staff of teachers. The other school, A1, had a more central location in Palermo, and strongly resented the competition from neighbouring schools. Although there was a lack of green spaces and playgrounds in this area, the proximity to central Palermo still made it less isolated, and perhaps its school less central to students' private lives.

Another explanation for students' level of generalised trust refers to their personal experiences. Were students who had had negative experiences less inclined to trust people they did not know? Were students who had had positive experience more trustful? However, students' letters did not give any clear answer on this. Personal experiences mattered for some students' trust in other people, but not for everybody. The letters showed that many students had a personal commitment to trust others, while others based their generalised trust on personal experiences. Students' generalised trust may be related to Uslaner's distinction between strategic and moralistic trust. While strategic trust is an effect of a person's previous experience, moralistic trust is more of a moral commitment to treat people as if they are trustworthy.

Nevertheless, students' narratives about their neighbourhood suggest that their trust in some categories of citizens was based on personal experience. Differences between areas were important on only four items: trust in relatives, neighbours and classmates, and people in the area (see Tables 7.3–7.6). The differences were striking for trust in neighbours and trust in classmates. In 2002, only 46 per cent of the students in the low-ranked areas trusted their neighbours, compared with 55 per cent in the intermediate areas and 72 per cent in the high-ranked area. Only 60 per cent of the students in the low-ranked areas trusted their classmates, compared with 71 per cent in the intermediate areas and 90 per cent in the high-ranked area. These differences diminished over time, however, as students in the lower-ranked categories gained trust, and students in the high-ranked area lost trust. Students' letters suggested that their degree of trust might be based on their perceptions of the area where they live.

Many students in the low-ranked areas expressed concern about the presence of drugs, criminality and people who should not be approached, while students living in more well-off areas felt secure and at ease with their neighbourhood. Students' answers from the low-income areas were balanced and no obvious general distrust in people was visible. Their reasoning showed that they knew perfectly well how to distinguish between honest people and those of ill-will. Some of the students' reactions during the questionnaire survey also pointed in this direction. When asked whether they trusted the president of Italy, for example, many looked confused and explained: 'I don't know. I haven't met him yet!' When I confronted some students who said they did not trust foreigners, and asked if they did not trust me (a foreigner) they often answered, 'Yes, I do, but I have met you'. However, there are also indications that contradict this analysis. Some students participating in the Letter Project seemed to have a personal commitment to trust other people, regardless of their personal experiences.

If you live in dangerous or hostile surroundings, it may be wise to not trust everybody, at least not persons in the local environment. The students' letters clearly showed that they were careful when dealing with strangers, which is understandable if your neighbourhood does not consist of honest people. Students seemed to be very aware of which persons to avoid in their local environment. They were also attentive to dangerous or difficult students. The quantitative analysis in Chapter 7 showed that differences between socio-economic areas were significant for trust in neighbours, people in the area, relatives and classmates, that is, persons in the students' immediate environment. However, this did not affect trust in people living elsewhere – Palermitans, Sicilians, Italians or foreigners.

Notes

1 More in-depth studies of the content of the letters would have been possible, of course, analysing the different themes in the letters by using different methods of content analysis. One Swedish study, for example, used the repertory grid technique. Skolverket [Swedish National Agency for Education], *Den rimliga skolan: livet i skolan och skolan i livet* (Stockholm: Liber, 1995), pp. 20–9.

2 The accounts are translated from the original Italian by the author, and are provided in the original Italian only for extracted quotes.

3 I am indebted to Christian Lundahl for important inspiration and input for the Letter Project. Pasqualino Ferrarotto organised the project in close cooperation with schools and motivated students to participate. Cono Ferrarotto helped with the collection of the third and fourth letters. Without their help, advice, organisational and motivational skills, and good faith, this project would never have been realised.

4 Twenty-two boys and 24 girls participated in the Swedish study, which stretched over two years, and they were 10, 12 or 14 years old when the project started. During these two years, the Swedish students were asked to write 15 letters on different themes. About half the letters related to their school life, half to their lives outside school (for example, the importance of music in their lives, self-confidence, important events, personal strategies to achieve personal goals).

5 No. 59, B2, 1st letter.

6 No. 78, C1, 2nd letter.

7 No. 83, C1, 2nd letter.

8 No. 3, A3, 2nd letter.

9 No. 39, A1, 2nd letter.

10 No. 3, A3, 1st letter.

11 No. 41, A1, 2nd letter.

12 No. 59, B2, 2nd letter.

13 No. 63, B2, 2nd letter.

14 No. 64, B2, 2nd letter.

15 No. 66, C1, 4th letter.

16 Between 2002 and 2005 five students dropped out from the class in A3 and seven students from the class in B2. Newcomers were few in all classes (none, one or two).

17 No. 76, C1, 4th letter.

18 No. 70, C1, 1st letter.

19 No. 3, A3, 1st letter.

20 When visiting the schools for the third letter, we saw posters with the photographs stuck to the wall in two of the classes, one entitled 'Carina in the world' ('Carina in mondo') and the other one 'The letter project and who created it' ('Il progetto lettera e chi l'ha creato').

21 No. 14, A3, 3rd letter.

22 No. 24, A3, 3rd letter.

23 No. 41, A1, 3rd letter.

24 No. 31, A1, 3rd letter.

25 No. 44, B2, 3rd letter.

26 No. 55, B2, 3rd letter.

27 No. 57, B2, 3rd letter.

28 No. 1, A3, 4th letter.

29 No. 20, A3, 1st letter.

30 No. 45, B2, 1st letter.

31 No. 33, A1, 1st letter.

32 No. 37, A1, 1st letter.

33 No. 7, A3, 1st letter.

34 No. 46, B2, 1st letter.

35 No. 55, B2, 1st letter.

36 No. 48, B2, 1st letter.

37 No. 88, C1, 1st letter.

38 No. 47, B2, 1st letter.

39 No. 41, A1, 1st letter.

40 No. 75, C1, 1st letter.

41 No. 79, C1, 1st letter.

42 No. 41, A1, 1st letter.

43 No. 88, C1, 1st letter.

44 No. 76, C1, 1st letter.

45 No. 13, A3, 1st letter.

46 No. 51, B2, 1st letter.

47 No. 68, C1, 1st letter.

48 No. 72, C1, 1st letter.

49 No. 88, C1, 1st letter.

50 'Arrivati in classe il lunedì a prima ora, abbiamo … con la professoressa L: lei non è cattiva, anzi con noi è molto gentile ed è brava a spiegare le cose. A seconda e terza ora abbiamo … con la professoressa M: lei è severissima non ci fa uscire neanche per andare in bagno, e se ci comportiamo male non ci fa fare neanche la ricreazione…. Dopo la ricreazione abbiamo … con la professoressa C: lei è gentilissima con lei facciamo discorsi molto belli ed interessanti. A quest ora noi ce ne dobbiamo andare e abbiamo … con la professoressa G: secondo me è la più brava di tutta la scuola è molto gentile e non mette mai note e ci fa fare un sacco di cose.' No. 87, C1, 1st letter.

51 No. 68, C1, 1st letter.

52 No. 81, C1, 1st letter.

53 No. 11, A3, 4th letter.

54 'Una cosa che riflettendoci è sbagliato è che nei tre anni tutti noi non portiamo rispetto all'insegnante e ci pigliamo gioco di loro questo fino dalla prima ma in modo più leggero, ora siamo arrivati in terza e le cose continuano a peggiorare. Continuando così quindi non studiando come dovremmo, ci troveremo in un mare di guai alle superiori.' No. 34, A1, 4th letter.

55 No. 36, A1, 4th letter.

56 'Lì mi arrabbiai e riuscii a respingere il gruppo con tutta la mia forza ... (sembrava stessi spingendo una flotta di marinai di 80 kg ciascuno). M.T. scappò di gran corsa e io scoppiai a piangere e corsi in bagno. La cosa che mi irritò di più fù che la prof. (che assistì a tutta la scena) né le mie compagne (specialmente R.) fecero niente. Allora chiamai singhiozzando mio padre che potè venire alle 13.35, con mia madre a scuola.' No. 39, A1, 4th letter.

57 No. 40, A1, 4th letter.

58 No. 1, A3, 4th letter.

59 No. 10, A3, 4th letter.

60 No 20, A3, 1st letter.

61 No. 11, A3, 4th letter.

62 No. 79, C1, 1st letter.

63 No. 3, A3, 4th letter.

64 'Di solito parlo con i miei compagni, sono molto felice perché mi posso confidare con i miei compagni e loro con me. Parliamo anche di come va la classe, dei miei compagni monelli, a proposito di compagni monelli ce n'è uno che si chiama X., ha dei problemi psicologici ed è molto pericoloso. Ogni giorno si litiga con i miei compagni ed io soffro perché non voglio che succeda che si litighino. L'altro giorno si litigò con un mio compagno che si chiama A. si litigò con lui dandosi botte, calci, spintoni e pugni; allora il mio compagno A. gli disse che lo buttava dalla finestra e allora X. di scatto si sedette sul davanzale della finestra e gli disse ora mi butto io. Le professoresse corsero verso di lui e lo tirarono verso l'interno io in quel momento dissi: X. perché fai questo. Eravamo tutti sconvolti e il mio compagno A. pianse perché se X. cadeva non se lo poteva permettere. Finita questa storia e i due fecero pace ricominciarono a parlarsi ed io ero molto fiero di loro due.' No. 64, B2, 1st letter.

65 No. 37, A1, 4th letter; no. 31, A1, 4th letter.

66 '[S]iamo una classe vivace e facciamo esasperare i professori e quindi anche per il nostro comportamento. Rischiamo quasi tutti la bocciatura così magari posso rimanere ancora con loro ma poi voglio realizzare il mio sogno, voglio diventare grande e sapere parlare con le altre persone e che le persone mi apprezzino per il mio modo di fare, sono molto confusa, ho paura di lasciare la scuola e di lasciare anche i miei compagni loro mi fanno sentire bene e poi ci aiutiamo tutti anche sulle verifiche ci passiamo tutti i bigliettini, poi mi vogliono bene e io voglio bene a loro tanto.' No. 3, A3, 4th letter.

67 No. 22, A3, 4th letter.

68 No. 13, A3, 1st letter.

69 'Sono stato preso in giro dai miei compagni che mi dicevano Nino D'Angelo, perché avevo i capelli lunghi come lui e mi cantavano sempre le sue canzoni. Un giorno me li sono tagliati e tutti sono rimasti male perché non sapevano chi prendere in giro. Dopo due ore di silenzio abbiamo preso in giro un nostro compagno che ha le orecchie molto più grandi di quelle nostre e lo chiamavamo "orecchie di jumbo" "ricevitore satellitare di sky", che poteva andare nello spazio e fare da parabola satel-litare per il digitare terrestre. Dopo questi insulti lo ha detto ai professori e hanno fatto il rapporto a tutta la classe. Noi non lo potevamo più prendere in giro e abbiamo prese in giro un altro compagno che si portava pane con la marmellata e noi gli dicevamo "carcerato, oggi pane e acqua" li

hanno in carcere lui se la prendeva sempre, ora glielo diciamo ancora, ma lui non ci fa più caso, perché è bravo e tutti gli vogliamo bene anche se ci prendiamo in giro a vicenda, ma ci conosciamo tutti dal primo giorno di scuola media e ci vogliamo molto bene, lui è anche molto basso e gli diciamo anche nanetto e lui se la prende. Poi una nostra compagna ha le basette molto lunghe e la chiamiamo Lupatelli come il giocatore che ha le basette lunghe ed è senza capelli. Lei fa finta di non sentire e dopo un po' si mette a piangere. Tutti ci prendiamo in giro a vicenda ma ci vogliamo molto bene.' No. 5, A3, 3rd letter.

70 '[M]i prendono in giro perchè ogni volta che vengo a scuola mia madre mi fa sempre il panino con la nutella e dal quel momento in poi mi chiamano "carcerato". Quando mi prendono a volte in giro io provo a perdonarli ma non ci riesco, non so perchè mi prendono tanto così in giro, forse lo fanno, io capisco che forse mi vogliono tanto così bene.' No. 14, A3, 3rd letter.

71 No. 13, A3, 4th letter.

72 No 3, A3, 4th letter.

73 No. 93, A3, 4th letter.

74 Many students seemed shocked when reading the question, and many of them asked us during the test whether they had understood the question properly or not.

75 Results from the 2005 panel study showed that the proportion of students who agreed with the statement 'real friendship does not exist' varied by 23 percentage points between schools in low-ranked areas: in school A2, 32 per cent of the students said they agreed with the statement, compared with 9 per cent in school A3. In school A1, 18 per cent of the students agreed with the statement.

76 No. 63, B2, 1st letter.

77 No. 9, A3, 4th letter.

78 No. 35, A1, 4th letter.

79 'Nel corso dei 3 anni di questa scuola tanti eventi hanno segnato la mia vita particolarmente, uno di questi è avvenuto recentemente e si tratta del viaggio di istruzione in Toscana. Per la prima volta sono stata fuori di casa per 6 giorni senza la mia famiglia e in un certo qual modo mi ha dato un senso di responsabilità, trascorrere queste giornate con i miei compagni mi ha dato modo di poter dialogare e vivere dei bei momenti con loro…. Tutto si stava transformando, i nostri ritmi quotidiani si erano persi e tutti noi abbiamo tirato fuori una personalità tutta nuova.' No. 9, A3, 4th letter.

80 No. 15, A3, 4th letter.

81 No. 9, A3, 4th letter.

82 No. 75, C1, 3rd letter.

83 No. 9, A3, 3rd letter.

84 'Io non credo molto al proverbio che dice: "fidarsi è bene ma non fidarsi è meglio" perché sono convinta che la gente merita fiducia. Nella vita ho avuto delle fregature ma penso che questo sia normale e faccia parte della vita.' No. 68, C1, 3rd letter.

85 Uslaner, *The Moral Foundations of Trust*, pp. 162–5.

86 No. 33, A1, 3rd letter.

87 No. 74, C1, 3rd letter.

88 No. 77, C1, 3rd letter.

89 '[S]i sono stata aiutata da due signore quando sono svenuta per strada che hanno chiamato mia mamma per farmi venire e prendere; quando mi hanno aiutata mi sono sentita molto contenta perché non pensavo che qualcuno mi aiutasse. Tu mi hai anche detto se penso, se la maggior parte delle persone siano disponibili ad aiutarmi e penso proprio di si, grazie all'esperienza che mi è successa.' No. 55, B2, 3rd letter.

90 No. 88, C1, 3rd letter.

91 'Un giorno, veramente tutti i giorni, vengo preso in giro. Loro lo fanno per scherzare ma lo fanno pesante. Mi hanno preso in giro con parolacce e offese ... quando faccio amicizia io sto sempre attento con chi la faccio. Le uniche volte che sono stato aiutato sono state quelle in cui mi ha aiutato la mia famiglia nello studio a fare dei lavori con l'elettricità e altre piccole cose. Io non sono stato aiutato *mai* da amici e conoscenti.... In fine solo dei familiari ti puoi fidare pienamente e mai degli amici e dei conoscenti. Perché le persone (amici e conoscenti) non sono mai disponibili sono disponibili solo se ricevono qualcosa in cambio, altrimenti niente.' No. 36, A1, 3rd letter.

92 No. 2, A3, 2nd letter.

93 No. 3, A3, 2nd letter.

94 No. 9, A3, 2nd letter.

95 No. 11, A3, 2nd letter.

96 No. 16, A3, 2nd letter.

97 No. 12, A3, 2nd letter.

98 No. 20, A3, 2nd letter.

99 No. 20, A3, 2nd letter.

100 No. 13, A3, 2nd letter.

101 No. 9, A3, 2nd letter.

102 No. 28, A1, 2nd letter.

103 This may partly be explained by the turbulence within that class: many students had left the class and new students had arrived who were not acquainted with the project.

104 No. 52, B2, 2nd letter.

105 No. 55, B2, 2nd letter.

106 No. 66, C1, 2nd letter.

107 No. 94, C1, 2nd letter.

108 No. 69, C1, 2nd letter.

109 No. 80, C1, 2nd letter.

110 No. 75, C1, 2nd letter.

111 No. 78, C1, 2nd letter.

112 No. 67, C1, 2nd letter.

113 'La gente del mio quartiere vive nel turbine stressante della quotidianità lavoro, scuola, hobby, e altre occupazioni normali di vita media spesa, figli da accudire, cani da passeggiare ecc ... la maggior parte sono come lupi solitari immersi nel loro problemi e nella loro vita frenetica.' No. 95, C1, 2nd letter.

114 No. 95, C1, 2nd letter.

115 No. 96, A2, questionnaire, 2002.
116 No. 106, A2, questionnaire, 2002.
117 No. 86, A2, questionnaire, 2002.
118 No. 88, A2, questionnaire, 2002.
119 No. 55, B2, 1st letter.
120 No. 34, A1, 4th letter.

10

Conclusion

A high level of generalised trust is a desirable value in any society. Generalised trust is positively correlated with economic growth and democracy, and is more advantageous for income redistribution between rich and poor citizens. Trust leads to better government, less corruption, less crime and happier citizens. Generalised trust is also important for donations or benevolence to other people. When trust declines, people's willingness to make contributions to people different from themselves declines as well.[1] This study has raised the question of whether it is possible to fight persistent values of distrust and non-cooperation. *Is it possible to support the development of trust between citizens through public action from above, through civic education?*

While an important part of the literature has focused on the importance of associations, there is increasing interest in institutional and political explanations for the development of trust. A general criticism of Robert Putnam's *Making Democracy Work* is that he neglected state agency in his analytical model, when explaining the lack of trust in southern Italy. Another agency that was not sufficiently taken into account in Putnam's analysis of differences between the north and the south is the Mafia. In this book, we have understood the Mafia as a promoter of distrust, as an actor that diffuses values of distrust. In contrast to cultural explanations for the Mafia, our argument is that it actively hinders the development of trust by the plantation of an ideology that is based on a culture of fear and anxiety. Researchers on the Mafia have in recent years increasingly challenged cultural explanations for its power. In accordance with Gambetta's analysis of the Mafia (see Chapter 4), I have argued that culture has been used as a functional tool by the Mafia because it has been useful for its activities. Values that are part of the Sicilian cultural heritage have been distorted or exaggerated by the Mafia as a way of rendering its violence more legitimate.

This book has focused on institutional explanations and has analysed more recent political efforts to break the heritage of the past, that is, to turn the vicious circle of non-cooperation into a virtuous circle based on trust and cooperation. The primary aim of the project is to contribute to theories on social capital, and particularly to analyse whether institutions matter for the development of generalised trust.

In the book, we have studied the impact of educational institutions on students' generalised trust. There are strong theoretical reasons for focusing on schooling. School represents the first encounter with public institutions during some of the most formative years in a young citizen's life. Despite the central role of school in young people's lives, it has for a long time been neglected as a research focus by researchers on social capital. Scholars in the educational field have of course studied the impact of educational efforts. From these disciplines we borrowed theory and methods to measure the impact of school factors on students' levels of generalised trust. We found there was an important bridge to build between the two discourses. While research on social capital acknowledges the importance of education on generalised trust, school as a socialising agent has not yet been studied. On the other hand, research on civic education has not looked at the possible effects of civic education on generalised trust. Empirical evidence indicates that trust is established early in life, which is why we have endeavoured to concentrate our analysis on young citizens, during their last years of compulsory schooling.

The project focused on the 'legality programme' at schools in four of Palermo's most deprived areas. The selected areas share several characteristics: high density of criminality or dominance by the Mafia, low scores on social and economic indexes, and weak presence of government agencies or other associations.[2] Three of these poor areas are on the outskirts of Palermo, while one is closer to the city centre. Two schools in areas with more mixed profiles and one school in a high-income district were included in the study as a way of enabling comparisons between different socio-economic settings. The schools that were part of the study were selected according to 'the snowball method', that is, after discussions with numerous interlocutors in Palermo. These schools were all renowned for their anti-Mafia programme, or legality programme as it later became known. The classes were selected in cooperation with the schools. We endeavoured to include a blend of different educational orientations in the sample. Efforts were made to identify a variation as regards teachers' experience, motivation and degree of cooperation in the class council (*consiglio di classe*) across classes.

Describing trust

Researchers from different fields have argued that some dominant characteristics of Sicilian culture are egoism, suspicion and distrust of others, strong attachment to the family, an instrumental view of friendship, a strong belief in honour, fatalism, pessimism and a negative view of the state and its representatives.[3] In the literature on Italy it is frequently claimed that the citizens of southern Italy express less social trust and less confidence in their fellow citizens than do the citizens of northern Italy. Gambetta argues that the Mafia can be understood as a response to the lack of trust in southern Italy: the 'endemic distrust is the crucial difference, which explains why the mafia did not emerge elsewhere in the Mediterranean world'.[4] An important part of the English-speaking literature continues to refer to Banfield's 1958 work *The Moral Basis of a Backward Society* when discussing the Italian political system, without presenting new data.[5]

A starting point for the study was therefore to examine students' values by describing their trust in political institutions and their degree of trust in other citizens. We based the study on two surveys of students' values. A first questionnaire was handed out at the beginning of the first year in lower secondary school (2002) and a second questionnaire during the last semester of compulsory schooling (2005). The first sample consisted of 386 students; the second sample was somewhat smaller, of 315 students. The response rates were high: 89 per cent in 2002 and 76 per cent in 2005.

The descriptive analysis showed that students' trust in political representatives and political institutions was low.

Comparisons of the 2005 results with the Italian results from the IEA international study showed that the students' degree of trust was lower than the Italian average student. Trust in the national government reached 28 per cent among our students, compared with 53 per cent for Italy in the IEA study. Trust in the political parties was 14 per cent in the Palermo study and 26 per cent for the average Italian student. Students' trust the national parliament was 40 per cent, compared with 62 per cent in the IEA study. Further, students' trust in political representatives and political institutions had decreased over time. In 2005, students' expressed less trust in their political representatives – the Italian president, the Sicilian president and Palermo's mayor – than in doctors, athletes and lawyers. An interesting finding was that the students expressed a high level of trust in the police. A majority of students also agreed on the importance of reporting to the police after witnessing a crime, that is, to break *omertà*. These results ran counter to what we expected to find considering the current literature on southern Italy, which emphasises a distrust of the state in general, and of the police in particular. There were important differences between the three socio-economic areas, however, and also between schools.

Interesting for this study was the students' high level of trust in school. The students in the Palermo study expressed more trust in the Italian educational system than in any other public institution. In 2002, an average of 84 per cent of the students answered they had complete trust or a lot of trust in school. Trust continued at a high level in 2005 (80 per cent), even if students in the high-ranked socio-economic area had lost some of their trust in the schooling system between the two surveys.

The analysis of students' generalised trust started with the most abstract question, 'Generally speaking, do you believe that most people can be trusted or that nobody can be trusted?' We found that students leaned somewhat towards the statement 'most people can be trusted'. Students in the low-income areas were more distrustful than those in the intermediate and high-ranked areas. Different scaling renders comparisons with other studies difficult. We were also unable to compare our results with data on students of the same age as those in the Palermo study. The results seem to suggest, however, that the level of generalised trust was lower among the students in the Palermo study than elsewhere in Italy. Still, this tentative conclusion has to be treated with great caution.

We thereafter continued our search with an analysis of questions that asked about students' trust in different categories of citizens. Starting with people who were not personally known to students, we found that students made quite important distinctions between different categories of citizens. The lowest levels of trust were expressed for foreigners, followed by Palermitans and Sicilians. Italians enjoyed the most trust. In the 2005 survey, 30 per cent said they had a lot of trust or complete trust in foreigners, 36 per cent expressed trust in Palermitans, 40 per cent trusted Sicilians and 50 per cent had trust in Italians.[6]

This finding is interesting. If Putnam were right in his conclusions, Sicilians should not trust anyone they do not know personally. They would not trust Palermitans in general, Sicilians, Italians or foreigners. When comparing our results with those from Sciolla's survey of six Italian cities, we also found that students expressed more trust in inhabitants of the same city and in Italians than (adult) respondents did in other cities. Thirty-six per cent of the students in the Palermo study expressed trust in their co-inhabitants, in comparison with 10–11 per cent in Turin and Milan in northern Italy.[7]

The empirical findings (presented in Chapters 6 and 7) suggest that the situation may not be as bad as Banfield suggests. Students had different levels of trust in different public institutions. There were also some important differences between socio-economic areas. Students' lack of trust in other citizens was not general, but varied between different categories of citizens, sometimes apparently for good reasons. Our analysis also showed that the students' trust was not always lower than in other Italian regions; their level of trust was sometimes lower, sometimes higher, and occasionally on an equal level.

Explaining generalised trust

The descriptive statistics did not permit an analysis of change on an individual level, nor of the causes of individual change. We therefore turned to our panel data in order to explore possible change on the individual level between the two waves. We chose to perform several multivariate regression analyses. This is the standard research approach to measure the effects of a number of independent variables (each being controlled for the others) on a dependent variable of a continuous (or close to continuous) nature.

There are a number of different ways in which we can measure trust. The survey included several questions to gauge the level of trust among the students. These questions have been summarised into five different indexes of students' degree of trust in various categories of people. Factor analysis confirmed a common dimension between the variables in each index.[8] Index 1, 'Trust in known people', is an additive index based on questions about the level of trust in family, relatives, neighbours and people from the district (*il quartiere*). Index 2, 'Trust in the school environment', is an additive index based on questions about the level of trust in classmates, teachers, the school principal and school staff. Index 3, 'Trust in unknown people', is an additive index for the level of trust in Palermitans, Sicilians, Italians and foreigners. Index 4, 'Trust in people in general', is an additive index based on three general questions: 'Do you believe that most people can be trusted or that nobody can be trusted?'; 'Do you believe that most people try to be helpful or do you think that people only think about themselves?'; 'Do you believe that most people try to be honest, or do you think that most people are not honest?' The fifth index, again additive, was based on Sicilian sayings and proverbs on trust, sincerity or co-operation: 'To live well it is better to mind your own business'; 'If you need something, it is better to rely on yourself'; 'When people cooperate they never achieve positive results'; 'Real friendship does not exist'; and 'Nobody does anything for free'.

Index 1 was used as an example of so-called 'bonding social capital', illustrating trust in people already known to students. Index 2 measured the students' trust in persons in the school environment. Index 3 represented generalised trust, which is trust in people who are not personally known. Index 4 analyses generalised trust, too, but was based on three questions that are frequently used in national and international surveys. Index 5 was based on Sicilian sayings that in different ways expressed views on trust. In the regression analysis, we used the third index, measuring generalised trust, as our main dependent variable. The reason why we chose index 3 instead of index 4 (or 5) is that it is more precise and more easily comprehended.

As mentioned above, we are interested in the effects of a number of school variables on students' generalised trust. First, one hypothesis suggested a positive correlation between open school structures and levels of trust. Openness of school structures was measured by asking students about the ease with which they felt they could confide in teachers, the school psychologist or the school principal. A second hypothesis was that the more fair the school institutions were perceived to be, the higher would be the level of trust. Fairness of institutions was measured by asking students whether they estimated their teachers to be 'fair', whether teachers were interested only in the best and most intelligent students, and whether the students felt 'badly treated by teachers'.

Another theory was that a caring environment should foster trust. Whether the school environment was deemed to be caring was measured using two indicators: 'Teachers pay attention to my situation' and 'Teachers make me feel at ease'.

The nature of social interaction between students was also expected to affect their levels of generalised trust. Peer interaction was measured by asking students about their school environment: was swearing frequent among students, were there often quarrels between students, or did they feel badly treated by other students?

Openness of the classroom climate was measured by using questions that had previously been used in the IEA international study. The questions asked to what extent teachers encouraged students to express their opinions; to what extent students felt encouraged to develop personal ideas and opinions on various topics; and whether they felt free to express their thoughts in class, or to propose discussions on current problems. In all cases, the different items were included in a simple additive index.

We also endeavoured to include variables that covered each school's particular curriculum. These questions were constructed in discussion with schools when the project began and by studying the different educational programmes established by the institutional council of each school. Activities included both individual activities and activities based on teamwork. They included activities that were part of the formal curriculum as well as the extracurricular activities. Examples of activities belonging to the formal curriculum were the production of a school journal and engagement in sports, cooperatives, environmental groups or an artistic group of any kind (music or theatre). Examples of extracurricular activities were visits to the gym, photography, ceramics, computers, games, dancing, painting, music, theatre or woodwork.

The control variables that were included in the regression analyses were family-related variables such as the parents' educational level, the families' socio-cultural level (measured as the number of books at home), the parents' involvement in school-work (participation in meetings at school and engagement in homework) and the families' interaction with neighbours (help, visits, discussions). Various individual features of the student were also included as control variables, including participation in organisations, personal ambitions in school (degree of interest in his/her studies), interest in society (reading news articles, watching news on television, listening to news on the radio) and gender. An explicit ambition at all the schools in this study was to stimulate increased cooperation between students, to increase trust and to promote values of solidarity, tolerance and respect for diversity. These objectives were expressed both in school programmes and by school principals.

The research question was analysed through a panel study of two waves. Panel designs are rare in the literature on social capital and civic education, as they are time-consuming and resource-demanding enterprises. The panel design increases the opportunity to deal with issues of selection bias, as we know the students' level of trust when they started lower secondary school. The panel design also permits a better assessment of the direction of causality between different forms of activities and the dependent variable, which is here generalised trust. A total of 246 students participated in both tests, which represents 64 per cent of the original sample of 386 students.

The empirical analysis gave strong and consistent support for our school hypotheses. The analysis clearly showed that students had become more inclined to trust other people if the school structures were open, fair and caring, relations between students were friendly, the classroom climate was open, and the school organised school excursions.

Our analysis also identified three variables that seemed to be more important for students' development of generalised trust, namely: open school structures; fairness of school structures; and friendly peer interaction. In comparison, having a caring school climate, an open classroom climate and programmes aimed at enhancing the students' civic engagement seemed to be less important.

The Letter Project

Letters from the Letter Project gave some keys to a better understanding of why different variables were important, if not all of them. Peer interaction, including peer conflict, was a theme that was frequently discussed in students' letters. Students wrote about their interaction with friends during breaks. They wrote often of the joy of being with their classmates. Some narratives also told us about conflicts, harassment or violence between students. Many students particularly enjoyed the time before and after school, when they had time to talk and play with their friends. Several students wrote passionately about their school breaks. The importance accorded to breaks was striking in all classes in all schools. Several students regretted the shortness of the break, though: 'we hardly have the time to put something to eat in our mouths and then the bell rings'. Sometimes the students were restricted in what they could do during breaks: 'the teachers do not allow us to go out in the corridor'. There were also examples of incidents with peer interaction causing trouble and anxiety in class. Nevertheless, several of the students' final letters were littered with descriptions of their affection for their friends and referred to their experiences together: 'I don't want to leave my friends, I am very attached to them because with them I have had fun, I have laughed, cried, made a lot of jokes … the simple thought of leaving them makes me feel bad.' Results from the two surveys indicated that students valued friendship even more in 2005 than in 2002.

Few letters mentioned any particular interaction between teachers and students. It was evident that students were attentive to variations in teachers' characters and styles, however. There were few examples of students who described their own participation or active involvement in discussions. Students' letters revealed that the teachers behaved differently towards students, and in particular the degree of authoritarianism was noted to vary considerably. Sometimes even the daily mood of the teacher was accounted for: 'as soon as the teacher enters I observe her carefully in order to see if she has got out of bed on the right side'. Different teachers also had different standards of toleration. One student described her teachers' different characters during a normal day at school: 'Professoressa L … is not mean; on the contrary she is very gentle and good at explaining things.… Professoressa M … is very severe and we are not even allowed to go to the toilet, and if we don't behave she doesn't even allow us to have a break. Professoressa C … is very kind and with her we have a lot of good and interesting discussions. Professoressa G … is the best of the whole school and she is very kind and never give us notes and she makes us do a lot of things'.

Positive experiences of excursions were vividly described in the fourth letter the students were asked to write, about important events during their years of schooling. Apart from school journeys, some students enthusiastically described private trips in Italy or abroad with their families or clubs. Many students wrote about the places they had visited, but most of all they were enthusiastic about their interaction with friends and teachers during their excursions. It was evident that these represented important breaks to the daily routine as well as occasions when informal interaction with teachers and classmates was possible. Several students in one of the schools wrote about the school trip to Tuscany. One said, 'During the 3 years in this school a lot of events have marked my life, one of them … was the school trip to Tuscany.… we were away from home for 6 days …with my friends.… Everything changed, our daily routines were lost.' 'It was a beautiful experience', exclaimed one of her classmates, 'because I had the chance to know my friends better and to establish true friendship.… Even the teachers seemed changed, they seemed better.' This variable thus approached the two variables discussed above, peer interaction and interaction between students and teachers.

In contrast to the school factors, the students' family conditions or personal ambitions did not seem to affect their changing tendency to trust others. Another important conclusion is that we did not see any effect of the students' engagement in voluntary associations on generalised trust. In fact, the link we saw was slightly negative, that is, engagement in associations seemed to lead to less trust. This finding contradicts theories that emphasise the importance of membership of associations.

How should we understand the negative effect of associations on trust? A first reflection is that we studied young people, and not adults, which may be an explanation of the difference. Young people do not necessarily react in the same way as adults to organisational engagement. There may also be some selection bias, as the students' engagement may be a result of the influence of parents' choices or desires, and unwilling students may be forced or convinced by their parents to join an association. We also suggest that the explanation may be found in the character of the organisations or their internal dynamic. The impact of social interaction found in this study – that peer conflict negatively affects generalised trust – is an aspect that may also be considered when studying different interaction patterns *within* groups or associations. If the social interaction within a particular group is aggressive, these factors will probably negatively influence a person's inclination to trust people in general. Moreover, leadership within these associations may have an important impact on students' attitudes. A story told by one of the boys participating in the Letter Project suggested that participation in an organisation was not always linked to positive experiences: 'I practise water polo. Unfortunately my trainer is not the best one. [He] swears at us.... instead of encouraging me he teased me ... my trainer ... said I was a woman and that I should stop playing water polo.' As this letter suggests, leadership within these associations may have an important impact on students' attitudes. Young citizens are probably more exposed, more influenced and more forced to obey leaders within these organisations than are adults. If adults disagree with the leadership or the working methods, exit is always a possibility. Young people may not have this option. More empirical research is needed on the impact of associations on young citizens.

Further findings

We were also interested in examining the gendered nature of the impact of various school factors. The experiences of social workers in Palermo indicated that women were more inclined to visit the social centres and participate in the activities offered there. We found that the explained variance for the control variables did not differ between boys and girls, while the variation explained by the school variables was higher for girls than for boys. This indicates that school has more impact on girls' levels of trust than it does on boys'. This finding is thus in line with practitioners' experience: women do seem to be more inclined to be influenced by government institutions.

We also examined whether the effects of various school factors on children depend on their socio-economic position. Empirical research on the impact of schooling suggests that it may have a particularly strong effect on socio-economically disadvantaged students, whereas relatively well-off students seem to be more affected by their families and other socialising agents. On the basis of work by Hess and Torney, as well as Almond and Verba, Ehman argues that 'it appears that schooling may be relatively more important than home or other socializing agents for lower socio-economic groups than for higher status groups'.[9] However, when we analysed the effect of the school factors on students in socio-economically disadvantaged and wealthy areas, respectively, we could not establish any substantial differences in this regard.[10]

An important theoretical conclusion is that it is possible to stimulate the development of generalised trust by state action at the grass-roots level, for example through schools and civic education. The results thus support institutional explanations for the development of trust. It has also been shown that it may be possible to encourage the development of trust within a shorter time frame than Putnam suggests. Trust does not need centuries to develop: it may do so within two or three years.

Some reflections

Some caution is needed in the interpretation of the results, however, as the effects found were small. It should be recalled that this study was conducted in poor areas where the presence of the Mafia was often strongly felt. There was thus an over-representation of schools in poor neighbourhoods in the chosen research design. Despite the difficult circumstances that these schools are facing in their daily work, we found that several school factors had an impact on students' generalised trust.

Furthermore, the school programme in Palermo also had other aims, apart from that of creating trust. It also aimed to make students aware of Palermo's cultural heritage, to increase their knowledge of the territory and to encourage their engagement with the city and its monuments. Another objective was related to citizenship: to learn the principles of citizenship, to encourage students to break the traditional *omertà* and to cooperate with law enforcement agencies, to learn about lawful behaviour, and to increase students' tolerance and co-operative skills. The programme also had more knowledge-based objectives: to increase students' knowledge of the Mafia, protection rackets and the state witness programme. Generally, school policy in Palermo particularly focused on education for citizenship, control of the territory and of the city's collective memory.

Some factors we were unable to explore in this study, including different programmes, timing of classes and the content of discussions. It may also be asked which specific elements of civic education actually matter, and to what extent it may be more desirable to provide students with the necessary skills – knowledge and intellectual capacity – to make critical assessments themselves.

Were there any changes within the schools during these years that may have affected students' levels of generalised trust? Four schools changed principal during this period (A2, A3, B1 and C1). In two cases (A3 and B1) this was in the autumn of 2004, shortly before the second survey, and their possible effects on students' attitudes or perceptions were therefore likely very small. In A2 and C1, the school principal changed when students started their second year at lower secondary school, and their leadership had probably some effect on the schools' legality programme. Although these changes, in some cases, may have been dramatic for the teachers in the schools, they did not seem to affect the orientation of the school programmes. Interviews with the new school leaders confirmed that they preferred to respect the general outlines of their predecessors rather than introducing revolutionary change.

What events outside school may have affected students' responses between 2002 and 2005? We were not able to discern whether gains or losses of trust were related to changes in families' economic situations. The Italian economy fared rather poorly during our study. Italy's position in the world economy and in Europe was eroded, and public finances deteriorated. Family-owned companies are the backbone of Italy's economy; while they were successful during the 1970s and 1980s, by the turn of the century they were facing increasing difficulties adapting to a global economy and strongly felt the competition from lower-cost producers in Asia. Italy's share of global trade fell from 4.6 per cent in 1995 to 2.7 per cent in 2005. Thus, general economic development could not be an explanation for the improvement in students' level of generalised trust. However, more information would be needed about individual families' incomes in order to test economic explanations for the development of students' individual levels of trust.

There were no assassinations of politicians, police officers or other officials in Palermo during the three years I followed the classes. In one of the areas, the police made an important intervention and 84 Mafia dependants were arrested. This resulted in headlines and numerous articles in the national, regional and local press. However, it occurred one week after the second questionnaire had been collected and could therefore not have had any effect on students' attitudes. The arrest of the Mafia boss Bernardo Provenzano took place more than a year after the second survey, in April 2006.

A positive event for the city in general, and for the students participating in the study, was the Palermitan soccer team's success during the year 2004/05. The team was promoted to Serie A of the Italian football league in May 2004, for the first time in 33 years, and the event was celebrated throughout the streets of Palermo. When visiting Palermo in February–March 2005 one could still see decorations in black and pink hanging from trees and over the streets from the celebrations the year before. The soccer team's further success in Serie A (Palermo finished in sixth position that year) had a clear effect on students' answers. Many wrote, in answer to the question about whether they liked Palermo or not, 'Yes, I like Palermo because we have a very good soccer team!' As the soccer team performed better than expected, this may have had an effect on students' perception of Palermo in general, creating a greater sense of pride and attachment to the city compared with two years earlier.[11] According to one of the school principals, the event had affected not only students' attitudes but people in general. The team's success in Serie A simply surpassed many Palermitans' wildest dreams.[12] In a long-term perspective, the soccer team's success may have an important positive impact on Palermitans' perceptions of themselves and their city. Palermo is talked about on national television, the most important football teams visit Palermo, and there is the possibility of the team's participation in the European Champions' League.

The change of the Italian government in 2002 was probably the most important event to affect school policy. The reforms launched by Letizia Moratti, minister of public education, were probably some of the most debated and contested reforms of Silvio Berlusconi's government. While the previous centre-left government had tried to bring greater homogeneity across the education system, Moratti's reform aimed to strengthen differentiation. It proposed the introduction of a combination of courses, to transfer educational decisions to the regional level and to increase funds for private schools. One of the most important innovations was to lower the age of access to school.[13] The reforms divided Italian schools in two. The consequences of the reform on the panel study were limited, however, as reforms were introduced only for students starting lower secondary schooling in 2004/05. School principals said that reforms were introduced step by step and with great care, as a way of avoiding confusion.

On the international level, there were several important events that may have had an effect on students' values.[14] The United Nations was given a lot of exposure in the media during the first test, in November 2002, as a result of the situation in Iraq and the discussions in the Security Council. This may have affected students' answers on international events in particular. Another event that may have affected students' perceptions, during the second survey, was the capture of the Italian journalist Giuliana Sgrena in Iraq in 2005. The fate of the journalist made headlines in most newspapers and across the media for several weeks. The Beslan drama in Chechnya in September 2004 and the tsunami catastrophe in Asia in December 2004 both happened when schools were closed for holidays. Several school principals and teachers said, however, that students had closely followed these events, and in some cases discussions about the events were organised when students returned to school. One school had organised a commemoration for the events in Beslan as an act of solidarity.

The need for further research

A clear conclusion of this study is that institutions are a factor that needs to be increasingly addressed in future research on social capital and generalised trust.

Will the improvements made by schools participating in this study endure over time, or will they be lost, as students grow older? Or do their experiences at lower secondary level constitute an important formative moment in life, as we have suggested in this study? It has not been possible to examine whether the impact of school at the lower secondary level will cause a long-term change in the students' values. Research by Uslaner shows that generalised trust is established early in life and is stable over time. Even if changes occur during adulthood, as an effect of job experiences, family events, social experiences or changes in society, it has been found that they do not in general interfere with the basic pattern established early in life. Nevertheless, it is possible that age, life experiences or external events will affect the change obtained thus far. A new outburst of Mafia violence may mobilise or destroy students' trust. While the violent years of the 1970s and 1980s led to a withdrawal of citizens from public life and into private life, the murders of the two judges Falcone and Borsellino in 1992 led to massive public demonstrations and mobilisation against the Mafia.

This study did not analyse students' behaviour, but rather their expressed perceptions and attitudes. During our visits to the schools, many teachers complained about the gap between expressed values and behaviour in practice. For example, in theory students knew perfectly well that they should not throw paper on the floor, or anywhere else; nevertheless, a teacher said that it was always necessary to spend some time before every lesson cleaning up the classroom.

The importance of the implicit or hidden curriculum is a factor widely recognised in the literature on civic education. White points to the importance of trust in school, arguing that one of the primary tasks of school is to *show* trust. Negative signals such as distrust in students, or different categories of students, should be avoided, even if there is reason to distrust some individual students. Although control systems are necessary in all schools, there is always a risk that these will be perceived negatively by students.[15] The qualitative approach used by Niemi and Niemi is interesting in this regard. In their study, six high-school classes in government and American history were observed during the autumn of 2004. Niemi and Niemi spent four months observing six classes, taking note of the topics discussed in the classroom, analysing how these topics were presented, and what attitudes to politics teachers and students expressed. Their aim was to study values relating to political parties, political leaders and the political system in general. Niemi and Niemi observed that, overall, 'all teachers expressed opinions directly, despite their intent to do otherwise. In five of the six cases, this was not an everyday occurrence, but neither was it highly unusual.'[16] The ways of expressing political attitudes were manifold, and included giving a direct opinion about politics and government, giving advice to students about their or others' political behaviour, expressing exasperation or frustration with the political system and politicians, and name-calling of politicians or government officials. An open and unexplored question is to what extent the Palermo teachers themselves expressed distrust in unknown people. It would also be of interest to include teachers' interaction patterns with students and study more in detail what values they consciously or unconsciously transmit to students. One of the school principals involved in this study admitted that teachers were often themselves suspicious and distrustful towards strangers. More qualitative research on interaction patterns between teachers and students are therefore warranted.

Few studies of gender differences and trust have been reported in the literature on social capital and generalised trust. The discussion appears to have focused more on differences between types of organisations rather than between the sexes regarding levels of trust. Nonetheless, it has been shown that women tend to engage in peripheral organisations that are smaller and focused on domestic and community affairs, while men engage in core organisations which are large and related to economic institutions.[17] There are also important differences between men and women in terms of their voluntary engagement: while men engage in voluntary work related to sports and recreation, women engage in the fields of health, education and social services. Often women engage in informal networks.[18] Economists analysing gender differences in game theory have found that men exhibit greater trust than women do, while women show higher levels of reciprocity.[19] Experience suggests that women are more active and more open to change than men. All the regressions in this study demonstrated a significant effect of gender, with boys being more inclined than girls to trust other people. As it is still rare to highlight gender differences regarding trust in the social capital literature, these findings will also be interesting to follow up in future studies. An analysis of variance showed that school factors explained more of the variance of generalised trust for girls than for boys.

It was not the purpose of this study to analyse whether students' generalised trust was based on strategic or moral calculations. While strategic trust is an effect of a person's previous experience (and relates to people you already have met), moralistic trust is more of a moral commitment to treat people as if they are trustworthy. It is difficult to apprehend to what extent students' negative perceptions of southerners correspond to reality, that is, whether their negative perception of Palermitans and Sicilians is based on experience, prejudice, negative press coverage that focuses on the Mafia, or any other explanation. One of the girls participating in the Letter Project described an incident that illustrates how negative perceptions of the south may colour southerners' attitudes towards themselves. The incident happened during a school trip to Tuscany. She described how a person who said he was collecting money for HIV victims had fooled her and her classmates. The students eventually learned they had been fooled and she concluded: 'from this experience we understood that there are cheaters not only in Palermo, but also in a well-to-do area such as Florence'.

There was some evidence, however, that students' trust in some categories of citizens may be based on personal experiences (i.e. strategic trust). Differences between areas were important on only four items: trust in relatives, neighbours and classmates, and people in the area (*quartiere*). The differences were striking for trust in neighbours and trust in classmates. In 2002, only 46 per cent of the students in the low-ranked areas trusted their neighbours, compared with 55 per cent in the intermediate areas and 72 per cent in the high-ranked area. Only 60 per cent of the students in the low-ranked areas trusted their classmates, compared with 71 per cent in the intermediate areas and 90 per cent in the high-ranked area. These differences diminished over time, however, as students in the lower-ranked categories gained trust and students in the high-ranked area lost trust. Students' letters suggested that their degree of trust may be based on their experiences in the area where they live. Many students in the low-ranked areas expressed concern about the presence of drugs, criminality and people who should not be approached, while students living in more well-off areas felt secure and at ease with their environment. Their degree of trust seems to be close to Uslaner's reasoning about strategic trust. Some of the reactions during the test also pointed in this direction. When asked whether students trusted the president of Italy, for example, many said 'I don't know. I haven't met him yet!' When I confronted some students who said they did not trust foreigners, and asked if they did not trust me (a foreigner), they often answered, 'Yes, I do, but I have met you'. The logic is, consequently, that if you live in dangerous or hostile surroundings, it may be wise not to trust everybody, at least not persons in the local environment. Students' letters clearly showed that they were careful when dealing with strangers, which is understandable if your neighbours are not honest people. The letters showed that students seemed quite aware of which persons to avoid in their locality. They were also attentive to dangerous or difficult students in their school environment. However, there are also indications that contradict this analysis. Some students participating in the Letter Project seemed to have a personal commitment to trust other people, despite their personal experiences.

An important methodological insight from the project is that questionnaires can successfully be used with very young people. Most studies on young people's attitudes start at age 14; however, as illustrated by this study, the attitudes and perceptions of younger students can be recorded via questionnaire. Questionnaires for young citizens require a different approach, however, from questionnaires for adults. Special attention to layout and design of the questionnaires and wording of questions, provision of pedagogic examples, a 'pep talk', personal presence and availability to answer questions are some examples of the endeavours made in this study.[20]

The qualitative part of the study, the so-called Letter Project, was also interesting, as it showed that young people are capable of giving interesting and colourful descriptions of their lives and thoughts. Open questions and letters from the respondents permitted fuller accounts of their reasoning about vague concepts like trust and helpfulness, and other matters of concern. Students' narratives about their neighbourhood and those living there gave interesting and valid information about their perceptions of other people.

A strong recommendation for future studies on generalised trust is to use more specific questions on trust, because of the significant variance in the respondents' degree of trust in different categories of people. The fact that students had more trust in Italians than in Sicilians and Palermitans is an interesting and unexpected finding. According to Putnam, Sicilians should not trust anybody they did not know personally, be they Palermitans, Sicilians, Italians or foreigners. Moreover, the expressed high levels of trust in the family are far from unique to this survey, as they apply to other areas in Italy and abroad as well.

For practitioners in civic education, we would recommend that teachers and school principals pay great attention to the openness of their school structures, the fairness of teachers, the caring aspect and stimulating open discussions in the classroom. The good news is that these measures may be implemented in every school without great cost. Pedagogical training, good leadership and cooperation between teachers are most likely required, in order to give teachers and school staff the necessary skills and motivations to create an open, fair and caring school. An interesting finding from the Palermo study was the positive impact of school trips on generalised trust. As described in Chapter 5, excursions to the city of Palermo were one of the hallmarks of Orlando's school policy as well as the project 'School adopts a monument', which aimed to increase students' interest and engagement in Palermo.

Cultural warfare

The Mafia uses different strategies to establish and maintain its power: organisation, violence, networks, territorial and mental control. In the present study, the focus was on the Mafia's territorial and mental control, as important power resources for the Sicilian Cosa Nostra. In spite of the increasing internationalisation of Mafia activities, Sicilian Mafia groups are still firmly rooted locally and dependent on local resources. Controlling the territory means imposing certain types of behaviour and ways of thinking on citizens in that very area. A Mafia leader who controls a territory is free to act as he chooses within it. Controlling the territory includes the extortion of local firms. It enables the Mafia to establish local monopolies in sectors of the economy, often through threats and violence towards competing companies, or to mobilise votes for political candidates. For citizens living in areas dominated by the Mafia, life can be harsh. Siebert has described everyday life in such areas as a civil war. She continues by quoting the mayor of a small town in Calabria, commenting on the mental control of the Mafia:

> such total control is a terrible thing; even more terrible than the criminal acts themselves or the fighting between different bands. It is like a door towards the future that has been shut in front of you, because there is no way out, you don't grow ... you're cut out ... you have to fight for your own rights.[21]

The programme launched for Palermo by Mayor Leoluca Orlando after the assassinations of Falcone and Borsellino in 1992 was an institutional answer to the Mafia's territorial and mental control. Important aspects of Orlando's policy for Palermo were to recapture the territory from the Mafia and to break its control of citizens' minds. As described, Orlando's policy had a threefold focus: infrastructure, culture and school. The major aims of his political programme were to reclaim the state's control over the city's territory, to restore citizens' rights and to promote a civic consciousness based on the rule of law. Many consider the school policy one of the most successful parts of that programme. Schools were constructed or the renting conditions of school buildings were changed, enrolment procedures were improved, efforts to fight school drop-out were reinforced, the use of 'double turns' was ended, new didactic methods were introduced, the 'School adopts a monument' project was launched, and more attention was given to education in good citizenship and the rule of law. Efforts were also made to open up a discussion on Sicilian cultural values and to contrast them with Mafia values. A central part of the programme was also to stimulate cooperation and trust between students and to instil a belief in the possibility of *change*.

The efforts made by teachers to change students' values were often in conflict with the Mafia's values and power. Different cultural models are here at play, one that favours change and one that strongly opposes change. In these areas, school represents a cultural battlefield, where the dominant role model offered by the Mafia is challenged. This struggle is not just a theoretical construction. The assassination of the priest Padre Pino Puglisi in Palermo in 1993 was a consequence of his opposition to a local Mafia group and his work related to civic education of children. In the same area, the attempt to establish a sports ground, named Centro sportivo Padre Puglisi, was strongly opposed by the local Mafia. The signpost bearing the name was destroyed three times and then 'someone' started a fire in the sports ground. Many social workers in these areas were aware that they constituted a threat to the Mafia. They still continued with their work. Their coping strategies were varied. These included not confronting or challenging the Mafia openly, establishing networks in the area that were favourable to their activities (for example with mothers) and not having too much success in their work (i.e. continuing with their work but always within certain limits). Schoolchildren in these areas may similarly experience conflicting pressures from different socialising agents – family, school, peers and the Mafia. The struggle is about competing models for how society should be organised: through the state or through the Mafia. This cultural warfare is also about state-building and nation-building, the establishment of the state's control over its own territory, the monopoly of the state over the use of violence and the establishment of state legitimacy.

The Italian case shows how a Mafia group that establishes its control over a specific territory enjoys several advantages: a place where criminals can find a safe haven from law enforcement agencies, a territory where recruitment of new members is possible, an area where money may be laundered, and where people's loyalty, or fear, offers protection against law enforcement agencies. Control over a specific population also represents a power resource, especially in relation to the political establishment. Votes may be mobilised to increase the political influence of criminal groups. The control of a territory is thus an important power resource that may be used in different ways.[22] Breaking the Mafia's territorial power may consequently constitute an important element of the fight against organised crime.

Territorial control is also a threat to civil society in many different ways. It is a threat to legal business and the economic development of the area, since the penetration of Mafia groups distorts market mechanisms. Legal businesses receive threats, are forced to pay protection money and cannot compete on equal terms with Mafia-backed businesses. Trade in hazardous waste is a good example of an industry in which the Mafia has become increasingly involved. The territory controlled by the Mafia may be used as a dumping for industrial waste, with important consequences for citizens' health.[23] The Mafia also undermines citizens' ability to express their legal, civic and democratic rights. As described by Siebert, the Mafia creates a culture of fear that leads to conformist behaviour, which itself implies mental surrender to the Mafia's exercise of power.[24]

Research tells us that generalised trust is necessary for the establishment of civil society, as it makes people more inclined to participate voluntarily in different kinds of collective institutions, for example political parties, trade unions and, indeed, any other kind of organisation that is generally beneficial for democracy. Creating generalised trust between citizens therefore represents one way of undermining the Mafia's power.

The fight against organised crime is, however, much broader than the scope of this book. The work done by schools must be coupled with efforts in many other fields. Political awareness, appropriate laws, adequate support for the law enforcement agencies, coordination of the different police forces, engagement by civil society, press coverage, strategies against unemployment, special programmes for young citizens 'at risk', well functioning and non-corrupt public institutions, and coordinated international responses are other strategies that need to be added to efforts in civic education. But that is another story.

Notes

1 Uslaner, *The Moral Foundations of Trust*, pp. 204–5.

2 The selection of areas was based on comparisons of statistics on employment, unemployment, educational level, the literacy rate, the number of foreigners per 1,000 inhabitants, youth unemployment and employment rates, number of square metres per person, number of square metres per apartment and frequency of higher education in the 14–29-year age group.

3 See Arlacchi, *Mafia Business*; Banfield, *The Moral Basis of a Backward Society*; Fukuyama, *Trust*; Hess, *Mafia and Mafiosi*.

4 Gambetta, *The Sicilian Mafia*, p. 77.

5 For a criticism of Banfield's work, see A. Pizzorno, 'Familismo amorale e marginalità storica ovvero perché non c'è niente da fare a Montegrano

(1967)', in L. Gallino and P. Ceri (eds), *La società Italiana. Cinquant'anni di mutamenti visti dai 'quaderni di sociologia'* (Turin: Rosenberg and Sellier, 2001); Sciolla, *Italiani*; F. Sabetti, *The Search for Good Government* (Montreal: MacGill–Queen's University Press, 2000).

6 Differences between the three socio-economic areas were small and not significant.

7 In the two cities in southern Italy, Teramo and Caltanisetta, the figures for 'trust in inhabitants' were 16 per cent and 24 per cent, respectively. In central Italy, they were 22 per cent in Modena and 20 per cent in Vicenza. Sciolla, *La sfida dei valori*, p. 196, table 7.1.

8 Analysis of Cronbach's alpha for each index was based on the total sample from 2005. For details, see Chapter 8.

9 Ehman, 'The American school in the political socialization process'.

10 In order to answer this question, we divided the students into two major groups based on the overall socio-economic conditions of their respective residential areas. Since we are mainly interested in the poor areas in comparison with the non-poor ones, we collapsed the intermediate and high-ranked areas into one category, thereby making a distinction between low-ranked and wealthier areas. We thereafter conducted separate regression analyses for these two categories.

11 One boy had written a poem about his love of the soccer team:

'Riccordo quand'ero fanciullo sognavo una maglia e un pallon,
Guardavo la curva cantare io provo la stessa emozion,
E quando Palermo è in campo fortissimo batte il mio cuor,
La voce che prende il soggetto Palermo sei l'unico amor...
Forza Palermo.'

'I remember when I was a boy, I dreamt about a shirt and a ball,
I watched the curve [in a stadium] sing and I shared the same emotion,
When Palermo is in the arena, my heart beats very fast,
The name of the subject is Palermo, you are my only love...
Forza Palermo.'

12 Palermo finished in sixth position in their second year in Serie A.

13 K. Jones, 'Remaking education in Western Europe', *European Educational Research Journal*, 4:3 (2005), pp. 228–42.

14 The following section discusses international, national and local events that may have influenced students' attitudes. The discussion is based on informal discussions with school principals and teachers in March 2005, shortly after the finalisation of the second survey.

15 White, *Civic Virtues and Public Schooling*.

16 R. G. Niemi and N. S. Niemi, 'The content and focus of high school civics teaching', paper presented at the 3rd General Conference of the ECPR, Budapest, Hungary, 8–10 September 2005, p. 10.

17 Miller McPherson and Smith-Lovin, 'Women and weak ties'.

18 Lowndes, 'Women and social capital'.

19 Chaudhuri and Gangadharan, 'Gender differences in trust and reciprocity'.

20 For a discussion of issues related to the distribution of the tests and the questions' reliability, see the Appendix.

21 Siebert, 'Mafia and anti-mafia', p. 40.

22 Williams, 'Transnational crime and corruption', p. 250.

23 For an analysis of business with industrial waste, see M. Massari and P. Monzini, 'Dirty businesses in Italy: a case-study of illegal trafficking in hazardous waste', *Global Crime*, 6:3/4 (2004), pp. 285–304.

24 Siebert, 'Mafia and anti-Mafia', pp. 39–40.

Appendix: the distribution of the questionnaires

The students participating in this study were 10–11 years old when the first questionnaire was handed out. The schools were asked to inform students about the survey the day before as a way of preparing and motivating them for the test.[1] Of the total of 436 students in the classes selected, 394 participated. Six students did not complete the questionnaire and two questionnaires were excluded from the analysis for other reasons. A total of 386 questionnaires were coded, giving a response rate of 89 per cent. The questionnaires were distributed in class and collected immediately after the test. In the second wave, 315 out of 410 students participated and completed the questionnaire, a response rate of 77 per cent. The panel consists of the 246 students who completed the test on both occasions.

A general problem with questionnaires is that most people tend to try to give a positive image of themselves. We tried to minimise this problem by emphasising the importance of giving honest answers before the students started the questionnaire. They were asked to answer what they really thought and believed. In our presentation we particularly underlined that the information gathered would be entirely anonymous. This was repeated in writing on the questionnaires themselves. The purpose of the study was also carefully explained and examples of questions were provided to students as a way of improving their comprehension of the items. Teachers were asked to wait outside the classroom, or else to remain passive during the test, as a way of enhancing students' integrity. I distributed the questionnaires personally, with the help of a research assistant from Palermo.

It was evident that completing the second questionnaire was much easier for students. They had of course matured during the intervening two and a half years. We were recognised by most students on arrival. While the first questionnaire had taken about two hours for students to complete, the second was completed in about one hour. When they were asked after completing the questionnaire, many students said that the questions were appropriate and easily answered. In many cases classes were smaller at the second survey and we were better prepared to help students with difficulties. In some cases, where students advanced slowly through the questionnaire, we asked them to complete only a part of it, or not participate at all. However, the ambition was to include as many students as possible, and in fact most students insisted on participating. It was obvious that students worked more independently at the second survey.

Another difference between the two surveys was that teachers were permitted to remain in the classes for the second. Their presence had positive disciplinary and calming effects. Teachers' information about the surveys seemed to vary between schools.

Reliability

During completion of the questionnaires, it was evident which questions the students found hard to understand. This was particularly clear in the first wave. Questions on trust and confidence were the ones that worked best: students asked few questions about them and they did not seem to have problems in understanding their meaning.

Following the experiences from the first survey, the second questionnaire was somewhat improved to enhance students' understanding of the questions. The dependent variable remained exactly the same, but some minor changes were made for the independent variables, such as to the wording of the questions. For instance, a question about parents' origins was somewhat changed as the Italian word used in the first questionnaire was ambiguous and could have referred to origins in another Italian region as well as another country: 'Qualcuno dei tuoi genitori è nato in un altro paese' was changed to 'Tua madre/tuo padre à nato all'estero?', since the word *paese* may refer to another Italian region and not solely another country.

Generally, political questions worked less well. With the exception of students in the high-ranked area, students had weak conceptions about politics. We received many questions like 'What is "politics"?' or 'What is a political party?', particularly in 2002, when the students were only 10–11 years old. However, differences were important between the areas. When asked whether students had trust in political parties, one of the boys in the high-ranked area said: 'Well, it depends. I have complete trust in the Left, but not in the Right.' The high rates of 'Don't know' answers on political questions are a clear indication of students' difficulty expressing their personal opinions on politics.

Another section that caused some problems was the section 'Other values', based on Sicilian sayings, which appeared to be too abstract for many students. Moreover, the negative wording of the statements may have hindered their understanding of the questions.

Some open-ended questions were removed after the first survey as it took students too long to answer them. Several open questions were changed to closed form. One example was the open question on good citizenship ('Make a list of four characteristics that you consider most important for a good citizen'). Another deleted question was the open question 'Write down five places in Palermo that are important for you'. Three questions relating to environmental concerns were also removed. The main reason for not including too many open questions was time and space, and the need to concentrate on questions of more theoretical relevance to this study.

Some other questions were also dropped after the first survey, for example two questions related to the schools' internal democracy, as they were not relevant in an Italian context. As internal democracy is not introduced until higher secondary level, these questions were excluded in the second questionnaire. Although many students tried to answer these questions, their reliability is low and the items are not used in the analysis.

Questions about parents' professions were included in the first questionnaire, but excluded in the second wave, since students had little (if any) knowledge of their parents' professional lives. Answers like 'My father works in a company with computers' or 'in an office' were not possible to classify. We had added a follow-up question asking students to describe the tasks their parents were performing ('come si svolge il suo lavoro'), but many students just answered 'he does his work very well' or filled in information that was difficult to interpret and use. As in the IEA international study, I therefore decided to exclude the question in the second test.

The visual format of the questionnaire was somewhat improved in 2005 in order to facilitate the reading of the questions (there were fewer of them on each page and the line spacing was increased). Some questions on students' study habits at home were also added ('Do you have a place where you can study at home?', 'Do your parents make sure that you have a place to study?', 'Are there a lot of discussions and quarrels at home?'). The phrasing and presentation of the questions were also improved. For example, single questions that asked for two responses were were split into two separate questions.[2]

Generally, students had good comprehension of the questions. However, they were very young and sometimes forgot to answer some questions or even missed whole pages. In order to reduce this 'internal drop-out', we introduced checks within the questionnaires such that we could prompt students to make sure they had not forgotten to answer questions or missed pages.

Drop-outs and newcomers

It was obvious that students would drop out of school somewhere between the first and second surveys. We knew that school drop-out was high in lower secondary school, averaging 10 per cent per year. Substantial drop-out was expected, therefore, and furthermore this would be non-random, affecting in particular the samples from the low and intermediate socio-economic areas. According to statistics from the National Board of Education in Palermo for the year 2000/01, the average drop-out was 9.7 per cent for the low-ranked socio-economic areas (this varied from 1.8 per cent to 19.0 per cent across the four study areas), 10.2 per cent for intermediate areas and 2.1 per cent for the high-ranked socio-economic district.

The statistics presented in Table A.1 are based on class lists provided by the schools for the school years 2002/03 and 2004/05. It shows the numbers of students in the classes that

Table A.1 Changes in student numbers between 2002 and 2005

School[a]	Number of classes included in survey	Total student numbers 2002	Number of leavers, 2002–05	Number of newcomers, 2002–05	Total student numbers 2005	Drop-out rate[b] (%)	Newcomer rate[c] (%)
A1	4	82	9	3	76	11	4
A2	3	67	20	15	62	32	24
A3	3	73	14	6	65	19	9
A4	4	67	17	18	68	25	26
B1	2	49	2	7	54	4	13
B2	2	48	13	4	39	27	10
C1	2	50	3	2	49	6	4

[a] A1–A4 = low-ranked areas, B1–B2 = intermediate areas, C1 = high-ranked area.
[b] The denominator used is the total number of students in 2002.
[c] The denominator used is the total number of students in 2005.

were part of the study, as well as the numbers of students leaving and joining those classes, and the drop-out rates. The first column indicates the school and the second column shows how many classes we selected from each school.[3]

The table shows that changes were particularly important in one of the schools in one of the low-ranked areas, A2, which is situated in a very difficult neighbourhood. One-third of the students in 2002 were no longer in their classes two years later, and a quarter of the students were newcomers. Classes were particularly stable in one school in an intermediate area, B1, and the school in the high-ranked area, C1.

It has not been possible to estimate how many of the students who are true school drop-outs (as opposed to study drop-outs), since some students may have moved to another school or changed class. New students have also entered the classes, for the same reasons. Still, the information presented above gives an idea of the *stability* of the classes at each school.

Notes

1 Schools were provided with written instructions in order to enable teachers to give similar presentations to students.

2 For example: 'Have you ever met one of the following persons at school; if yes, what impression did you get of him/her?' was replaced with 'Have you ever met one of the following persons at school?', with the presentation of a series of alternatives, and then 'What impression did you get of him/her?' followed by possible answers.

3 The drop-out rate is calculated from the number of students in 2002, for example for A1, class 1A–3A, $3/22 = 0.136$. The 'newcomer' rate is calculated from the total number of students in 2005, for example for class 1A–3A, $2/21 = 0.095$.

References

Adman, P., *Arbetslöshet, arbetsplatsdemokrati och politiskt deltagande*, Uppsala: Acta Universitatis Upsaliensis, 2004.

Almond, G. A. and S. Verba, *The Civic Culture. Political Attitudes and Democracy in Five Nations*, Boston: Little, Brown, 1963.

Arlacchi, P., *Mafia Business: The Mafia Ethic and the Spirit of Capitalism*, London: Verso, 1986.

Armao, F., 'Why is organised crime so successful?', in F. Allum and R. Siebert (eds), *Organized Crime and the Challenge to Democracy*, London: Routledge, 2003, pp. 27–38.

Baldini, G., 'The direct election of mayors: an assessment of the institutional reform following the Italian municipal elections of 2001', *Journal of Modern Italian Studies*, 7:3 (2002), pp. 364–79.

Banfield, E. C., *The Moral Basis of a Backward Society*, New York: Free Press, 1958.

Beck, P. A. and K. M. Jennings, 'Pathways to participation', *American Political Science Review*, 76:1 (1982), pp. 94–108.

Boix, C. and D. N. Posner, 'Social capital: explaining its origins and effects on government performance', *British Journal of Political Science*, 28:4 (1998), pp. 686–93.

Braithwaite, J., 'Institutionalizing distrust, enculturating trust', in V. Braithwaite and M. Levi (eds), *Trust and Governance*, New York: Russell Sage Foundation, 1998, pp. 343–75.

Bricker, D. C., *Classroom Life as Civic Education. Individual Achievement and Student Cooperation in Schools*, New York: Teachers College Press, 1989.

Campbell, A., G. Gurin and W. E. Miller, *The Voter Decides*, Evanston: Row, Peterson, 1954.

Carlestål, E., *La Famiglia: The Ideology of Sicilian Family Networks*, Uppsala: DiCa, 2005.

Casarrubea, G., *Gabbie strette. L'educazione in terra di mafia: Identità nascoste e progettualità del cambiamento*, Palermo: Sellerio editore, 1996.

Cavadi, A., 'Sull'attuazione della legge 51/80', in A. Cavadi (ed.), *A scuola di antimafia: Materiali di studio, criteri educativi, esperienze didattiche*, Palermo: Centro siciliano di documentazione Giuseppe Impastato, 1994, pp. 143–6.

Chaudhuri, A. and L. Gangadharan, 'Gender differences in trust and reciprocity', Working Paper, Department of Economics, University of Melbourne, 2003.

Chubb, J., *Patronage, Power and Poverty in Southern Italy: A Tale of Two Cities*, Cambridge: Cambridge University Press, 1982.

Circolo Didattico Borgo Nuovo 2, *The Brave Mayor Against Marco the Mafioso*, video, 1994/95.

Città di Palermo, *Relazione generale Palermo città di città*, Palermo: Città di Palermo, 1994.

Comune di Palermo, *Abitare Palermo: Guida al nuovo piano regolatore*, Palermo: Assessorato al Territorio, 1998.

Della Porta, D. and A. Vannucci, 'The "perverse effects" of political corruption', *Political Studies*, 45 (1997), pp. 516–38.

Della Porta, D. and A. Vannucci, *Corrupt Exchanges: Actors, Resources and Mechanisms of Political Corruption*, New York: Aldine de Gruyter, 1999.

Di Maria, F. and G. Lo Verso, 'La donna nelle organizzazioni mafiose', in *Donne e mafie: Il ruolo delle donne nelle organizzazioni criminali*, Palermo: Università degli Studi di Palermo, Dipartimento di Scienze Penalistiche e Criminologiche, 2003, pp. 90–103.

Dino, A., 'Cosa Nostra si inabissa e cambia pelle', in *La Mafia esiste ancora*, Giorni di Storia, 26, Turin: Alicubi SRI, 2004, pp. 6–8.

Eek, D. and B. Rothstein, 'Exploring a causal relationship between vertical and horizontal trust', QoG Working Paper Series No. 4, Quality of Government Institute, Göteborg University, 2005. QoG Working Paper series are available at www.qog.pol.gu.se.

Ehman, L. H., 'The American school in the political socialization process', *Review of Educational Research*, 50:1 (1980), pp. 99–119.

Falcone, G. and M. Padovani, *Men of Honour: The Truth About the Mafia*, London: Fourth Estate, 1992.

Finkel, S. E., *Causal Analysis with Panel Data*, London: Sage, 1995.

Fiore, I., *Le radici inconsce dello psichismo mafioso*, Milano: FrancoAngeli, 1997.

Fukuyama, F., *Trust: The Social Virtues and Creation of Prosperity*, London: Hamish Hamilton, 1995.

Gambetta, D., *The Sicilian Mafia: The Business of Private Protection*, London: Harvard University Press, 1993.

Gentile, M., 'The drop-out preventing project in Palermo', in M. Valkestijna and G. van de Burgwal (eds), *New Opportunities for Children and Youth: Good Practices and Research Regarding Community Schools*, a report on the European conference, EDE, The Netherlands, 2001, pp. 112–15.

Gibson, J. L., 'Social networks, civil society, and the prospects for consolidating Russia's democratic transition', *American Journal of Political Science*, 45:1 (2001), pp. 51–68.

Ginsborg, P., *Italy and Its Discontents 1980–2001*, London: Allen Lane, Penguin, 2001.

Graziano, L., 'Center–periphery relations and the Italian crisis: the problem of clientelism', in S. Tarrow, P. Katzenstein and L. Graziano (eds), *Territorial Politics in Industrial Nations*, New York: Praeger, 1978, pp. 290–326.

Hess, H., *Mafia and Mafiosi: Origin, Power and Myth*, London: C. Hurst, 1998.

Holland, A. and T. André, 'Participation in extracurricular activities in secondary school: what is known, what needs to be known?', *Review of Educational Research*, 57:4 (1987), pp. 437–66.

Hooghe, M. and D. Kavadias, 'Determinants of future willingness to vote. A comparative analysis of 14 year olds in 28 countries', paper presented at the 3rd ECPR General Conference, Budapest, 8–10 September 2005.

Hooghe, M. and D. Stolle, 'Introduction: generating social capital', in M. Hooghe and D. Stolle (eds), *Generating Social Capital: Civil Society and Institutions in Comparative Perspective*, New York: Palgrave Macmillan, 2003, pp. 1–18.

Huysseune, M., 'Institutions and their impact on social capital and civic culture: the case of Italy', in M. Hooghe and D. Stolle (eds), *Generating Social*

Capital: Civil Society and Institutions in Comparative Perspective, New York: Palgrave Macmillan, 2003, pp. 211–30.

Inglehart, R., *Culture Shift in Advanced Industrial Society*, Princeton: Princeton University Press, 1990.

Inglehart, R., *Modernization and Postmodernization: Cultural, Economic and Political Change in 43 Societies*, Princeton: Princeton University Press, 1997.

Jamieson, A., *The Antimafia: Italy's Fight Against Organized Crime*, London: Macmillan, 2000.

John, P. and Z. Morris, 'What are the origins of social capital? Results from a panel survey of young people', *British Elections and Parties Review*, 14 (2004), pp. 94–112.

Jones, K., 'Remaking education in Western Europe', *European Educational Research Journal*, 4:3 (2005), pp. 228–42.

Katastrofkommissionen, *Sverige och tsunamin – granskning och förslag*, SOU 2005:104, Finansdepartementet: Stockholm, 2005.

Knack, S. and P. Keefer, 'Does social capital have an economic payoff? A cross-country investigation', *Quarterly Journal of Economics*, 112:4 (1997), pp. 1251–88.

Leone, G., *Cultura della persona e senso della legalità oggi a Palermo*, Palermo: Cooperativa Grafica Siciliana, 1994.

Levi, M., 'A state of trust', in V. Braithwaite and M. Levi (eds), *Trust and Governance*, New York: Russell Sage Foundation, 1998, pp. 77–101.

Lipsky, M., *Street-Level Bureaucracy: Dilemmas of the Individual in Public Services*, New York: Russell Sage Foundation, 1980.

Lo Presti, C., C. Morrocchi and M. Pezzini, *Quali valori tra i giovani: Risultati di un'indagine tra gli studenti di Palermo*, Milan: FrancoAngeli, 1999.

Lorenzi A., C. Morrocchi, M. Pezzini and A. Savoja, *Obiettivo: Coscienza civile*, Palermo: La Zisa, 1990.

Losito, B., 'Italy: educating for democracy in a changing democratic society', in J. Torney-Purta, J. Schwille and J.-A. Amadeo (eds), *Civic Education Across Countries: Twenty-Four National Case Studies from the IEA Civic Education Project*, Amsterdam: International Association for the Evaluation of Educational Achievement, 1999.

Losito, B. (ed.), *Educazione civica e scuola. La seconda indagine IEA sull' educazione civica: Studio di caso nazionale*, Milan: FrancAngeli, 1999.

Losito, B. and A. D'Apice, 'Democracy, citizenship, participation. The results of the second IEA civic education study in Italy', *International Journal of Educational Research*, 39 (2003), pp. 609–20.

Lo Verso, G. (ed.), *La Mafia dentro. Psicologia e psicopatologia di un fondamentalismo*, Milan: FrancoAngeli, 2002.

Lo Verso, G. and G. Lo Coco (eds), *La Psiche mafiosa. Storie di casi clinici e collaboratori di giustizia*, Milan: FrancoAngeli, 2003.

Lowndes, V., 'Women and social capital: a comment on Hall's "Social capital in Britain"', *British Journal of Political Science*, 30:3 (2000), pp. 533–7.

Massari, M., 'Transnational organized crime between myth and reality. The social construction of a threat', in F. Allum and R. Siebert (eds), *Organized Crime and the Challenge to Democracy*, London: Routledge, 2003, pp. 55–69.

Massari, M. and P. Monzini, 'Dirty businesses in Italy: a case-study of illegal trafficking in hazardous waste', *Global Crime*, 6:3/4 (2004), pp. 285–304.

Mastropaolo, A., 'Tra politica e cittadinanza', in *La mafia esiste ancora*, Turin: Alicubi SRI, 2004, pp. 43–8.

Miller McPherson, J. and L. Smith-Lovin, 'Women and weak ties: differences by sex in the size of voluntary organizations', *American Journal of Sociology*, 87 (1982), pp. 883–904.

Mishler, W. and R. Rose, 'Trust, distrust and scepticism: popular evaluations of civil and political institutions in post-communist societies', *Journal of Politics*, 59:2 (1997), pp. 418–51.

Misztal, B. A., *Trust in Modern Societies*, Cambridge: Polity Press, 1996.

Niemi, R. G. and J. Junn, *Civic Education: What Makes Students Learn*, New Haven: Yale University Press, 1998.

Niemi, R. G. and N. S. Niemi, 'The content and focus of high school civics teaching', paper presented at the 3rd General Conference of the ECPR, Budapest, Hungary, 8–10 September 2005.

Norris, P. (ed.), *Critical Citizens: Global Support for Democratic Government*, Oxford: Oxford University Press, 1999.

Oppenheim, A. N., *Civic Education and Participation in Democracy: The German Case*, London: Sage, 1977.

Orlando, L., *The Mafia: 150 Years of Facts, Figures and Faces*, City of Palermo: Cliomedia Officina, 1999, CD-ROM.

Orlando, L., 'Preface', in *Darsi una mano: Educazione alla cittadinanza. riflessioni, percorsi, scelte di gemelaggi*, Firenze: Edizioni della Giunta Regionale, 2001, p. 10.

Orlando, L., *Fighting the Mafia and Renewing Sicilian Culture*, San Francisco: Encounter Books, 2001.

Pantaleone, M., *Mafia e politica* (2nd edn), Turin: Einaudi, 1972.

Pasquino, G., 'The politics of civic tradition eclipsed', *APSA-CP* (newsletter of the American Political Science Association's Organized Section in Comparative Politics), 6:2 (1995), pp. 8–9.

Petersson, O., A. Westholm and G. Blomberg, *Medborgarnas makt*, Stockholm: Carlssons, 1989.

Pizzorno, A., 'Familismo amorale e marginalità storica ovvero perché non c'è niente da fare a Montegrano (1967)', in L. Gallino and P. Ceri (eds), *La società Italiana. Cinquant'anni di mutamenti visti dai 'quaderni di sociologia'*, Turin: Rosenberg and Sellier, 2001, pp. 349–62.

Putnam, R., *Making Democracy Work: Civic Traditions in Modern Italy*, Princeton: Princeton University Press, 1993.

Putnam, R., 'Tuning in, tuning out: the strange disappearance of social capital in America', *Political Science and Politics*, 28:4 (1995), pp. 664–83.

Putnam, R., *Bowling Alone: The Collapse and Revival of American Community*, New York: Touchstone, 2000.

Raudenbush, S. W. and A. S. Bryk, *Hierarchical Linear Models: Applications and Data Analysis Methods* (2nd edn), Newbury Park: Sage, 2002.

Rokkan, S., *State Formation, Nationbuilding, and Mass Politics in Europe: The Theory of Stein Rokkan*, Oxford: Oxford University Press, 1999.

Rothstein, B., *Just Institutions Matter: The Moral and Political Logic of the Universal Welfare State*, Cambridge: Cambridge University Press, 1998.

Rothstein, B., 'Social capital and institutional legitimacy', paper presented at the Annual Meeting of the American Political Science Association, Washington, DC, 31 August–3 September 2000.

Rothstein, B., *Social Traps and the Problem of Trust*, Cambridge: Cambridge University Press, 2005.

Rothstein, B. and D. Stolle, 'Social capital and street-level bureaucracy: an institutional theory of generalized trust', paper presented at the ESF Conference, Exeter, 15–20 September 2001, and also at the 1st General Conference of the European Consortium for Political Research (ECPR), Canterbury, 6–8 September 2001.

Rothstein, B. and D. Stolle, 'Social capital, impartiality and the welfare state: an institutional approach', in M. Hooghe and D. Stolle (eds), *Generating Social Capital: Civil Society and Institutions in Comparative Perspective*, New York: Palgrave Macmillan, 2003, pp. 191–209.

Rothstein, B. and J. Teorell, 'What is quality of government? Impartiality in the exercise of political power', QoG Working Paper Series No. 6, Quality of Government Institute, Göteborg University, 2005. QoG Working Paper series are available at www.qog.pol.gu.se.

Rovelli, R., *Valori e modelli di comportamento: Un indagine sugli studenti dell'università di Palermo*, Palermo: I.l.a. Palma, 1997.

Sabetti, F., *The Search for Good Government*, Montreal: MacGill–Queen's University Press, 2000.

Santino, U., *La Mafia interpretata: Dilemmi, stereotipi, paradigmi*, Messina: Rubbettino, 1995.

Santino, U., *L'Alleanza e il compromesso. Mafia e politica dai tempi di Lima e Andreotti ai giorni nostri*, Soveria Mannelli: Rubbettino Editore, 1997.

Santino, U., *Storia del movimento antimafia: Dalla lotta di classe all'impegno civile*, Rome: Editori Riuniti, 2000.

Santino, U., 'La Sicilia dopo la disfatta: Cu vinciù?', *La Rivista del Manifesto*, No. 20 (September 2001), www.larivistadelmanifesto.it/archivio/20/20A20010911.html.

Santoro, M., 'Mafia, cultura e politica', *Rassegna Italiana di Sociologia*, 39:4 (1998), pp. 441–76.

Santoro, M., 'Mafia, cultura e subculture', *Polis*, 14:1 (2000), pp. 91–112.

Schneider, J., 'Educating against the Mafia – a report from Sicily', *Civnet's Journal for Civil Society*, 3:3 (1999), p. 4.

Schneider, J. and P. Schneider, 'Mafia, antimafia, and the question of Sicilian culture', *Politics and Society*, 22:2 (1994), pp. 237–58.

Schneider, J. and P. Schneider, *Reversible Destiny: Mafia, Antimafia and the Struggle for Palermo*, Berkeley: University of California Press, 2003.

Sciarrone, R., 'The dark side of social capital: the case of mafia', paper presented at the Workshop on Social Capital and Civic Involvement, Cornell University, 13–14 September 2002.

Sciarrone, R., 'Forza e persistenza delle mafie', in *La Mafia esiste ancora*, Giorni di Storia 26, Turin: Alicubi SRI, 2004, pp. 2–5.

Sciarrone, R., 'Le relazioni esterne: il capitale sociale della mafia', in *La Mafia esiste ancora*, Giorni di Storia, 26, Torino: Alicubi SRI, 2004, pp. 30–3.

Sciarrone, R., 'Corleone Italia: la cultura civica dei giovani', in P. Viola and T. Morello (eds), *L'associazionismo a Corleone: Un inchiesta storica e sociologica*, Palermo: Istituto Gramsci Siciliano, 2004, CD-ROM.

Sciolla, L., *Italiani. Stereotipi di Casa Nostra*, Bologna: Il Mulino, 1997.

Sciolla, L., *La sfida dei valori. Rispetto delle regole a rispetto dei diritti in Italia*, Bologna: Il Mulino, 2004.

Scuola Elementare G. Daita, *I colori della speranza*, Palermo: Comune di Palermo, Assessorato Pubblica Istruzione, 1996.

Scuola Media Statale Giuseppe Piazzi, *Palermo è nostra*, Palermo: Citta di Palermo, Assessorato Pubblica Istruzione, 1998.

Siebert, R., 'Mafia and anti-mafia: the implications for everyday life', in F. Allum and R. Siebert (eds), *Organized Crime and the Challenge to Democracy*, London: Routledge, 2003, pp. 39–54.

Siragusa, A., *Per una nuova identità cittadina. L'esperienza educativa di Palermo apre le porte la scuola adotta un monumento*, Palermo: Città di Palermo, 2001.

Skolverket [Swedish National Agency for Education], *Den rimliga skolan: livet i skolan och skolan i livet*, Stockholm: Liber, 1995.

Skolverket, *Attityder till skolan 1997*, Rapport 197, Stockholm: Liber, 1997.

Smith, T. W., 'Factors relating to misanthropy in contemporary American society', *Social Science Research*, 26 (1997), pp. 170–96.

Stenesöta, H., *Den empatiska staten: Jämställdhetens inverkan på daghem och polis 1950–2000*, Statsvetenskapliga Institutionen, Göteborgs Universitet, 2004.

Stolle, D., 'Communities, citizens and local government: generalized trust and the impact of regional factors: a study of three regions in Sweden', paper presented at the 95th annual meeting of the American Political Science Association, Atlanta, 2–5 September 1999.

Stolle, D., 'The sources of social capital', in M. Hooghe and D. Stolle (eds), *Generating Social Capital: Civil Society and Institutions in Comparative Perspective*, New York: Palgrave Macmillan, 2003, pp. 19–42.

Strömblad, P., *Politik på stadens skuggsida*, Uppsala: Acta Universitatis Upsaliensis, 2003.

Tarrow, S., 'Making social science work across space and time: a critical reflection on Robert Putnam's Making Democracy Work', *American Political Science Review*, 90:2 (1996), pp. 389–97.

Torney-Purta J., J. Schwille and J-A. Amadeo (eds), *Civic Education Across Countries: Twenty-Four National Case Studies from the IEA Civic Education Project*, Amsterdam: International Association for the Evaluation of Educational Achievement, 1999.

Torney-Purta, J., R. Lehmann, H. Oswald and W. Schulz (eds), *Citizenship and Education in Twenty-Eight Countries: Civic Knowledge and Engagement at Age Fourteen*, Berlin: International Association for the Evaluation of Educational Achievement, 2001.

Tyler, T. R., *Why People Obey the Law*, New Haven: Yale University Press, 1990.

Uslaner, E. M., 'Trust as a moral value', paper presented at the conference Social Capital: Interdisciplinary Perspectives, University of Exeter, 15–20 September 2001.

Uslaner, E. M., *The Moral Foundations of Trust*, Cambridge: Cambridge University Press, 2002.

Uslaner, E. M., 'Trust, democracy and governance: can government policies influence generalized trust?', in M. Hooghe and D. Stolle (eds), *Generating Social Capital: Civil Society and Institutions in Comparative Perspective*, New York: Palgrave Macmillan, 2003, pp. 171–90.

Vannucci, A., 'Politicians and godfathers: mafia and political corruption in Italy', in D. Della Porta and Y. Mény (eds), *Democracy and Corruption in Europe*, London: Pinter, 1997, pp. 50–63.

Weber, E., *Peasants into Frenchmen: The Modernization of Rural France, 1870–1914*, Stanford: Stanford University Press, 1976.

White, P., *Civic Virtues and Public Schooling: Educating Citizens for a Democratic Society*, New York: Teachers College Press, 1996.

Widmalm, S., 'The utility of bonding social capital', *Journal of Civil Society*, 1:1 (2005), pp. 75–95.

Williams, P., 'Transnational crime and corruption', in B. White, R. Little and M. Smith (eds), *Issues in World Politics*, New York: Palgrave Macmillan, 2005, pp. 235–56.

Newspapers

'Dispersione scolastica, allarme in Sicilia', *Giornale di Sicilia*, 25 March 2005.

'Italy's once-plucky little factories now complicate its battle with "Made in China"', *New York Times*, 14 May 2006.

Camilleri, A., 'When a Godfather becomes expendable', *New York Times*, 21 April 2006

Lerner, T., 'Vi uppmuntras att inte ta ansvar', *Dagens Nyheter*, 23 February 2006.
Martirano, D., 'Ecco perché il padrino viveva da povero', *Corriere della sera*, 15 April 2006.

Statistics

Censimento generale della popolazione e delle abitazioni (Rome: ISTAT, 20 October 1991).
Statistiche della scuola media inferiore. Anno scolastico 1996/97 (Rome: ISTAT, 1999).

Ministry circulars

Ministry of Public Education, circular 302, prot. 23608/JR, 25 October 1993.
Ministry of Justice, circular no. 364764, 10 September 1991.

Quoted interviews and personal communications

Anonymous prosecutor, Palermo Court of Justice, 15 March 2002.
Maurizio Artale, director, Centro Padre Nostro, 22 February 2002.
Attilio Bolzone, journalist, *La Repubblica*, 1 March 2002.
Enrico del Mercato, journalist, *La Repubblica*, 13 March 2002.
Maria Falcone, Fondazione Falcone, 9 February 2000.
Giovanna Granata, school principal, Scuola Oberdan, 12 February 2002.
Gianluca Lo Coco, researcher, Department of Psychology, University of Palermo, May 2005.
Ivana Manone, Centro Padre Nostro, 2 February 2000.
Alfio Mastropaolo, municipal commissioner for citizens' rights 1992–94, 14 March 2006.
Nino Rocca, Centro Sociale di San Severio, Albergheria, 26 February 2000.
Alessandra Siragusa, municipal commissioner 1993–2000, City Department for Education, 2 February 2000.

Index